BARBARY
AND
ENLIGHTENMENT

BRILL'S STUDIES IN INTELLECTUAL HISTORY

General Editor

A.J. VANDERJAGT, University of Groningen

Editorial Board

M. COLISH, Oberlin College
J.I. ISRAEL, University College, London
J.D. NORTH, University of Groningen
R.H. POPKIN, Washington University, St. Louis — UCLA

VOLUME 2

BARBARY
AND
ENLIGHTENMENT

*European Attitudes towards the Maghreb
in the 18th Century*

BY

ANN THOMSON

E.J. BRILL
LEIDEN · NEW YORK · KØBENHAVN · KÖLN
1987

Library of Congress Cataloging-in-Publication Data

Thomson, Ann.
　Barbary and enlightenment.

　(Brill's studies in intellectual history; v. 2)
　Bibliography: p.
　Includes index.
　1. Africa, North—Foreign opinion, European.
2. Europe—Relations—Africa, North.　3. Africa, North—
Relations—Europe.　4. Europe—Intellectual life—18th
century.　5. Public opinion—Europe.　I. Title.
II. Series.
DT197.5.E8T46　1987　　　961'.03　　　87-706
ISBN 90-04-08273-5

ISSN　0920-8607
ISBN　90 04 08273 5

CONTENTS

PREFACE

This study arose from several unexpected discoveries on my part, thanks to the state of almost total ignorance in which I originally approached the Maghreb. After working on several aspects of eighteenth-century thought, centred around the question of the natural history of man and materialistic explanations of the mind, I was led on to take an interest in the emergence of anthropology. This coincided with my removal to Algiers and my discovery of the Maghreb. I was therefore naturally curious to see what had been written about North Africa in the Eighteenth Century in Europe. Here it was that I noticed several things which surprised me. Firstly, in writings about anthropology and the European discovery of the world during this period, North Africa, or Barbary, is generally absent; this is notably the case of Michèle Duchet's *Anthropologie et Histoire au Siècle des Lumières* (Paris, 1971), which has a very comprehensive bibliography of travel literature; the works concerning the African continent cover only sub-Saharan Africa. In the second place, most writing about French views of North Africa begins in 1830, and P. Lucas and J.C. Vatin's extremely interesting work *L'Algérie des Anthropologues* (Paris, 1979) gives the impression that nothing was known about Algeria, or the Maghreb in general, before that date; they even begin with the sentence, "Au commencement règne l'inconnu". This seemed to me to be contradicted by the large number of books and reeditions listed in Playfair's *Bibliography of Algeria from the Expedition of Charles V in 1541 to 1887* (London, 1889). I was further intrigued to find that many attitudes which are commonly considered to be constants of French — and more generally European — thinking about this region and its inhabitants were absent in the Eighteenth Century. This struck me most forcibly in connection with racial attitudes. Such factors whetted my curiosity to go further into what had been written about North Africa in eighteenth-century Europe; I immediately noticed that Barbary presented a particular problem for enlightened thinkers, as it did not seem to fit neatly into the classificatory systems they developed to deal with the rest of the world. By 1830, however, this problem had vanished. This is therefore the starting-point of my book, in which I have attempted to analyse the way in which Barbary was perceived by enlightened Europe, and how these perceptions were transformed to culminate in the colonialists' clichés, which have still not totally vanished.

I have been preceded in this field by Denise Brahimi, whose thesis *Voyageurs français aux XVIII° siècle en Barbarie* (1976) covers some of the same ground; however, her interesting and detailed study concerns French travellers in Algeria, whereas my aim is rather to seize the contours of European, and not only French, thinking about Barbary as a whole and the way in which it integrates into the general framework of writings about non-European peoples. I have not therefore been concerned to assess the accuracy of accounts, nor have I limited myself to writers who visited the region, although I can in no way claim to have included all that was written on the subject. My project is therefore at the same time more limited and wider than hers.

Unexpected events meant that I had enough time at my disposal to complete the writing of this book; those who unwittingly made it possible are hereby given their due. The large number of friends and students whose support and encouragement have been invaluable makes it unfortunately impossible for me to thank them all by name; they know who they are. I would also like to thank the staff at the Bibliothèque universitaire in Algiers, without whom I could not have written this book. And of course Karim, who put up with everything.

INTRODUCTION

This is not a history of the Maghreb in the Eighteenth Century, nor is it a study of the relations between Barbary and Europe; such studies have already been made. It is rather an investigation into the way in which enlightened Europe perceived the Maghreb in the period which stretches up to the French conquest of Algiers in 1830. In other words, it is a study of 'Western attitudes' towards Barbary. There has been, in recent years, a growing interest in the study of attitudes, particularly those of Europe towards the rest of the world; it is thus not an uncharted field. But the term 'attitude' is extremely vague, and such a study lacks an established theoretical framework within which to operate. It is therefore necessary, at the outset, to define precisely what I am trying to do and the limits of my investigation. I am not studying government policies, nor am I attempting simply to present travellers' accounts of Barbary. Instead I wish to look at the way educated Europeans during the period known as the 'Age of Enlightenment' perceived North Africa, and the framework within which they interpreted what was known about it. I am only concerned with what was written, and of course read, by the educated élite during *grosso modo*, the Eighteenth Century. Small as this educated élite was, it is nevertheless the body of knowledge constituted by them that has come down to us and influences to some extent our perceptions of the rest of the world, despite later developments.

But why North Africa? One might say, quite simply, because such a general study does not exist[1]. This reason is not as frivolous as it may appear at first sight, because the very reason why, in my opinion, it does not exist, reveals the inherent interest of the subject. North Africa was not, in 'civilised' European eyes in the early Eighteenth Century, a savage region; it was not an area to which Europeans travelled in search of marvels and mysteries, or even in the main to find primitive peoples, as they went to North America or afterwards to the South Seas. It was not, in short, a land for exploration. At the same time, it was not for them an immediate example of an ancient civilisation from whose philosophy they could learn, as were China or India. It was instead a region with which Europe had numerous and continuous contacts throughout history and was an integral part of Mediterranean civilisation. It was the site of Carthage, had been part of the Roman Empire and had had a flourishing Church that produced Saint Augustine. In addition it was inhabited by peoples who, if they were very different and even hostile, were known to have had a brilliant past and to have occupied the Iberian peninsula. Depite their decline, they still possessed an urban civilisation, navies, engaged in trade and so on. However much hostility might be felt towards the Barbary states, with which the European nations were engaged in perpetual wars, they were precisely that: states with which the Europeans maintained diplomatic relations and signed treaties, and to which they even paid tributes. Such states could not therefore be primarily objects of ethnographical interest. They did not at first sight, to Europeans acquainted with their towns, provide examples of 'savage' peoples living in a primitive state of social evolution, from whom European thinkers could draw lessons about their own past, as they believed they could from observation of the North Americans. We never find the North African used as an example in ethnographical, sociological or philosophical works in the Eighteenth Century. Nor did Barbary exercise the exotic fascination of civilisations like that of China or even of oriental towns like Constantinople. The Barbary states were in many ways part of the world that was familiar to Europeans but they were not, like European lands, countries in which one travelled easily and naturally (if uncomfortably). They thus fell between several stools and tend to become invisible to present scholarship, although this does not mean that they were not present in European thought. And this is precisely why it is in my opinion interesting to look more closely at the way Barbary was perceived, and how the categories present during the Enlightenment for interpreting the rest of the world made it difficult to find a place for this region and for the knowledge concerning it.

We may, however, wonder as to precisely what knowledge there was concerning Barbary. By the time that the French landed in Algiers in 1830 there was, according to most writers, complete ignorance on their part concerning the state they had defeated, and North Africa in general. They saw it as not only hostile but also as barbaric, as "the wilds of Africa", an uncharted territory waiting to be opened up and explored. The inhabitants had become objects of ethnographical curiosity, and even 'savages' needing to be civilised. There is a general feeling in writings on Algeria in this period that the author is embarking on virgin soil. What had been a familiar part of the Mediterranean world, comprised of states with which long-standing relations existed, became a primitive and frightening African wilderness peopled by wild barbarians. Since the French were so fond of comparing themselves to the Romans, previous conquerors of North Africa, we can find a classical parallel to such amnesia concerning both previous knowledge about the Maghreb and the realities of its past: this obliteration of the past can be compared to that of the Romans deliberately destroying the slightest vestige of Carthage and its civilisation, which had dared to challenge Roman power. But how did it come about? How did knowledge and awareness of a complex reality give way to ignorance and simplification? This is what I propose to study in this book.

But is there anything to study? If we read what has been written by most commentators concerning what was known of North Africa before 1830 there is ample reason to be discouraged. L. Valensi talks of a few poor books gathering dust on library shelves, unread and of little intrinsic interest[2], and this is the general impression, apparently borne out by the ignorance of the men of 1830 and the fact that works such as those by Peyssonnel and Desfontaines were not published until 1838[3]. But this opinion is, I believe, not totally accurate, as we can see from the following account. An anonymous author published in 1834 a refutation of Hamdan's *Miroir*, a work by a 'Moor', which criticized many aspects of French policy after the conquest. Amongst other things, the French author rejects Hamdan's claim that the French were ignorant as to the interior of the country (notice that he is talking about the interior, not the capital, much better known); he refers to both Poiret and Desfontaines (proving that the latter's notes were known before the edition of 1838) and claims that many Frenchmen had journeyed from Algiers to Oran. He also refers to the contacts between the French factory at La Calle and the town of Constantine, and the commercial contacts with Tlemcen and Mascara thanks to the traders from Gibraltar living at Oran[4]. If we are to believe this author, Algeria was far from unknown and eighteenth-century literature on Barbary was read. We could also mention Bory de Saint-Vincent's note for the War Ministry on the Commission of exploration in 1838; he too remarks that Algeria had hitherto been much visited despite all obstacles[5]. And as to the works on Barbary, were they merely a few poor volumes gathering dust unread? On the contrary, there is a considerable body of literature concerning North Africa that was published, translated and reedited throughout the Eighteenth Century, and that appears to have circulated[6]. Readers seem to have been as curious about the Maghreb as about the rest of the world. And it was not only travellers who visited Barbary who wrote about it; some authors simply plagiarised earlier publications[7]. Particularly interesting is the case of the 'philosophe', the marquis d'Argens, who included a certain number of letters concerning Barbary in his *Lettres juives* (1736), purporting to be letters sent by Jewish travellers in various parts of Europe and the Mediterranean. (Imaginary travellers' letters constituted a peculiarly eighteenth-century semi-journalistic literary genre, being a way of introducing criticism of society and discussion of contemporary issues.) D'Argens was from Provence and had perhaps stopped off in one of the Barbary ports on his way to or from Contantinople where he spent five months in 1723—4[8]; but if this journalist with a keen eye for the reading public's taste chose to write at some length about the Maghreb, we can infer that there was a market for such accounts. In addition, the very example of the abbé Raynal who in the late century, after the brief passage on North Africa in the *Histoire des Deux Indes*, undertook a detailed investigation into the Barbary states, should make us think about the interest they held for European intellectuals. His "Mémoires" on Barbary were published posthumously by Peuchot in 1826, another proof that information about North Africa, including works by famous authors, was available in 1830[9]. Such works by people who had never set foot in Barbary — or, for example, the passages in Voltaire's *Essai sur les moeurs* or Gibbon's *Decline and Fall of the Roman Empire* — are for my purpose as relevant as the more numerous accounts by travellers. For my aim is not to draw conclusions as to the reality of life in Barbary in the Eighteenth Century, nor to judge the accuracy of accounts. Instead I am attempting, I repeat, to discover the structure of the Enlightenment's perceptions of Barbary, the way such perceptions were inserted into the framework of thinking about the rest of the world and about the human race in general, and the way they were modified. In this perspective second-hand accounts are equally, if not more, revealing than descriptions by people who had actually been there. Denise Brahimi remarks that travellers in Barbary failed to discover or understand the essential and interpreted what they saw in terms of preexisting prejudices[10]; this could hardly have been otherwise, and it is precisely this aspect which I intend to study, for what influences later attitudes is less what was than what was thought to be.

The period covered in this study — roughly the century before the conquest of Algiers — is particularly interesting as it corresponds to the flowering of 'enlightened' thought, which led to a transformation of ways of seeing the world, despite the ultimate failure of enlightened aspirations. The term 'Enlightenment' (or *Lumières* or *Aufklärung*) is of course one which, although consecrated by usage even during the period itself, is not completely devoid of ambiguity. As an attempt at definition, we could say that it denotes a desire to judge by experience and reason rather than according to authority and tradition (which does not mean that this aim was always achieved)[11]. The corresponding openness to different forms of thought and customs is evident if we compare its representatives with those of the following century, despite the latter's greater achievements in science and technology. But we should be careful of a tendency to idealize the Enlightenment. It is true, for example, that enlightened travellers' aims were not to 'open up' unknown regions for European penetration, like the nineteeth-century explorers; instead they were curious to understand human nature, the evolution of language and ideas and the working of human society, which they considered to follow universal laws. The 'savage' was thus not a radically different or necessarily inferior being, simply 'Man' in an earlier stage of evolution or rather in his infancy[12]. But this should not blind us to the Europocentrism inherent in their attitude and to their belief that 'enlightened' European society constituted a higher state of development and the one towards which the others were striving. There was only one possible model of development. In addition, the racist attitudes so widespread in the following century developed from eighteenth-century roots. The white man's burden to civilise the backward nations flowed also from enlightened beliefs.

It may, though, be argued that 'enlightened Europe' is not a coherent entity and that it is a mistake to treat together works written by Frenchmen, Englishmen, Germans or Italians. These thinkers lived in countries with very different economic, social and political realities; indeed, most modern studies treat only one country. But I think it is possible to speak of a European 'république des lettres' during the Eighteenth Century, uniting the intellectual élite. Works circulated in different countries, were rapidly translated or were read in French by educated people of different nationalities; men of letters corresponded and travelled, ideas circulated. One has only to look at inventories of private libraries to see the extent to which books travelled about Europe. In the field we are concerned with here, this is equally true: the Englishman Shaw's work was rapidly translated into French; Laugier de Tassy's was plagiarised in English; there were personal contacts between Peyssonnel, La Condamine and Shaw; the German Rehbinder, reviewing the literature on Algiers, discusses works published in several countries, normally referring to the French edition, and he himself met Venture de Paradis. These few examples are enough to show, I think, that it is legitimate to speak of 'European' attitudes provided it is clear that we are referring to the educated élite. It is also possible to include American writers for they were as yet still influenced by European thought and had not yet asserted a distinctive intellectual character or tradition.

Similarly, can we talk about the Maghreb as a whole? I think that it is possible to discern a set of attitudes and reactions concerning Barbary in general. It was felt to possess a certain unity, despite the differences which were seen to exist between the different Regencies, as will be made clear. On the whole I shall pay more attention to Algiers and Tunis, more frequently discussed and more 'visible' than Tripoli; the Empire of Morocco was more closed to outsiders and unwelcoming. It is finally Algiers which will loom largest, as it did in European consciousness, being the most powerful and aggressive of the Barbary states. It was also the one that was to be conquered by a European country. The fact that it was the French who launched the 1830 expedition resulting, not altogether expectedly, in the French colonisation of Algeria, has meant that it was the French who were most concerned with the region; as a result, French attitudes have been explored in more detail. We shall see, though, that such hindsight has tended to some extent to deform our perception of European awareness of North Africa. In general, to understand eighteenth-century reactions to the Maghreb (or to anything else for that matter) we must make an effort to forget what was to follow; we must try to see the texts on their own terms if we are to understand the structure of the thought behind them. This is, as we shall see, particularly relevant to the question of racism; identical remarks made in a totally different context do not necessarily imply the same things.

I must finally explain clearly the nature of the texts under study. Works on Barbary fall into different categories. There were firstly, of course, consular reports and diplomatic correspondance, which fall outside my concern. There are, next, accounts written by former slaves, a flourishing genre, but as they are more often than not highly romanced, they are normally of little use[13]. An exception is the book on Algiers by the Italian Pananti who had spent several years in slavery[14]. A different category concerns the works written by the monks (mainly French) who went to Barbary to redeem the Christian slaves, the 'pères Rédempteurs'[15]; their narratives are motivated by the need to arouse sympathy for the slaves and hence money to buy them back, and as a result they tend to depict the Barbary states in the worst possible light and insist on the suffering of the prisoners. This is the accusation made by many writers, from d'Arvieux and d'Argens to Rehbinder. Their narrowly apologetic point of view makes them of little use for my present purpose and I have not taken them into account. More interesting are accounts written by people who had visited or resided in Barbary in an official capacity and afterwards wrote accounts for the general public. Such works are those of the chevalier d'Arvieux who travelled widely in the Levant in the middle of the Seventeenth Century and who visited the Barbary states in order to negotiate the liberation of Christian captives. His *Mémoires* and travels were written up and published posthumously in the first half of the following century[16]. Amongst the most notable eighteenth-century visitors of this sort are: Laugier de Tassy, for some time at the French consulate in Algiers, whose history of that Regency was reedited several times and plagiarised by Le Roy in French and Morgan in English; La Condamine, who visited Barbary on a scientific expedition in 1731; Shaw, chaplain to the British community in Algiers who spent twelve years in the country and whose *Travels* concerning both Barbary and the Levant were generally recognised in the Eighteenth Century (and later) as one of the main sources of information on the region; Peyssonnel, a geographer later famous for his research concerning coral, whose letters were published only in 1838; Venture de Paradis, whose career as a diplomat and interpreter took him all over the Levant and Barbary before his death during Napoleon's expedition to Egypt, and whose notes on Barbary, left among his manuscripts, were published a century after his death; Rehbinder, who spent four years in Algiers and whose anonymously published and comprehensive work on Algiers also reviews previous writings on the subject; Mordecai Noah, sent to Barbary as American consul in Tunis in 1813—15 before being revoked by the American Secretary of State because of his Jewish religion; William Shaler, American consul in Algiers, author of a very perceptive book on that Regency published in 1826. There was also the occasional isolated traveller, visiting Barbary out of curiosity; such are the abbé Poiret, whose letters on 'Numidie' were published in 1789 or the botanist Desfontaines, who was sent by the Académie des Sciences during the same period and who met Poiret, but only left written fragments, published in 1838. These are merely the most well-known and frequently consulted writings; I have also referred on occasion to other works, which are indicated in the Bibliography. It is perhaps worth mentioning here the *Mémoire* written in 1781 for de Castries, the navy minister, by Césaire-Philippe Vallière, vice-consul (later to be consul) in Algiers; although he, in the main, reproduces the same details as other observers, his notes are interesting for the unremitting hostility he displays towards everything Algerian. All these works, well-known and more obscure — as well as references contained in books on other subjects — can be interrogated to give us an idea of how enlightened Europe saw Barbary. There is however one regret that I must express; all of them were written by men and give us a masculine view of things. It is a pity that Mary Wortley Montagu, for example, did no more than stop off at Tunis on her way back from Constantinople.

I have decided to treat these texts as a whole; instead of discussing each individual writer's point of view separately, I have attempted to extract a common outlook from the mass of the works taken together. My aim is precisely to see the structure and workings of this system of thought and the common outlook concealed behind the individual expression of a point of view. Hence I have chosen to proceed, as it were, in a circular manner, isolating one by one different problems and the pattern of thought concerning them that emerges from the texts. This approach means that I look at the texts as a group from successively different angles and in a different light; by this means I hope to lay bare the attitudes common to different authors. But first we must have a look at the pre-conceptions existing in European minds concerning Barbary, which is the subject of the first part of this work.

PART ONE

PRECONCEPTIONS

The area with which we are concerned is that part of Africa which was called Barbary in the Eighteenth Century. We should first be clear as to exactly what is meant by this term. First of all, the term 'Barbary' referred, not to the whole of the area north of the Sahara which we now call North Africa or the Maghreb, but only to the northern part of it, that is the coastal plain and the mountains or, in other words, the ports and their hinterland. To the south of this area was what was called the 'Bildegerud' and then south of that the Sahara, mainly unknown to foreigners. Interest in, and knowledge of, Barbary was therefore mainly concentrated on the towns with which the Europeans traded and against which they fought; their surrounding countryside was less known, but there are enough accounts and descriptions for us to have an idea of how the Europeans perceived it and its inhabitants. The other factor that should be pointed out at the beginning is that there was more contact with that part of Barbary that was under Turkish control, in other words the Regencies of Algiers, Tunis and Tripoli, than with the Empire of Morocco which remained more closed to outside influence and commerce. Indeed, on occasion, Morocco is not included in the designation of Barbary, although this is not always the case. In what follows I shall, as I have already said, be mainly concerned with the Regencies and in particular Algiers, which figured more prominently in European consciousness than the others.

These Regencies, under the nominal control of the Sultan in Constantinople, were ruled by the Turkish militia which was completely separated from the rest of the population who had no influence or say in the government. The policy of these states was largely independent of their nominal overlord and they behaved to a certain extent as independent states, which caused the Europeans difficulties in their relations with them. As far as these relations are concerned, I do not propose to go into them, as the political and diplomatic history has already been recounted by other historians[1]. What is relevant for my purpose is the fact that such relations existed; there was a series of wars between the Barbary states and different European countries, there were naval expeditions against the North African corsairs and, when all else failed, treaties for

the return of captives (on both sides, for there were 'Turkish' captives in
Christian galleys as well as Christian 'slaves' in Barbary) and the pay-
ment of tributes to protect commercial shipping. The existing series of
treaties, periodically broken by both sides, is sufficient proof of the continuity of these relations. There were also long-standing commercial relations, going far back into Mediterranean history, although they were in
the Eighteenth Century not as important as those with the eastern end
of the Mediterranean. But the presence of a French factory at La Calle,
belonging to the Compagnie royale d'Afrique, and of a certain number
of foreign merchants in the towns, indicate that it was not negligable. We
should also not forget the particular Spanish ties with Barbary and the
episodic, but very real, Spanish presence at Oran.

Hence it is clear that the northern shore of the Mediterranean was far
from ignorant of its southern counterpart. It did not constitute, as I have
already said, simply a barbaric and mysterious land, even if the countryside and interior were largely unknown to foreigners. The Europeans
were well aware of the states of Algiers, Tunis and Tripoli and even of
the more forbidding Empire of Morocco, of their history, government
and inhabitants. In this respect these North African states played a very
different role in eighteenth-century European consciousness from that
played by the rest of Africa, about which practically nothing was known
and, consequently, the wildest stories circulated. Barbary was not a part
of the world waiting to be discovered or even explored. It was rather part
of the Ottoman Empire, comprising a number of states with which the
European powers had maintained relations, frequently strained. Hence
it constituted a preeminently political problem, and it is from this angle
that the question of the relations between Europe and the Barbary states
has tended to be approached. The history of these relations has been
studied on the basis of treaties, consular reports, foreign office archives
and diplomatic correspondences. The interpretations of this history have
varied, ranging from the traditional one of persistent bad faith on the
part of the barbarous North African 'pirates' to Fisher's attempt to view
the question from a more impartial point of view, even if he has rather
a tendency to exonerate the Barbary states completely, so that he has
been accused of attempting a whitewash, however welcome a less biased
perspective may be.

These very differences of opinion, which sometimes constitute
diametrically opposed interpretations, point to the problems that I wish
to deal with in this work. For the authors of such works are all, in one
way or another, products of the attitudes towards the Maghreb that
emerged in Europe, not only in the colonial period, but also long before.
For many reasons the preconceptions and even prejudices which are

brought to a study of North Africa are in some ways more complex than those concerning other parts of the world. These prejudices — and reactions against them — have informed the writing about the region that made it known to European readers. Such writing has thus helped to reinforce European preconceptions. It is unfortunately not always true that more knowledge means greater understanding, as is abundantly clear from a reading of the works devoted to Algeria during the colonial period. Much has been written about such works, and the influence of the colonial context is evident. But in the preceding period, too, much can be learnt from a study of relations on a level other than political and diplomatic; the preconceptions revealed by pre-colonial writings betray a different relationship between the writer and the object of study, and also bring to light certain constants in European attitudes. In this first part, I shall try to show what were the presuppositions which a European writer brought to a description of Barbary. Even if some aspects of these prejudices have not changed throughout the colonial period and up to the present day, they did not always function in the same way in the Eighteenth Century. They were in general long-standing, built up through the past history of European relations with the Maghreb and even though some were re-worked in the context of 'enlightened' ideas, the force of ancient prejudices remained. I shall not deal here with one emotion-charged topic that I have already mentioned, namely the question of Barbary 'piracy'; this will be discussed in the last part of the book as it was more of a political problem and provided one of the main arguments for conquest by Europeans. But it should not be forgotten that it was one of the clichés conjured up in European minds when North Africa was mentioned, and the terror aroused by the very name of the corsairs should not be underestimated.

The first problem I shall consider is that constituted by the very name 'Barbary', a word which is so overlaid with adverse connotations in European minds that it must immediately have provoked hostile reactions among most people. This is, I think, even more true of the French word *Barbarie* than of the English version. We can see that it did present a problem by looking at the number of discussion of the word's origin and true meaning. There were a certain number of more or less far-fetched attempts to explain the origin of the name without having to introduce connotations of barbarism; d'Herbelot, in his *Bibliothèque orientale* edited by Galland in 1697, gives, following Marmol and subsequent authors, several different etymologies, including one concerning a certain 'Bar', son of an Egyptian king; all refer also to the word 'bar' meaning desert[2]. Despite such attempts at more 'innocent' derivations, Gibbon, in his *Decline and Fall of the Roman Empire*, shows us the true force of the unplea-

sant connotations of the word. Although he reviews the different
etymologies proposed, going back to the Greeks and, after them, the
Romans, whose use of the word 'barbari' to refer to all foreigners outside
the empire was extended to the inhabitants of North Africa, he concludes:

> In every sense it was due to the Moors; the familiar word was borrowed
> from the Latin provincials by the Arabian conquerors, and has justly settled
> as a local denomination ... along the Northern coast of Africa[3].

Here is erudition linked to a perceptible prejudice concerning the barbaric nature of the inhabitants of North Africa.

Whatever attempts at explanation were given, the adverse prejudice
visible in Gibbon's account persisted, with the constant linking of the
name 'Barbary' to barbarian or even barbaric. This led certain writers,
better disposed to the Barbary states, to attempt, apparently in vain, to
combat their readers' prejudices. They were at some pains to demonstrate that the name had nothing to do with the behaviour or degree of
civilisation of the inhabitants. Particularly insistent on this score was
Laugier de Tassy who here, as elsewhere, tried to provide a more balanced view of Algiers in particular, and the whole region in general. He
writes in his first chapter:

> L'idée que nos préjugés attachent à ce nom renferme celles de cruauté, d'in-
> justice, d'irreligion, d'inhumanité. Les ignorants s'imaginent qu'un Barbare
> ne diffère point des bêtes sauvages de l'Afrique et qu'il n'agit que par in-
> stinct et par férocité. Ils croient que c'est là ce qui a fait donner le nom de
> Barbarie au pays, d'où celui de Barbares a passé à ses habitants. Mais les
> relations de plusieurs voyageurs dignes de foi détruisent ces notions in-
> jurieuses. On y apprend qu'il y a plusieurs peuples dans le monde,
> quelques-uns même en Europe, plus ignorants et plus sauvages, et dont les
> coutumes tiennent plus de la férocité que celles des habitants de la Barbarie.
> La plus grande partie de ces peuples sont aujourd'hui fort humains et
> gouvernés par des lois[4].

> (The idea that, due to our prejudices, we associate with this name includes
> those of cruelty, injustice, irreligion, inhumanity. The ignorant imagine
> that a Barbarian is no different from the wild beasts of Africa and that he
> only acts from instinct and ferocity. They believe that this is what gave the
> name of Barbary to the country, whence that of Barbarians passed to its in-
> habitants. But the accounts of several travellers worthy of confidence belie
> these injurious ideas. We learn that there are several peoples in the world,
> some even in Europe, who are more ignorant and more savage and whose
> customs are more ferocious that those of the inhabitants of Barbary. The
> greatest part of these peoples are today very humane and governed by
> laws.)

And he continues by reviewing the different derivations that we have already seen, from Marmol's 'desert' to the Romans' 'foreigners'.

This passage is interesting in several ways. It confirms the existence of prejudices in the minds of Europeans, created by the very name used to refer to North Africa; it also shows a desire on the part of Laugier to combat these prejudices, but not necessarily by giving a more rational explanation of the name as others had already done. Unlike, for example, Gibbon, who gives the same etymology, he refers to travellers' accounts to show that as a description it is untrue, and that the inhabitants are not barbarians at all, but civilised people. He also tries to introduce a more balanced note by pointing out that there are certain inhabitants of Europe itself who are much more deserving of the epithet 'barbarian' than the so-called barbarians of Barbary. This attempt to combat Europocentric prejudice and provide a classification in terms of the country's degree of social evolution and behaviour rather than in terms of national origin, is indicative of a willingness to approach these regions and peoples with an open mind. It is interesting to observe a similar reaction from a very different source, which bears witness both to the persistence and widespread nature of the prejudice and to the continuation of attempts to combat it in the Eighteenth Century. It is the reaction of a Russian naval officer, M.G. Kokovtsov, who wrote a journal of his visits to the Barbary coast in 1776 and 1777. We read, at the entry for 21st June 1776:

> The Romans called this people 'Barbarians' as they did all those whom they had conquered, and the Europeans have conserved the habit until today, although these peoples do not at all deserve such a contemptuous name. It is true that they are not cultivated but, like all other peoples, they have their own origin, which cannot be criticised, and their customs. The name of Barbarian only suits a ferocious, lawless and cruel people, but the Barbaresques seem to me in general to have mild manners and to be more welcoming to strangers than many Europeans, in particular the Sicilians, the Calabrians and some parts of the Spanish people[5].

It is interesting to note, in passing, the hostility of a Northerner towards the Southern Europeans.

I shall be returning later on in more detail to the question of barbarism and civilisation, and the way North Africans were perceived in this context. For the moment, I merely wish to point out that despite learned explanations of the origin of the name 'Barbary', the image it evoked could not easily be eradicated from European minds and inevitably coloured all approaches to the Maghreb and its inhabitants.

The other word that was certain to provoke immediate hostility in the European reader's mind, and which was commonly used to refer to the

Barbaresques was 'Turk'. There was a certain amount of confusion as to the meaning of the term and its applicability to the inhabitants of the Regencies; as we shall see below, there was an awareness that the mass of their population was not Turkish. But to the extent that these states were formally part of the Ottoman Empire and that the rulers, the militia and naval captains were of Turkish or Levantine origin, the Barbaresques with whom the Europeans had most contact were seen to be, and referred to as, Turks. In fact, they were more often of Greek or Armenian origin, but as they were Levantines and subjects of the Ottoman Empire, such subtleties did not usually bother Europeans. Now the very word 'Turk' was calculated to strike fear into the heart of all inhabitants of Christendom, for they had been for centuries its chief enemies, representatives of the Antichrist and the very personification of cruelty and ferocity. This image is so well-documented as to need little illustration; suffice to say, with P. Coles, that they were "the object of loathing and fear"[6]. Although this remark refers to sixteenth-century Europe and there were, as he explains, a certain number of attempts to provide a more balanced picture of this radically different and menacing civilisation, this popular image of the Turk remained unchanged in the Eighteenth Century; as Earle writes in his book on the Corsairs, "the very word 'Turk' in English was an epithet meaning barbarous, savage and cruel"[7]. Galland sums up the general attitude towards the Turks in the 'Discours pour servir de Préface' to d'Herbelot's *Bibliothèque orientale*, which attempted to present a more balanced picture:

> par leur nom seul, les Turcs sont tellement décriés, qu'il suffit ordinairement de les nommer pour signifier une Nation barbare, grossière et d'une ignorance achevée, et sous leur nom l'on entend parler de ceux qui sont sous la domination de l'Empire ottomane[8].

> (by their very name, the Turks are so decried that it is usually sufficient to name them in order to denote a barbarian, rude and completely ignorant Nation, and by this name we mean those who are under the domination of the Ottoman Empire.)

Equally telling is a remark to be found in the works of the chevalier d'Arvieux, who visited different parts of the Ottoman Empire in the Seventeenth Century; the accounts of his travels, published in the early Eighteenth Century, were much read and quoted. He explains that, in general usage, the epithet 'Turk' or 'barbare' (apparently interchangable terms) is given to those whose cruelty and 'mauvaises inclinations' are to be emphasized[9]. As d'Arvieux is concerned to give a more impartial account, he remarks immediately afterwards that as soon as one gets to know these people, one discovers the falsehood of such ideas. But this was the remark of someone who had travelled extensively in the Turkish

Empire and who spoke its languages, and it was far from being the opinion of the majority of Europeans, whose prejudices d'Arvieux so well describes. Thus we find Volney writing in 1788 in his *Considérations sur la Guerre des Turcs* of the Turks' fanaticism, ignorance and prejudices. He even goes as far as to accuse them of being responsible for the plague, saying that before the Ottomans there was no plague in the Mediterranean and that lazarettos were unheard-of: "C'est par ces barbares que sont venus ces fléaux; ce sont eux qui, par leur stupide fanatisme, perpétuent la contagion en renouvellant ses germes"[10]. He almost seems to be equating the Turks themselves with the plague! It is true that Volney was above all attacking the French government's policy towards the Ottomans and that this condemnation of the Empire was accompanied by sympathy for the peoples under their control, including the Moors of Barbary; nevertheless I do not think that one can deny that he is here voicing the common, long-standing prejudice existing in European minds. The stereotype of the Turks, which had been that of a barbarian but warlike and threatening civilisation had by now become, as their dynamism had somewhat waned and the threat they presented to European states diminished, that of ignorant, fanatical and cruel barbarians under whose despotic rule the peoples of their empire had sunk into misery and stupidity. The question of the image of the Turk in the Eighteenth Century has been studied, in the case of France, by Werner Krauss who discerns a changing attitude with the Enlightenment, particularly in the case of Voltaire[11]; it would however be a mistake to believe that the old hostility had totally vanished, as the case of Volney shows.

Part of this hostility can be accounted for by their supposed fanaticism, which brings us to another aspect of the problem; the word 'Turk' was frequently simply a synonym for 'Moslem' or, to use the eighteenth-century term, 'Mohammedan'. Thus 'to turn Turk' was the usual expression to describe the action of the 'renegade' who converted to Islam. It is, as a result, difficult to distinguish, in European prejudices, how much of the hostility to the Turks simply reflects the traditional Christian hatred for Islam. To give another example of this confusion, we could quote again from Laugier de Tassy's *plaidoyer* for a greater understanding of the Barbaresques; he refers to the excessive nature of the Christians' hostility towards "les Turcs, et tous les autres Mahometans", which would seem to indicate that the hostility he is describing towards the Turks is largely conditioned by their religion[12].

The question of Christian attitudes towards Islam is in fact a more complex phenomenon, and we must look at it in greater detail, as it played a very important role in conditioning European perceptions of

Barbary. For these Turks, barbarians, or whatever other epithet was
chosen, were indisputably 'Mohammedan'. However ignorant a European might be about North Africa, at least he knew that it was Moslem
long before it was part of the Ottoman Empire. It was from here that the
conquest of Spain had been launched and it was here that the Spanish
'Moors' retreated after the Reconquista of the Peninsula by the Catholic
rulers. Blood-curdling accounts of the Islamic conquest of North Africa
and their supposedly destructive and fanatical fury abounded.

Islam had for centuries been the enemy, whether personified in the
Turk, its contemporary manifestation, or in its earlier shape, the
'Saracen' or Moor. It was the force which had threatened Christendom
from the East, the South and the West, which had controlled the
Mediterranean Sea, and against which a permanent crusade had been
launched. It figured, consequently, largely in the popular imagination
despite general ignorance as to its exact nature. But this force was no
longer, by the Eighteenth Century, what it had been in the Middle Ages
when, while Christendom was in a state of ignorance and squalor, the
Moslem Empire had known a rich civilisation whose superior learning
had been recognised and from which Europe had a lot to learn, and had
learnt a lot. It was now, in the form of the Ottoman Empire, generally
perceived to be in a state of decline and hence less of a threat. It was
precisely now that Islam became an object of study with attempts at a ge-
nuine comprehension of this strange and different world. This new attitude can be seen in the translations of the Koran into French, English
and other European languages, in the vogue for the *Thousand and One
Nights* and in works such as d'Herbelot's *Bibliothèque orientale*[13]. But at the
same time there persisted an image of Moslems as fanatics and of
Mohammed as an imposter. This latter theme was particularly
widespread in the Eighteenth Century and is found both in Christian
works of propaganda and in anti-religious tracts such as the famous *Traité
des trois imposteurs* which circulated clandestinely and figured the Prophet
in the company of Moses and Jesus[14]. The development of European attitudes towards Islam during this period has already been studied by
several authors and it is not the place to go into it here in great detail,
for the subject is complex and attitudes varied greatly. The popular view
of Islam can be summed up with a remark by H. Djait in his book
L'Europe et l'Islam:

> La vision populaire oscille entre l'image d'un Orient splendide et
> merveilleux, celle d'un Oriental lascif et cruel, d'un Barbaresque fruste et
> violent, le tout coiffé par la vision d'un Islam religieux fanatique, agressif,
> simple, élémentaire[15].

(The popular vision oscillates between the image of a splendid and marvellous Orient, a lascivious and cruel Oriental, and a crude and violent Barbaresque, the whole spanned by a view of a fanatical, aggressive, simple and elementary Islamic religion.)

This was not necessarily the view of specialists or of enlightened thinkers, as we shall see; but it could not fail to play a role in influencing the way Europeans saw countries that were part of the Islamic world. What I would like to discuss here is the way in which such perceptions informed the image of Barbary held by Europeans. We must first see how the traditional popular prejudices subsisted, before looking for traces of a new understanding. It is evident that exacerbated Christian prejudices are to be found in the accounts by the 'Pères Rédempteurs' who, in addition to being monks, were concerned to present the North Africans in the worst possible light in order the arouse their readers' sympathies and to raise the money to buy back the captives who, in their eyes, risked not only their lives but also their salvation at the hands of the Infidels. But what of lay observers who had no such axe to grind?

The existence of anti-Islamic prejudice is confirmed by Laugier de Tassy's attempt to combat it. He writes in the preface to his work on Algiers:

On m'a demandé plus d'une fois s'ils avaient quelque idée de la Divinité. Mais je suis persuadé que si ces personnes venaient à converser avec des Mahometans deguisés en chrétiens, elles leur trouveraient autant de raison et solidité qu'à ces derniers; mais qu'ils reprissent le turban, aussitôt toutes leurs qualités disparaîtraient[16].

(I have been asked many times if they have an idea of the Divinity. But I am convinced that if these people happened to converse with Mohammedans disguised as Christians, they would find they had as much reason and solidity as the latter; but as soon as they put their turbans back on, all their qualities would immediately vanish.)

This incidentally confirms not only the prejudice which an impartial observer had to combat, but also the general ignorance concerning the Islamic religion to be found in Europe, despite the works which had tried to explain its dogmas. We would not expect the same ignorance from those who visited the countries of Barbary. There is nevertheless a persistent tendency to interpret what is seen in terms of the Christian religion, which in itself betrays a certain ignorance. Thus d'Arvieux in his description of Tunis talks of the 'clergy', and gives its hierarchy as follows: "mufti, cadi, imam ou Marabouts des Mosquées"[17]. In general, these writings do not go into great detail about the religion, preferring to refer the reader to existing works on the subject. But we do find reproduced a certain number of stereotypes concerning Islam and the Moslems. One of

the elements that constantly crops up concerns the supposed fatalism of
the Moslems (or 'Turks'), and their belief in predestination. This is one
of the first remarks made by d'Arvieux on his arrival in the Levant, at
Smyrna in 1653; he describes the reactions of the different nationalities
to an earthquake, and compares his own compatriots' fear to the
behaviour of the Turks, who wait fatalistically at home. Their belief in
predestination apparently persuades them of the futility of attempting to
escape their fate[18]. Over a century later Poiret, who goes into very little
detail as far as the religion is concerned, does insist at some length on the
Barbaresques' belief in predestination and their refusal to take adequate
measures to defend themselves from the plague, for example. He
describes their tranquillity in the face of all adversities, simply remarking
'Dieu le veut', and he recounts the stoical reaction of a father to the death
of his son. But he carefully explains that it is not, as we might think, a
heroic attitude, for such behaviour is only for the 'Arabs' a consequence
of their 'system'. He does not therefore find this stoicism admirable (not
surprisingly, in a man of sentiment), and he writes that it is little different
from the Christians' resignation in the face of Providence, but simply
taken to extremes and ill-understood[19]. Similar remarks concerning the
plague are to be found in a later work, Rehbinder's *Nachrichtungen*; when
discussing the deplorable state of medicine in Algiers, the German author
devotes quite some space to the plague which ravaged the country during
Poiret's visit, beginning in Tunis in 1784 and spreading westwards.
Referring to Poiret, Rehbinder ascribes the lack of proper measures to
combat the epidemic in part to the fatalism of the Turks, instilled in them
by their religion (although, it is true, he also mentions the Turkish rulers'
indifference to the fate of their Moorish subjects)[20]. Here again we meet
the plague which, as we have seen, Volney, writing soon after this
epidemic, seems to attribute to and almost equate with the Turks. It is
interesting to note that Venture de Paradis, despite the hostility which
he frequently displays towards Barbary and its inhabitants, has a different reaction; describing the same stoicism on the part of the Tunisians, he speaks of their 'fermeté héroïque' thanks to the doctrine of
predestination[21].

   A more serious accusation concerning Islam, of which traces are to be
found in writing on Barbary, is that its followers were ignorant. This is
a widespread opinion, despite European recognition of their past splendour and awareness of the learning associated with Moslem civilisation;
knowledge of this past does not prevent writers from attributing the ignorance they find to the Islamic religion, however paradoxical this may
appear. This is the opinion expressed by Shaw — who, it is true, was an
Anglican clergyman, although he was more interested apparently in

classical Antiquity than in Christian apologetics, and was certainly not a missionary. He writes, when discussing the 'Learning, Arts, Manufactures, Habits, Customs' of Barbary, that "The liberal Arts and Sciences continue to be as they have been for many Ages, in a low state and condition among the Mohametans", which implies that the ignorance he describes, and which is common to all Moslem countries, is due to the religion[22]. D'Argens, the anti-clerical 'philosophe' is even more specific. In his *Lettres juives*, he has his Jewish traveller describe the ignorance in Algiers and Tunis, and is moved to the following reflection:

> Le triste sort qu'ont eu tant de superbes villes, dont une partie a été détruite par les Mahometans, m'a souvent fait réfléchir aux Préjudices qu'ils avaient portés aux Sciences et aux Beaux-Arts. Combien d'Edifices n'ont-ils pas renversés, combien de statues antiques n'ont-ils pas brisés, dans quel Etat pitoyable n'ont-ils point reduit toute la Grèce[23]...

> (The sorry fate of so many proud towns, of which part has been destroyed by the Mohamedans, has often led me to reflect on the harm they have done to Science and the Arts. How many edifices have they not demolished, how many classical statues broken, to what a piteous state have they not reduced the whole of Greece...)

And he considers battles won against the Moslems, or Turks, as so many victories against ignorance. This accusation of — more than mere ignorance — deliberate destruction of learning and civilisation, was a long-standing one among Christians, and we here find it adopted by a representative of the Enlightenment. In this d'Argens differs from Voltaire, who explains that Barbary was civilised by the 'Arabs' and does not at all attribute its later decline to their religion. He gives no reason for the poor state of science in the Regencies, but in the case of Morocco he attributes it to the despotism of its Emperors and the character of the 'Moors'[24]. Nevertheless, d'Argens's accusation is further developed at the end of the century by the German Rehbinder, himself a product of enlightened ideas. He explains that Islam is not only responsible for the ignorance of the inhabitants of the Algiers Regency, but actively prevents any progress in learning, so that they have remained in a state of Mediaeval superstition and have been excluded from the general European *Aufklärung*[25]. Other writers on Barbary insist frequently on the ignorance of its inhabitants, although it is not always so clearly linked to their religion. The idea is doubtless present in their minds, however, for they couple such descriptions with remarks concerning the fanaticism of these peoples and their ridiculous superstitions. This insistence on superstition crops up frequently and is another trait associated with Islam. Not everyone, however, goes quite as far as Shaw, who writes, "No Nation in the World is so much given to Superstition as the Arabs, or even as the Mohametans in general"[26]. Most writers, like for example Poiret, content themselves with general remarks on the ignorance and superstition of the 'Arabs' without going into its causes or insisting at length on the connection with Islam[27]. Despite their belief in the fatalism, superstition and ignorance of Moslems, in general eighteenth-century writers do not express the same degree of unthinking hostility as Admiral Bauffremont in the report of his journey to the Mediterranean and the Levant in 1766; after giving a very hostile account of Algiers and its government, the Admiral concludes:

> Tous les peuples qui admettent l'Alcoran font naître plus ou moins les mêmes réflexions; c'est partout le plus odieux et le plus méprisable des gouvernements[28].

> (All the peoples who recognise the Koran give rise to more or less the same reflection; it is everywhere the most odious and despicable of governments.)

The same instinctive antagonism towards all things Moslem is found in the *Mémoire* written by the French vice-consul Vallière or in the letters of Alexander Jardine, sent on an official mission to the Emperor of Morocco in 1788, and who is unremittingly hostile. He talks of 'Mahomedism' as superstitious and fanatical, and considers its 'true spirit' to be 'perpetual War'[29].

A comparison of such hatred, shown by official envoys who were not men of letters, with the attitudes manifested by the majority of enlightened writers towards Barbary, does reveal a difference. While we have seen some evidence of more or less concealed preconceptions, indicating a tendency to interpret what they saw in Barbary through preexisting stereotypes of Islam, such remarks do not represent a systematic desire to denigrate or to condemn out of hand everything connected with Islam. Unlike Bauffremont, Vallière or Jardine, most eighteenth-century commentators do not see Islam primarily as the enemy. A greater willingness to understand the Moslem world is, I think, present, and it is most clearly evident in Laugier de Tassy's appeal to the reader. This greater desire for comprehension is an element of enlightened thought. According to H. Djait, "le 18° siècle européen, dans ses noyaux centraux, fut tout entier traversé par un souci de compréhension de l'Islam"[30]. Without going into the question of what is meant by the word 'core', we should perhaps be a little more circumspect; we have after all seen the hostility of d'Argens and Volney's ambiguous attitude, and Diderot shows few signs of a desire to understand Islam[31]. There is no denying, nevertheless, that the Enlightenment did bring a new attitude, perceived also by M. Rodinson who considers that the Eighteenth Century saw the Moslem world with understanding and sympathy[32]; This new attitude is evident in the writings of Boulainviller, Gibbon or Voltaire and traces of it can be found in works on Barbary. The spirit of the *Bibliothèque orientale* did bear some fruit.

To quote Laugier de Tassy again, the appeal for greater understanding contained in the preface to his work on Algiers repeats several typically 'enlightened' themes. He insists that all peoples are essentially the same, with the same defects, and that no one way of life is inherently more ridiculous than another; he expresses the hope that his book will diminish the prejudices of 'those who are capable of reflecting', and appeals to his readers not to hate and despise others simply because of their different religion or nationality. He claims that a traveller who judges seriously and impartially will recognise the injustice of 'des idées faites'[33]. There are signs that his appeal was heard, at least in part and that some observers of Barbary were permeated with something of the spirit of the Enlightenment, even though none could hope to free himself of all prejudices. Thus Poiret, despite his final disillusion with the people he finds in Barbary, declares in a note at the beginning of his first letter from Barbary, with a trace of the true 'philosophical' spirit, his belief in the injustice of hatred and wars based on religion:

> Les guerres les plus injustes auxquelles le fanatisme donnait le nom de *saintes,* portées tant en Orient qu'en Afrique, ont révolté contre nous d'immenses nations qui ne nous avaient fait alors d'autre mal, que celui de suivre le religion de Mahomet, tandis que nous suivions celle de Jésus[34].

> (The most unjust wars, given by fanaticism the name of *holy,* waged both in the Orient and in Africa, have turned against us immense nations who had done us no other harm than to follow the religion of Mohamed while we followed that of Jesus.)

The Moslems' hatred of Christians is hereby explained, and in part justified, by the fanaticism and cruelty of the latter in the past and in particular by the Crusades.

A similar attitude is present in Gibbon's *Decline and Fall of the Roman Empire*; the author's sympathy towards Islam is well-known and serves as a means of condemning the Christian religion by comparison. Thus not only does he give a long, favourable description of the learning and culture of the Arabs, but he also writes of their religion, "A philosophic Atheist might subscribe to the popular creed of the Mahometans; a creed too sublime perhaps for our present faculties"[35]. This is far from the image of Moslems as fanatical and superstitious. He also rejects the frequently repeated story of the destruction of the Alexandria library by the conquering Moslems, which even Voltaire repeats in the *Essai sur les Moeurs*; Gibbon points out that the story is both unlikely and unattested by contemporary sources[36]. He even considers that the Moors had contributed to the civilisation of inland North Africa, a remark which goes against the common view of them as spreading ignorance and desolation[37]. Such an attitude is still very perceptible at the beginning of the next century in the works of James Grey Jackson, who argues for a greater understanding of Barbary (even though his aim is mainly to further British trade and influence). In his *Account of the Empire of Morocco,* he attempts in one chapter to combat the general hostility towards Islam and the errors of most Christian writers on this subject, even observing that Islam "approaches nearer to the Christian religion in its moral precepts, than any other with which we are acquainted". He concludes,

> it will be perceived that the principles of the Mohammedan religion are neither so pernicious nor so absurd as many have imagined. They have sometimes been vilified from error or for the purpose of exalting the Christian doctrine; but that doctrine is too pure and celestial to need any such aids[38].

We can see in all of these remarks a preoccupation that we can qualify as typically enlightened, and that is the use of Islam as a means of criticizing the Christian religion, either openly, by comparison, or, more discreetly, by suggesting that the latter is too intolerant. It is in this way that the reference to Islam is frequently used by Voltaire (for example in the *Essai sur les moeurs*) who was willing to enlist any allies in the fight against the Catholic Church. Thus he uses as the mouthpiece of wisdom in *Candide* an old 'derviche', also referred to as a Turk, living in the suburbs of Constantinople where Candide, Cunégonde and the others end up after their travels and misfortunes[39]. But there was also another way of using Islam as a means of attacking Christianity, in which it played a totally different role: the supposed ignorance and fanaticism of the Moslems could become the symbol of all religions, including Christianity. This seems to be the aim of d'Argens, whose hostility to Islam we have already seen. His Jewish correspondent in Barbary speaks of the Christians massacred in Tripoli when it was conquered by the 'Turks'; but he uses this traditional accusation of Moslem ferocity not simply in order to attack Islam, but as a means of attacking all religions and particularly forced conversions and intolerance such as those practised by the Spanish, or even the work of the Christian missionaries in China[40]. For d'Argens's aim was not primarily to describe Barbary, of which he had, at most, little first-hand knowledge, but rather to lead his readers to reflect on the absurdities of their own society and in particular of the Catholic Church. We should thus be very attentive of the way Islam was used by 'enlightened' authors, whose motives in writing about this subject were frequently complex. Even d'Argens, despite the hostility towards Moslems and their superstitions that we have already seen, quotes a letter from Leibniz to La Croze in which 'Mahométisme' is described as a sort of Deism like natural religion and is thus considered to be a useful antidote to Paganism[41]. We shall have occasion to come back to d'Argens in more detail in different contexts.

To return to those with a less openly 'philosophical' motivation, there are here too indications of an attempt at presenting a more balanced view of Islam. One aspect of this is the insistence on Moslem toleration, as compared to the intolerance of Catholic nations. Even d'Arvieux remarks frequently on the tolerance and latitude in religious matters to be found in the nations he visited. It is for example interesting to see that when describing his discussions with his friend Mahmoud Effendi in Saida, a learned and interesting man, he goes as far as to write that they spoke of religion as freely as if they had been in England (the touchstone in matters of religious toleration in the early Enlightenment). Later, speaking of Tunis, for which he consistently shows much greater sympathy than for Algiers, he writes:

> Tunis est un Pays de liberté, la Religion n'y gêne personne, on prie Dieu quand on veut, on jeûne quand on ne peut faire autrement, on boit du vin quand on a de l'argent, on s'enyvre quand on en boit trop, et qui que ce soit n'y trouve rien à redire[42].

> (Tunis is a land of liberty; religion disturbs no-one; they pray God when they wish, fast when they cannot do otherwise, drink wine when they have money, get drunk when they drink too much, and no-one finds any harm in it.)

Here we see a willingness to present an image of a Moslem country which is at variance with the belief generally accepted in Islam's fanatical nature; d'Arvieux contributes to a view of its followers as tolerant and even 'enlightened', particularly when compared to Catholic nations. Such an opinion is further reinforced by evidence of their toleration of other religions and of their willingness to allow them to practise freely. Again concerning Tunis, d'Arvieux writes that those who practise the Christian religion have a 'liberté entière' as long as they observe a minimum of discretion and do not attempt to proselytise[43]. This is far from being an isolated remark. Laugier de Tassy makes the same point in connection with Algiers, emphasizing the fact that all religions are tolerated, as does Le Roy, writing of its rulers' "tolérance sans bornes" for all religions[44]. Similar remarks are found in a large number of accounts, including those by Desfontaines, Kokovtsov, or even Vallière, despite his hostility towards almost everything Algerian[45]. But Shaler in 1826 still needs to insist on the Algerians' toleration and to combat the persistent view of them as fanatics and bigots[46].

We find, then, in the writers on Barbary evidence of the more sympathetic eighteenth-century attitude towards Islam and a reflection of the typically enlightened concern with the question of toleration, which was an important issue in most European countries during this period. Those who argued for toleration in Catholic countries and particularly in France, could point not only to England (where toleration was not as unlimited as its admirers would have their readers believe), but also to the supposedly barbarian Turks, which was enough to put civilised countries to shame. Evidence for their tolerant attitude had already been provided by d'Herbelot's *Bibliothèque orientale*, in the article DIN (la foi), where the author writes that in the second chapter of the Koran, the Prophet forbade any forcible conversion to Islam, quoting the passage in question[47]. The same information is provided by English specialists on Islam who likewise refuted accusations of Moslem intolerance and cruelty[48]. This doctrinal evidence of Islam's tolerance was confirmed by accounts of practice in the Ottoman Empire similar to those we have quoted concerning Barbary; they enabled Voltaire, comparatively sympathetic to Islam as we have seen, to write in the *Essai sur les moeurs,* "Aucune nation chrétienne ne souffre que les Turcs aient chez elle une mosquée, et les Turcs permettent que les Grecs aient des églises"[49]. In this respect Voltaire, like Gibbon, was more enlightened than the *Encyclopédie*, which in the article TOLERATION continued to present the followers of Mohamed as converting by the sword. The *Encyclopédie's* general lack of sympathy for Islam indicated the limits of the Enlightenment's understanding of the Moslem world.

But the question of toleration was not the only one on which longstanding Christian and European prejudices were combatted by eighteenth-century thinkers in their attempt to reach a more balanced judgement of their own and alien cultures. A problem of particular concern to us here is that of the Barbary states' treatment of their Christian captives (or slaves as they were usually called). This subject was one which was charged with emotion and far-reaching political ramifications, and I shall have to come back to it later on. Here I would like to discuss it in the context of attitudes towards Islam. As I have already said, the 'pères Rédempteurs' who were sent to Barbary to redeem the corsairs' captives had a vested interest in presenting their condition in as harsh a light as possible in order to excite the compassion of the public who could thus be persuaded to contribute generously towards the prisoners' liberation; as an added bonus they hoped to excite Christian zeal against the

Infidel. However, the accuracy of their accounts was immediately called into question and their motives criticised. D'Arvieux is very direct on this subject when he refers to the common belief that the poor Christian slaves in Barbary suffered cruel and inhuman torments; after calling the monks' accounts 'pious lies' in order to encourage the charity of the faithful, he explains that he himself held the same erroneous belief until he travelled to Tunis and saw for himself that they were in general well-treated, despite individual exceptions[50]. A similar attack on the pious lies is made over a century later by the German Rehbinder, this time with reference to Algiers. In his introductory review of previous works on this Regency, he is particularly scathing about the Catholic priests and their bigoted writings[51]. In this respect we imagine that d'Argens is torn between his hostility towards the Turks and his desire to attack Catholic intolerance; apparently the latter wins, for he insists that the accounts of the slaves' sufferings are 'outrées' and that the torments which the Turks are supposed to inflict on their captives are largely imaginary. He seizes this opportunity to launch an attack on the Europeans' treatment of their own captives and the misery endured by the Turkish slaves in Christian galleys. He even declares that if the 'Africans' had orators who were able to move their listeners by such 'touching and pathetic' speeches, they would make just as many pompous declarations as the Christians about the sufferings of their own compatriots. He pours scorn on the pious monks with their accounts of burnings, impalings and cutting into pieces, calculating that according to them, more slaves have died in one short period than have ever been killed, or are ever likely to be killed until the end of time in the whole Islamic world![52] Voltaire shows something of the same preoccupation when he recounts in *Candide* how the 'vieille' met the corsairs, for he points out that the activities of the Turkish corsairs are paralleled by those of 'Messieurs les religieux chevaliers de Malte'[53]. Part of this passage concerning the Moorish pirates is quoted by L. Valensi as an example of eighteenth-century prejudices about the Maghreb, but she leaves out the comparison with the Maltese; while Voltaire's acceptance of certain false stereotypes (such as for example that the Moors are black barbarians) is undeniable, one should not, in all honesty, deny his attempt at giving a more balanced presentation of the facts[54].

Even among those less suspect of ulterior motives, we find descriptions of the condition of the Christian slaves in Barbary which belie the lurid accounts of the religious propagandists. La Condamine, for one, who shows scant sympathy for Algiers and its inhabitants, remarks that the slaves are not ill-treated[55]. A similar account is given by Desfontaines, and by Peyssonnel who also describes the slaves' liberty to exercise their religion, concluding "en un mot, c'est de toutes les esclavitudes celle qui est la moins rude"[56]. There are likewise denials of the Christian propagandists' accounts of forced conversions. Several writers, like Laugier de Tassy or Venture de Paradis later on, explain that the Barbaresques have no interest in attempting to convert their slaves, for they would thereby become free men and their owner would lose the ransom money paid by their government, their family or the monks (which was, of course, the main reason for taking slaves in the first place)[57]. The same fact comes out in Vallière's account, particularly interesting as, not being a work intended for publication, he had no need to score propaganda points[58]. Another diplomat, the Baron de Tott, author of a *Mémoire sur les Turcs et les Tartares* which is unremittingly hostile towards the Turks, was also favourably impressed when he stopped off in Tunis. He describes the slaves as well clothed, fed and treated, remarking that the Europeans are the only peoples who ill-treat their slaves; and he compares the lot of these Christian captives with that of the 'Nègres de nos Colonies' who are much worse off[59]. Such descriptions of the lenient treatment of captives are echoed as late as 1826 by the U.S. consul in Algiers, William Shaler, who writes that their condition is "not generally worse than that of prisoners of war in many civilized Christian countries", and like many before him he describes how many have become rich through the commerce in which the slaves engaged[60]. In 1809 James Grey Jackson made similar remarks about Morocco and made a favorable comparison with the situation of the slaves in the West Indies[61]. But despite numerous such testimonies, the myth of barbarity towards slaves, fostered also by the ever-popular romanced accounts written by ex-slaves, has had a tenacious existence; it was apparently corroborated by accounts such as that of another official American envoy, Mordecai Noah who described Algiers in 1819 as "a sink of iniquity and curse of humanity", calling for a crusade to end the horrors of slavery which he describes in pathetic detail[62]. The Italian Pananti, himself a former slave, displays the same attitude. As we shall see below, the existence of this slavery was one of the justifications frequently evoked for an invasion of Barbary, and even today the monks' accounts are sometimes taken at their face value. A recently published book called *Gunfire in Barbary* written by two naval historians gives lurid contemporary illustrations of the tortures supposedly undergone by the slaves in Algiers (although the text is slightly toned down) and purports to describe how the British bombardment of Algiers in 1816 "ended white Christian slavery"[63]. They are simply continuing a long-standing tradition which enlightened eighteenth-century writers had tried to combat but which reemerges in force in the early Nineteenth Century, despite a few exceptions. We shall have ample occasion to note later on in this book the changes in attitudes undergone around the turn of the century, which parallel that witnessed in the evolution of the European view of Islam. Concerning this particular question, the rise of an 'Orientalist' school, with the institutionalisation of studies of Eastern languages and religions in the late Eighteenth and early Nineteenth Centuries, has been brilliantly studied by E. Said in his controversial book *Orientalism*; the new attitude to Islam is part of this development. Islam could no longer be, as it was for certain enlightened thinkers of the Eighteenth Century, a civilisation which could be known — however superficially — sympathetically and used to show up the inadequacies of European civilisation. As the threat that it had presented to Christendom diminished, it declined in the European consciousness to become a rather barbaric and primitive object of study; until its teeth had been completely drawn, however, Christians still saw it as the enemy, albeit as now a rather more puny one. Rodinson sums up the change of attitude, following that of the Middle Ages which saw the Oriental as an enemy but an equal, and the Eighteenth Century for whom he was another human being; he now becomes 'un être à part', an alien being who is treated with patronising condescendence even when he is praised, and thus the concept of 'Homo islamicus' is born[64].

This changed approach to the Islamic world can, I think, be found in the writings of Venture de Paradis, an 'Orientalist' of the late Eighteenth Century who was, significantly, not only an Arabic scholar but also a diplomat and interpreter who travelled widely all over Barbary and the Levant and accompanied Napoleon's expedition to Egypt, during which he died. He was frequently quoted as an expert on all things Ottoman. In his manuscript notes on Barbary, published only a century later, there are traces of hostility towards Islam which verge on the 'crusading' spirit. In the notes that he wrote in answer to questions from the abbé Raynal, he remarks that the war against the infidel is one of the fundamental laws of Islam, quoting texts to prove it, and endorses the remark from the *Histoire des Deux Indes* that 'celui qui apprendra l'art militaire aux Turcs sera l'ennemi du genre humain'[65]. This is consistent with the stereotypes concerning the barbarous and fanatical Turks that many enlightened writers were attempting to combat, and seems to show, despite the author's erudition, a certain continuity with Christian prejudices which reemerged in force in the Nineteenth Century. We could also mention the parallel that Venture draws between Algiers and Malta, their constitutions, organisation and so on, in which he underlines the similarity between the two corsair states and shows how they were both instituted in order to further their respective religions and to carry on the holy war against the infidel. Although at one point he apparently criticizes such an

aim, in the Voltairean remark to the effect that they both cut men's
throats in the name of a clement and forgiving God, nevertheless the
main thrust of his argument does not appear to be a defence of enlightened ideas, for he terminates by regretting that the knights of Malta have
apparently forgotten their original motivation, while the Algerians are
still busy assuring Moslem triumphs over the Christian nations[66]. This
betrays more of the crusading spirit than of enlightenment, and shows
that at the end of the Eighteenth Century the Turkish Empire was far
from being universally considered as a spent force. Venture's ambiguity,
which reflects, I think, a persistent religious prejudice, is also apparent
in a remark by Poiret who was in many respects a 'philosophe' and influenced by Rousseauism; visiting the site of Hippone, he reflects on the
ruins of St. Augustine's town and remarks that in the place of a Christian
people led by their bishop in the paths of virtue, he finds a 'perverse and
wicked race of men' who execrate the very name of the Christians[67].

The most frequently found aspect of the traditional stereotype of the
Moslems which we find reemerging at the turn of the century is perhaps
the view of them as ignorant and of Islam as a religion which is a positive
hindrance to learning. Rehbinder's reflections on their exclusion from the
Aufklärung have already been noted and indicate that the attack came not
only from the Christians but also from those influenced by enlightened
ideas. 'Enlightened' hostility towards Islam can be seen in the writings of
Raynal; in the *Histoire des Deux Indes* we find the belief expressed that of
all the political and religious systems that afflict the human race, it is the
Moslems' which allows least liberty[68]. The same hostility is present in
Volney's remarks quoted above. The combination of long-standing
Christian prejudices concerning Islam and a new hostility deriving from
aspects of enlightened thought, despite eighteenth-century attempts at a
greater understanding of the Moslem world, is thus present in the more
aggressive attitude of the late Eighteenth and early Nineteeth Centuries.
It is this point of view which has, in the main, prevailed up to the present
day. It is found for example in J. Leyden's anonymously published
Historical and Philosophical Sketch of the Discoveries and Settlement of the Euro-
peans in Northern and Western Africa at the Close of the Eighteenth Century (a title
which, probably intentionally, recalls that of the *Histoire des Deux Indes*),
which contains a chapter on the character of the inhabitants of Barbary.
Here we can read remarks on "the intolerance and irrationality of the
Mahometan religion" which amongst other things "checks the progress of
truth"[69]. Particular hostility is to be found in the work on Algiers written
by the Italian Pananti, whose condemnation of almost everything he sees
is ferocious and who, at the outset, criticises the 'bigoted Mohametan'[70].
The American envoy Noah, unlike his later compatriot Shaler, finds

nothing good here and again attributes the lack of progress in all fields to the religion, which he sees as a barrier to advancement as it "teaches intolerance and justifies despotism"[71]. In 1826 Peuchot, who edited Raynal's unpublished texts on Barbary, adding his own comments to the text, presents in contrast to the 'Philosophe' a totally negative picture of Barbary. He goes much further than Raynal in his description of the degradation and misery brought about by despotism, considering that it is due to the Moslem 'invaders' who destroyed the (Christian) civilisation of North Africa by their genius for destruction and their fanaticism, and replaced it with slavery and tyranny. He frequently quotes Pananti, insists on the sufferings of the Christian slaves and calls for a Christian conquest to free Barbary from a 'handful of barbarians'[72]. Even the Scots poet Campbell, who shows in general a certain amount of sympathy towards Algeria, which he visited just after the French conquest (which he criticises), repeats the same old clichés about Moslem 'bigotry'; he does, nevertheless, admit that the inhabitants would be better civilised by making them 'good Mahometans', which would at least keep them sober, rather than attempting to convert them, for they would then only become bad Christians[73].

In general, we find by the time of the French landing in Algiers, that any attempt to understand the peoples of Barbary as equals, if very different ones, had vanished, and their religion could only be seen as leading to bigotry and fanaticism. It is interesting that the greater knowledge of Islam that is apparent in the Eighteenth Century ended in a strengthening of the most bigoted Christian stereotypes, accompanied by general ignorance and a refusal to understand. Thus Captain Rozet, who came to Algeria with the French army and published accounts of what he saw which are remarkably well-balanced when compared with later prejudices, nevertheless remarks as a matter of course in the concluding paragraph of his article in *L'Univers* on the 'fanatisme religieux' of the Algerians, despite the fact that this fanaticism had not been at all evident in the description of their way of life that had gone before[74]. It would thus appear that the Enlightenment's willingness to approach the Moslem world with an open mind and even to draw lessons from it for application in Europe (which willingness, even so, was not found in all the representatives of the Enlightenment) could do no more than push temporarily into the background long-standing prejudices against the traditional enemy. These prejudices finally reemerged, even partially reinforced by certain ideas of the Eighteenth Century which enhanced European belief in the superiority of their own enlightened society; by the early Nineteenth Century, despite a few notable exceptions, such prejudices were largely unquestioned. From then onwards, hostility and

contempt for Islam and the Turks have been the norm in the West[75].
This underlying current of hostility should not be forgotten when reading
eighteenth-century texts about Islamic societies, even if the authors frequently attempt to go beyond current stereotypes to achieve a juster
understanding of what they see.

PART TWO

CLASSIFICATION

INTRODUCTORY

We have seen in the first part of this study the preconceptions and pre-judices existing in European minds concerning Barbary which, despite attempts to overcome them, inevitably coloured eighteenth-century ac-counts. Bearing these in mind, I intend, in the main part of this book, to analyse the way in which 'enlightened' Europe viewed North Africa. It is a truism that educated minds during the Enlightenment — which can roughly, if schematically, be said to extend from the late Seventeenth Century until the end of the Eighteenth, despite regional variations — at-tempted a new understanding of the world and of humankind. Rather than being the 'Age of Reason' (which can be a misleading name if Reason is linked too closely to rationalism), the Enlightenment was an age of curiosity, of experiment, of observation of Nature, and of attempts to draw general conclusions from such observation. The principal object of curiosity was Man (that is, the human being), man in his diversity throughout the world and man as a physical being or, in other words, as part of the animal world. The age saw the beginnings of anthropology, called the 'natural history of mankind'. Such a study implied an attempt to envisage the human race as a whole (a conception supported by Biblical teaching, according to which all the human race was descended from an original couple); all the different varieties of mankind, living in radically different ways, were equally human and valid, simply in a dif-ferent stage of human development. For a new historical awareness (evi-dent in the term 'natural history') meant that human society was seen as passing through different stages of development, from the most primitive to the most civilised. In the same way there was a realisation that forms of life developed from the original, primitive ones to the most complex and highly perfected, which was man, and that human faculties, ideas and language had similarly evolved. The era of discoveries, which re-vealed if not the marvellous monsters of imaginative travellers' tales, at least a great variety of mankind with a great diversity of customs and beliefs, brought a realisation that Christian, European norms and beliefs were not the only ones possible and that Europe had perhaps something to learn from more 'primitive' societies living in a manner which was more in accordance with 'natural' principles. The subsequent questioning of Christian beliefs, which has frequently been studied, relied in part on the discovery that apparently universal truths were not so universal after all; it was paralleled by a more tolerant and less ethnocentric vision of other peoples. Instead of being condemned out of hand, they were now studied in their own right in an attempt to understand not only them but also the origins of European society. While it is true that the ultimate failure of the Enlightenment in this respect — evident in the unquestioning belief during the colonial era in 'white' superiority — can be explained not only by changed circumstances but also by certain aspects of the new ideas themselves, nevertheless this fact should not blind us to the importance and sincerity of the attempt. I hope, in what follows, to throw light both on the attempt and on its failure.

An important aspect of the observation of mankind was the desire to organise the mass of information that had been gathered and to produce a coherent body of knowledge. The main way that European thinkers attempted to master this knowledge and to dominate the conflicting, and even unsettling, information concerning the rest of the world was to impose their own order on it. Thus there developed, following the eighteenth-century passion for taxonomy, different systems of classification of mankind, on the lines of the classification of the plant and animal world, developed by Linnaeus[1]. The most significant of these, although it was not the only one, was a racial classification of man that paved the way for the racial theories of the Nineteenth Century. This is a glaring example of the way in which the enlightened search for knowledge ended finally with the imprisonment of European modes of thought in rigid, stereotyped patterns which justified their own prejudices. It is by seeing this process at work in the case of the Maghreb that I hope to clarify the evolution that resulted in the French amnesia concerning Barbary at the time of their conquest of Algeria; their supposed ignorance of the country and its history allowed the existence of the most simplistic clichés concerning them. First, however, we must pay tribute to the Enlightenment's attempts at understanding Barbary on its own terms; there is abundant evidence of attempts at what we could call 'cultural relativity', which parallel the more sympathetic attitudes to Islam that we have already seen.

Thus d'Arvieux (or his editor), whose attempts to understand Islam we have already noted, warns his reader against European prejudices concerning the 'Arabs' who are generally, he says, considered to be impolite, crude, brutal, unjust, violent, untrustworthy and unfeeling; he compares such false prejudices with those of the Romans who considered all other peoples as barbarians, and he points out that such vanity is quite rightly mocked by those very people who fall into the same trap themselves. He also remarks that Frenchmen have the same unthinking prejudices concerning Normans, Picards or Gascons. According to d'Arvieux, these prejudices are the result of a refusal to use one's reason, and of ignorance of history in the case of the Arabs, whose past learning is well attested. In his *Voyages*, edited by a different hand, La Roque, the author insists that a mixture of good and bad is to be found in all nations[2]. These particular passages refer to the Arabs in Syria rather than to the inhabitants of Barbary, but they bear witness to a willingness, at least in theory, to approach all nations with an open mind and as equals. Such was also the clearly stated aim of Laugier de Tassy, who hoped by his work on Algiers to 'diminish the prejudices' of his readers, as he declares in his Preface, from which I have already quoted his views on Islam, and to show that the customs of some European nations are just as ridiculous as those of the Algerians whom they detest[3]. This aim is apparent throughout his account of Algiers and is again explicitly spelled out in the conclusion. Here again he appeals for an enlightened understanding of the Barbaresques, whose way of life is, to them, more logical and rational than the Christians'. Laugier then reviews the accusations and criticisms made of the Algerians, refuting them one by one and frequently showing that the Christian nations are guilty of precisely those things for which they reproach the North Africans. Thus he is able to declare that there is no difference between Barbaresques and Europeans, and concludes by saying that everyone who is free from national or religious prejudices will agree that man ('le coeur humain') is the same everywhere[4]. It is perhaps from such a work that the marquis d'Argens obtained much of his information about Barbary which he used in his *Lettres juives*. As d'Argens's main aim is to criticise French society, he unavoidably displays a much more open attitude to Barbary than do most contemporaries and compares it with his own society on an equal footing. There are frequent comparisons between the Barbary states and classical antiquity which, for eighteenth-century Europe, was a model; thus, for instance, the governments of the Regencies, the characters of the rulers and the licence of the soldiers are compared to ancient Rome under Caligula or Nero while Tripoli, where he says theft is openly tolerated, is likened to Sparta[5]. Such comparisons would no doubt have shocked a certain number of his readers, whose prejudices he directly challenges. Even more significantly, having described the noble action of Ibrahim, bey of Tunis, in pardoning those who had revolted against him, d'Argens remarks that such behaviour, if recounted by a Latin author, would have become famous and universally acclaimed as a model by educated men; but as this noble action was performed in a 'barbarian country' by an unknown ruler, it is consigned to oblivion[6]. Such a plea for equal stan-

dards of judgement and criticism of Europocentrism are still relevant today. They are, interestingly enough, echoed at the end of the century by
the American poet and friend of the 'philosophes' Joel Barlow who was
consul in Algiers. He writes in a report to the Secretary of State in 1796
concerning the Dey, Hassan Bashaw who has 'a high sense of Barbarian
honour'; Barlow describes an honourable action of the Dey and comments, "Had the Romans done such a thing it would be known to every
schoolboy in our day"[7]. In a different context, d'Argens uses his descriptions of Barbary to criticise European behaviour; when he, inevitably,
talks of piracy and the enslavement of Christians, it is order to condemn
the Christian nations' harsh treatment of their Turkish galley slaves. In
the same vein, he discusses the frequent bloodshed and revolutions in the
Regencies, so often the subject of blood-curdling accounts by visitors, but
it is in order to compare these events to the bloodthirsty revolutions in
England and France, and to point out that in the same situation, Frenchmen or Germans would behave in the same way. He thus concludes that
if the throne were in Europe the prize for the rebels' leader, there would
be just as many 'tragic events' as there are in Africa[8]. It is clear then that
d'Argens's aims which led him, on the one hand as we have seen, to
criticise Islam, at the same time meant that he had a more open and
balanced view of other aspects of Barbaresque society. This should put
us on our guard against hasty condemnations of writers on Barbary, who
could express points of view that we might consider to be contradictory
but which are coherent in view of their aims. Some of d'Argens's concern
for equity is shown by his contemporary, the German traveller Hebenstreit who visited Tunis and Algiers in 1731. He too points out that the
activities of the Barbary pirates are no worse than those of their Christian
enemies who, if anything, treat their Turkish captives with greater
severity[9]. It is, I think, true that we find fewer such remarks as the century progresses, although there is continuing evidence of attempts at
honest descriptions of what visitors saw; these accounts provide a contrast with the lack of understanding and willingness to condemn
displayed by the vice-consul Vallière in his *Mémoire*[10]. The Rousseauiste
Poiret even went to the opposite extreme, expecting to find among the
peoples of Barbary, closer to the state of nature than the Europeans, examples of a sort of 'noble savage', practising simple virtues forgotten by
corrupt Europeans. In the face of the evidence, however, he was forced
to abandon this very different sort of stereotype and admit his error[11].

By the beginning of the Nineteenth Century, open-minded approaches
were much rarer. Cultural relativity does however linger on in Rehbinder's comprehensive survey of the Algerian state, dating from the turn
of the century. In many ways this German was a representative of the

Aufklärung as can be seen from his plea for tolerance contained in the Annexe to his work. Here he insists that, despite the general impression that
the reader will probably have received of the misery and suffering of the
population of North Africa, he should not judge other peoples by his own
standards; instead he should realise that different peoples have different
conceptions of happiness. This rather patronising passage contains overtones of the idea of the noble savage (which we shall come back to in
chapter 3) and refers directly to Poiret[12]. In general, nevertheless,
criticisms of the European nations arising from descriptions of Barbary
tended to concentrate on their unwillingness to act against the North
African corsairs, for whom there is ever less indulgence. This is even the
case of the author of the *Histoire des Deux Indes* who, while insisting on the
equality of all men and condemning the Europeans' treatment of African
slaves, accepts European prejudices concerning Barbary. This indicates
a changing attitude in the late Eighteenth Century that we shall have ample occasion to return to. Some years later, the most that James Grey
Jackson, who condemns the European ignorance of North Africa, can
find to say in favour of its inhabitants is, "These ignorant, barbarous
savages, as we call them, are much more sagacious and possess much better intellects than we have yet been aware of"[13]. Again there are overtones of the patronising condescension to be found in Rehbinder's
remarks; there is apparently no question of judging the North Africans
on their own terms. They are simply less primitive than has been
thought. Even William Shaler, who is comparatively sympathetic towards the Algerians and rejects a certain number of prejudices concerning them, displays no trace of the cultural relativity characteristic of
enlightened thought. The country is judged firmly by 'civilised' standards
and found lacking. Even if he considers that its people are 'on the very
brink of civilization', he also believes that they can only attain it by European colonisation[14]. A rare observer who attempts something of the
eighteenth-century even-handedness is the Scottish poet Thomas Campbell in his *Letters from the South* (1837) in which he decribes his impressions
of the early stages of French occupation, observed during his visit in
1834. He does attempt, in passing, to judge the 'Algerines' and the
French by the same standards, writing,

> Ages of despotism must, no doubt, have left some traces of barbarity in the
> Moorish character; but what right have the French to accuse them, as they
> universally do, of being fanatic and treacherous? Has a single Frenchman
> been assassinated by an Algerine Moor since the conquest of the country?
> and yet the Moors have seen their mosques, their churchyards violated by
> the French.

He even manages to put himself in their place:

> How would you like the French if they had come into England, dug up the
> bones of your parents and countrymen and sent off a shipload of them to
> be used by the sugar-bakers of France?[15]

It should not be forgotten that this was written by a British subject who
would *a priori* have little sympathy for the French; in addition, as a
Scotsman he might be expected to have more understanding of a nation
whose culture was being trampled underfoot by foreign conquerors. (It
is perhaps significant that he compares some of the Moors' habits and
customs to those of the Scots[16].) However this may be, his willingness to
judge conquered and conquerors by the same standards and to see the
Algerians as fellow human-beings was an exception during this period.
In the texts reproduced by Lucas and Vatin in *L'Algérie des Anthropologues*
we see no such willingness. Even a writer such as Tocqueville who, in
1837, criticised his government's policy towards Algeria and pleaded for
a better understanding of its people and customs, apparently considered
them to be part of an irremediably inferior culture[17]. To say nothing of
those like V.A. Hain of the 'Société coloniale de l'Etat d'Alger' who considered its people as beyond all redemption and fit only to be removed
from the land[18].

Although not everyone went as far as such fanatical advocates of colonisation, the difference between early nineteenth-century viewpoints
and those characteristic of the Enlightenment is, I think, clear. But the
Eighteenth Century's opening towards other cultures ended in this
Europocentrism and contempt for others, when the search for knowledge
was subordinated to the desire for conquest. In other fields the Enlightenment did lead to lasting progress. Why then, in the case of anthropology,
and relations with North Africa in particular, was the sympathy and even
knowledge present in the previous century almost totally forgotten? Why
did the old prejudices reemerge, enriched by new ones fed in part by
enlightened ideas? It is this problem that I intend to investigate in this
section through a consideration of the way in which perceptions of Barbary were integrated into the contemporary conception of the world and
the eighteenth-century system of classifying information about it. The
main questions which will be considered and which cover the principal
fields of knowledge concerning man in society during this period are
those, broadly speaking, of geography, natural history and social evolution. These divisions subsume others, such as language, which will be
dealt with in passing. In each of these areas we shall see that the case of
Barbary presents a problem whose solution was finally dictated by external considerations.

CHAPTER ONE

LOCATION

The first question posed by eighteenth-century writings on Barbary may at first sight appear strange; for there is, to begin with, the problem of knowing where Barbary is. Despite its apparent oddity, this question is a very real one and arises from Barbary's position in the west of the Mediterranean and as part of Africa. In writings on the European awareness of the rest of the world during the Enlightenment — such as Michèle Duchet's *Anthropologie et Histoire* or Marshall and Williams's *The Great Map of Mankind*[1] — as I have already said, the world beyond Europe is divided into America, Asia, the Pacific and Africa (which means Sub-Saharan Africa and more specifically the west coast). Nowhere does Barbary appear. In part this can be explained by the fact that Barbary had not been discovered; it was an integral part of Mediterranean civilisation, of the known world and, as Numa Broc says, travels in the Mediterranean were not voyages of discovery but 'un renouvellement périodique des connaissances'[2]. Since ancient times the northern shore of the Mediterranean Sea had been in constant touch with its southern shore, as is attested by tangible reminders on both shores, and in the Middle Ages such contacts remained important[3]. From one point of view, therefore, Barbary was not an alien, distant and unknown land but a familiar participant in Mediterranean history. This lasted as long as the Mediterranean was the centre of European culture; once the centre of gravity moved northwards and the Mediterranean became steadily more peripheral, its southern shore was increasingly consigned to oblivion. It could not, however, be totally forgotten as the activities of the Regencies' navies, or pirates as they were considered to be, provided a constant threat to European shipping. For Barbary was, it should not be forgotten, largely cast in the role of the enemy; it could thus not be counted as one of 'us' in opposition to the 'other' in the recently-discovered lands. The religion of its inhabitants alone was enough to exclude it from Christian Europe. The ambiguity of its position thus appears: part of the known world but irremediably alien, part of both Africa, the Mediterranean and the Islamic worlds. Hence the difficulty of deciding where to classify it, for each of these accepted divisions of the globe entailed a certain number of characteristics in the European imag-

ination, which North Africa did not fit perfectly. This will become clear
if we take them one by one.

Firstly, was Barbary part of Mediterranean civilisation and thus cen-
tral, and to some extent European, rather than peripheral? The main
form taken by such a conception of Barbary in our period was an awareness of it as having been, in a not too distant past, part of the Roman
Empire and part of Christendom. By ignoring the Islamic present it was
possible to see North Africa in this light. Thus we find in the English
clergyman Shaw a permanent concern with the classical past of the
Maghreb, which eclipses frequently his awareness of its present.
Throughout his travels he attempts to identify, following in the footsteps
of classical scholars, the ancient sites he visits and to record the inscrip-
tions on Roman ruins. Indeed, in his Preface he presents one of his aims
in his work as providing 'an Essay towards restoring the ancient
Geography', which is indeed borne out by the contents of his book[4].
This preoccupation frequently leads him to ignore the contemporary inhabitants of Barbary in favour of architectural information. It is also interesting to observe the terms in which he refers to the Arabs' fear of
strangers, whom they suspect of being spies sent to reconnoitre these
lands which 'are to be restored to Christianity'[5]. Can we conclude from
his use of the word 'restored' that for Shaw Barbary was rightfully Christian? It is true that Shaw, whose erudition was widely praised and whose
work served as a guide for those who followed him, was perhaps more
a representative of an antiquarian attitude rather than of the ethnographical and anthropological interests of the Eighteenth Century[6]. Nevertheless, this classical and 'Roman' view of Barbary subsisted in the
Enlightenment, despite its rather subterranean existence. It is hardly surprising that such an attitude should colour Gibbon's vision, as his subject
was indeed, not the present, but precisely the Roman Empire; it is equally unsurprising that his descriptions of North Africa should rely heavily
on Shaw's *Travels*. But traces of the same point of view are also to be
found in other writers, such as Shaw's contemporary Peyssonnel, who
discusses on occasion the Roman past of the countries he visits, again
referring to Shaw in this context. Later, Poiret too is particularly touched
by the vestiges of Roman civilisation that he finds and forgets his enthusiasm for natural man to lament on the decline of an ancient culture.
Such sentiments particularly come to the fore when he visits the ruins of
the ancient Hippone; he contrasts the civilisation of the past with the
'ferocious barbarians' whom he sees inhabiting the ancient site. It is
worth quoting the words he uses to describe his feelings here:

Tout ce que je vois me peint si vivement l'ancienne splendeur des Romains, me retrace si bien ce que j'en ai lu, ce que l'on m'en a raconté, qu'il me semble avoir été romain moi-même et que je renais pour gémir sur les ruines de mon ancienne patrie[7].

(Everything I see paints so vividly the former splendour of the Romans, retraces so well what I have read about them and what I have been told, that I feel as if I was once Roman myself and that I have come back to life to lament on the ruins of my former homeland.)

For all his Rousseauistic enthusiasm, Poiret nevertheless affirms unambiguously the specifically Roman past of Barbary and identifies himself with it and with the Romans who were, it should not be forgotten, Christians and not pagans in this case. The land becomes here not only Mediterranean, but also part of Christian Europe, and its present inhabitants are usurpers who have destroyed its European, Christian civilisation. Poiret here revives the traditional picture of the barbaric Moslem invaders, destroying all in their path and bringing to an end centuries of civilisation; it was precisely this false picture that Gibbon was trying to eradicate when he pointedly attributed the decline of North Africa to the Vandals and the Christians long before the Islamic conquest[8]. But despite his efforts and those of others, the glorification of the Roman past continued to be, as with Poiret, linked to a condemnation of the Islamic present. The two ideas are combined in Pananti's extremely hostile account of Algiers in which he calls for the conquest of the country by the Europeans, drawing a parallel with the Roman conquest of North Africa[9]. He constantly reflects, as others have before him, on the Roman ruins, contrasting them with the degradation he sees around him; thus he wishes to restore European civilisation in what had, he insists, once been its home.

This conception of Barbary as part of Europe and the belief in the Europeans' right, as inheritors of Rome and of the Christian civilisation supposedly destroyed by the Arabs, to occupy the country had a tenacious existence; it was one of the arguments constantly put forward by the French conquerors of Algiers. They claimed that the land was rightfully theirs and that the Moslem rulers (and even population) were the usurpers. The argument was used as an incitement to conquest and was reiterated by the French as soon as they landed. Thus Campbell, who visited Algeria in 1834, mocks the French who would be agreeable "if they would not so constantly and ignorantly boast of their resemblance to the Romans"; and he points out that the Romans left ruins of what they created whereas the French leave ruins of what they have destroyed[10]. (This implies, be it noted in passing, that the Romans destroyed nothing and hence that there was nothing here before they arrived.) The same justification — that the French were the Romans' inheritors — was tirelessly trotted out by the French colonial writers for long afterwards. They thereby totally ignored the very existence of the earlier Islamic civilisation. One has only to see the large place devoted to the description of Roman and Christian vestiges in the *Revue africaine* to understand the importance of this preoccupation[11]. And to give but one example of the persistence of this argument, we need only quote the colonial novellist and propagandist Louis Bertrand; in *La Cina* (1901) he has a *colon* evoke Rome, then Byzantium, Saint-Louis, Charles V, Louis XIV, the Restoration's armies and his father's campaigns, to conclude, "vraiment nous ne sommes point des étrangers ici"[12]. It is revealing to notice that an echo of this point of view is to be found as late as 1966 in an American work on the American-Algerian war of the late Eighteenth Century; the author writes, "It is one of the absurdities of history that North Africa and Europe should have drifted apart. The warm Mediterranean should be a bridge not a barrier"[13].

This insistence on the European and Christian essence of Barbary concerns exclusively, we might say, the land. The people who inhabited it before the arrival of the French were not the inheritors of Rome but quite simply intruders with no rights. Openly proclaimed in the early Nineteeth Century, it was more muted but nevertheless present in some eighteenth-century writers. Shaw's comparative neglect of its present inhabitants implies, as we have seen, the same belief. It is also remarkable that references to the beauty and fertility of the country are often accompanied by disparaging references to its inhabitants on whom it is, as it were, wasted. This commonplace of the colonial era in Algeria is already present in the previous century. Desfontaines, for example, visiting Blida and admiring its situation and climate, regrets that it does not belong to Europeans who would make it 'un séjour délicieux'[14]. And Vallière, describing the fertility of the land, remarks that in European hands it could produce great riches, enough to satisfy the whole population[15]. Given the lingering belief in the Mediterranean or European character of Barbary, which had never totally vanished, such remarks could easily lead on to the belief that the only development possible was a restoration of the past by the 'return' of the Europeans to rule the country. By the turn of the century this was more and more openly affirmed, with the relative decline of attempts to understand the civilisation of its inhabitants on their own terms. Once part of Barbary had been occupied, the very existence of this civilisation was denied, in the same way as the Romans had methodically destroyed all traces of the Carthaginian civilisation.

But despite the evident attraction of the argument that Barbary was rightfully Christian, such an image of the Maghreb was far from being the only one present. In the Eighteenth Century, few could totally ignore its contemporary aspect, and even among those who used the argument of its Christian past, another image of the region is also found. For, by this period, North Africa had become gradually more detached from Europe as the centre of European gravity had moved northwards, to Holland and then to England. The long decline of the Italian city-states was consummated and the Mediterranean tended to become peripheral to the main thrust of European interest which was, in the Seventeenth and much of the Eighteenth Centuries, the Atlantic. Mediterranean trade, although still important, was now subordinated to the Atlantic slave trade, and thus commerce with and interest in North Africa declined accordingly. It was not until the end of the century with the independence of the British colonies in America and the decline of the transatlantic slave trade that interest returned to some extent to the Mediterranean and that there was a greater interest in the penetration of the African continent from the North. The result of these shifts of interest was that in the Eighteenth Century Barbary played a progressively smaller role in European awareness and was consigned to the periphery, part of the other, non-European world. It tended to be more and more perceived as part of the African continent, of which it formed part, as had never been forgotten. After all, the name 'Africa' originally referred to part of Barbary, although by the Eighteenth Century it was normally used to designate the continent as a whole. What is interesting to observe is the fact that not all authors during this period were clearly aware of Barbary as specifically part of the African continent. I propose here to have a look at the reactions of different eighteenth-century authors, to try to see the pattern that emerges and the significance of references to Barbary's 'African' character.

One writer who persistently brings out the 'Africanness' of the region is the marquis d'Argens; from his arrival 'en Afrique' his Jewish traveller Jacob Brito persistently refers to this fact, speaking in general of African rulers and African states[16]. It is usually a way of emphasizing their barbarity and difference, for by qualifying what he describes as 'African', the author insists on its outlandishness as compared to Europe or even the Levant, whence d'Argens's travellers supposedly came. In the same way, a distinction is made between the Turkish rulers and their African subjects. Such a use of the word 'African' to convey an impression of barbarity and ignorance is very clear in S. Ockley's *Account of S. W. Barbary* (1713) in which he distinguishes carefully between the Moslems of North Africa and those of the Levant, insisting that the reader "ought not to take these African Moors for the standard by which he is to pass his Judgement upon the Mahometans in general", for although they have the same religion, "their Temper, Genius, Breeding is as much inferior to that of the Polite Asiaticks ..."[17]. It is hardly surprising that the word 'African' should be used to insist on the backwardness of the inhabitants of the Maghreb, for Africa at that time (and to a large extent ever since) conjured up images of an unknown and savage continent. This was particularly the case during a period when only the fringes of the continent were known to outsiders and when the great mass of the interior was marked as a blank on maps. Given these connotations of the word, it is interesting to observe that the majority of eighteenth-century writers did not insist on Barbary's 'Africanness'. And for Laugier de Tassy, even though the region is undoubtedly a part of Africa, this awareness does not carry any particular stigma; it is simply a way of defining Algiers's position. He speaks, for example of Algiers' policy towards the African powers (i.e. the other Barbary states) and compares it to her policy towards the European powers. He even, to some extent, excuses the Algerians' enslavement of Christians by saying that it is an 'immemorial' custom throughout Africa[18]. But Laugier is something of an exception in drawing no derogatory connotations from his references to the African site of the Barbary Regencies. More frequently, those who attempt an objective account of North Africa tend to avoid references to its African character. Gibbon even, despite the fact that he is writing about the Roman Empire in Africa, is at some pains to distinguish Barbary from the rest of the continent, for which he shows nothing but contempt. The North, conquered by the Romans, is set apart from the rest of Africa to the south, peopled by the 'unknown and uninteresting tribes of Africa.' These tribes of Negroes he considers to be inferior to the rest of mankind and incapable both of civilisation and of the military prowess of their neighbours to the north[19]. At the same time Gibbon also uses the adjective 'African' to underline the misery and abjection of the peoples of North Africa when compared to the Romans and the Vandals[20]. He thus displays a certain amount of confusion concerning the 'Africanness' of Barbary; it is seemingly apparent only in comparison with Europe. Otherwise this land has little in common with the region to the south.

The negative connotations associated with Africa are confirmed by Poiret's use of the word. In general he pays little attention to the fact that he is in Africa, and his rare uses of the word serve to convey an impression of outlandishness. Thus, as he approaches the coast with some apprehension he refers to it as the coast of Africa, which he expects to be sandy and sterile. Instead he is agreeably surprised to find green hills and flowers[21]. This does not however prevent him, when describing his heroic expedition into the countryside around the French enclave of La Calle, from insisting on the inhospitable nature of the terrain; he refers to the 'burning sands' of Barbary (hardly an accurate description and in contradiction with what he himself had written earlier), and writes that his face has become sunburnt like those of the Africans[22]. Africa is once more associated with wildness and inhospitability and also, significantly, it serves as a means to underline Poiret's own daring and sense of himself as an explorer penetrating unknown and dangerous territory. But there is a problem in this view of Barbary inasmuch as the African continent was at the time generally considered to be inhabited by black savages, an image which it is difficult to reconcile with visitors' descriptions of the Barbaresques and their towns. Thus what was known about the Regencies — essentially their urban civilisation, naval activities and so on — seemed to exclude it from Africa as the Eighteenth Century conceived it. (I shall come back to this question in the next chapter.) This is confirmed by the descriptions of visitors who, like Poiret, found most of what they saw un-African. As the century progresses, however, there appears a growing disparagement of Barbary, accompanied by increasing references to its African characteristics. This is evident first of all in the writings of official envoys. A. Jardine, sent by the British government to the Emperor of Morocco in 1771, holds most of the old European prejudices against North Africa; he consequently insists on its African nature, comparing European and African manners and considering, significantly, that the original inhabitants were probably Negroes[23]. He concludes his disparaging remarks on the barbarous nature of the inhabitants with the reflection that "to be conquered by a civilized and generous nation [by which he means the British] would be a happy event for these poor Africans"[24]. Likewise Vallière explains to some extent the harshness with which the Turkish rulers treat their Moorish subjects by the fact that the latter are 'un peuple africain'[25]. In a similar vein is J. Leyden's *Historical and Philosophical Sketch,* which begins by placing interest in Barbary in the context of the revival of interest in the African continent which had resulted in the foundation of the African Association[26]. Here again the author shows mainly hostility towards the inhabitants, their religion and way of life. But neither of these relatively minor works goes as far as the Italian Pananti's ferocious condemnation of Algiers. Significantly, he begins in his Preface by conjuring up the image of the unknown African continent which has 'terrified and baffled' explorers; Algiers is thus firmly situated in Africa, which is without doubt the 'dark continent' and is consequently barbaric, dangerous and, of course, in need of being civilised by the Europeans[27]. In contrast, William Shaler, whose attitude towards Algiers shows much more indulgence, makes little play with its African character. Indeed, he even writes, when speaking of the Kabyles — whom he identifies as the remnants of the ancient Numidians — that they have 'unafrican moral qualities'. This inclines him to extend to them Shaw's opinion concerning the inhabitants of the Auress mountains, namely that they are also partly descended from the Vandals[28]. It is true that such a remark could, by implication, condemn the other inhabitants to 'African' vices, but Shaler does not say this. Nevertheless, by the time he wrote, Barbary (or at least Algiers) was more or less definitively relegated to the African continent, and this is how it was seen by the invading French, for all their insistence on Roman civilisation. In 1829 the 'Deputé' for Marseille, Thomas, referred in the Chambre des Députés to the Dey of Algiers as 'ce potentat africain'[29], in which the contempt is unmistakable. And in 1834, Thomas Campbell is very much aware of venturing into darkest Africa and describes how, before he went there, he had imagined the French, 'opening, as it were, the northern gate of civilisation into Africa'. On his arrival he is very much excited by 'landing in Africa' and when visiting the British Consul's country house, he describes the beauty of the scenery, the streams and the flowers, all of which moves him to exclaim, 'Is it possible . . . that I am in Africa the torrid!'. Despite the discrepancy between such scenes and the African barbarity and wilderness that he had expected, he could not reject the ambient clichés concerning Algeria; thus, on finding an excessive number of gunsmiths in the town of Algiers, he exclaims, "What a singular circumstance, that the over competition of artisans should extend to the wilds of Africa"[30]. It is difficult to imagine an eighteenth-century traveller considering this town, however un-congenial he may have found it, to be the 'wilds of Africa'! Such a remark brings out, I think, the transformation that had come about in the image of Barbary by the 1830s. As it became more barbaric and ripe for 'civilisation' by the Europeans, so it became more African.

But there is another, more practical aspect of the 'Africanisation' of Barbary, to which the clue is given by an examination of the passage concerning North Africa in the *Histoire des Deux Indes*. In the context of its denunciation of the slave trade, this work gives a description of the home of the human cargo and thus of the whole of the African continent, including not only the Western slave coast but Barbary as well. It was as a result of criticisms of inaccuracies in the description of the latter area that Raynal went more deeply into the subject, consulting specialists such as Poiret and Venture de Paradis[31]. With this added information, he wrote his *Mémoires* on Barbary, left among his manuscripts conserved at the Bibliothèque nationale in Paris and partially published by Peuchot in 1826. What is interesting in this preoccupation with North Africa is the fact that it arose through a concern with the African slave trade and thus from an awareness of Barbary as part of the African continent. More

than this, however, Raynal's particular interest in trade can be seen in
the unpublished manuscripts at the Bibliothèque nationale which include
a discussion of the French African Company's factory at La Calle in the
East of the Algiers Regency[32]. There is thus in the abbé Raynal's
writings (for even if the authorship of the *Histoire des Deux Indes* remains
a subject of debate and research, the manuscripts seem to be by him) an
undoubted link between an awareness of Barbary as African and an interest in its trade. Raynal is representative of a growing interest in the
Maghreb precisely because of its trade links with the rest of Africa; the
Africanness of Barbary is for some authors therefore not simply a sign
of barbarity but instead a source of commercial interest. Already in the
Encyclopédie article BARBARIE, there is an account, following many
earlier authors, of the trans-Saharan trade via which the Moors obtained
the gold of Timbuctoo. The transaction was carried out without the two
parties meeting; they simply left the agreed amount of goods and gold in
a fixed spot. The anecdote, recounted by Shaw and others, was usually
told to show the honesty of the traders involved. What it also reveals is
the European awareness of, and interest in, the gold and in the reputedly
untold riches of the interior of the continent to which Barbary was supposedly the gateway. This aspect of interest in Africa appears in a contemporaneous work by Maupertuis entitled *Lettre sur le progrès des sciences;*
the author includes a section on Africa, praising its climate, its former
glory and 'superbes villes'. He insists on the necessity to penetrate its interior because of its riches and commercial possibilities[33]. The preoccupation with African trade, present in some eighteenth-century writing,
really came to the fore at the turn of the century when, as we shall see
in Part III, it was used as one of the arguments for a European expedition
to conquer Barbary. Thus Pananti, who speaks of the desirability of the
conquest of Algiers because it would lead to the civilisation of Africa,
rather gives the game away by his insistence on the inexhaustible
resources of the continent, its precious metals and subsequent riches of
the coastal cities[34]. Awareness of the Maghreb as essentially African
thus made it more barbaric, but also more desirable. The visitor who
goes furthest in this direction is James Grey Jackson, who wrote mainly
about Morocco and whose recurrent theme was the need for Britain to
obtain control of the trade into the interior of Africa, which would bring
her great wealth. He proclaims, in a letter signed 'Vasco da Gama', the
importance of conquering Algiers and expatiates on the riches this would
bring his country. He enumerates the advantages of control first of
Algiers and then, as a result, of its neighbouring states, in providing a
market for British manufactured goods and East Indian produce. And

Britain would obtain not only grain but also direct commerce with the interior of the continent. Hence:

> the fertile and populous districts which lie contiguous to the Nile of Sudan, throughout the whole of the interior of Africa would become, in a few years, as closely connected to us, by a mutual exchange of benefits as our own colonies; and such a stimulus would be imparted to British enterprise and industry, as would secure to us such a store of gold as would equal the riches of Solomon ...[35].

I shall discuss in the final part of this book the role played by such motives in the French conquest of Africa. For the moment I wish to emphasize the implications of such a conception of North Africa. As part of Africa, Barbary was not only more mysterious and barbaric but, perhaps more importantly, full of unexploited treasures that were apparently just waiting to be seized or at least, as Jackson writes of the Empire of Moroco (much more closed to foreign trade) opened up to European commerce. Thus the Barbary states were progressively perceived as ever less organised *states* and governments with which the European nations could treat, but as barbaric and backward regions in the hands (for the Regencies) of foreign ruffians who oppressed their African subjects (or with less regard for accuracy, as African potentates). The ruffians needed to be chased away to bring enlightenment and trade to the natives. These are the two aspects that are particularly in evidence in the famous appeal, in the *Histoire des Deux Indes,* for a European conquest of Barbary which begins, "Mais à quel peuple est-il reservé de briser les fers que l'Afrique nous forge lentement ..."[36]. As they became more African, the inhabitants of Barbary were perceived as progressively more unknown and primitive; to get to know them, the traveller had to become an explorer. This is very clear in the writings of Jackson or of Leyden who speaks of the renewed interest in African exploration aroused by the foundation of Banks's African Association which financed Mungo Park's expedition into the interior of the continent at the end of the century[37]. It is perhaps forgotten now how much fascination Timbuctoo exercised on the minds of Europeans during this period; this fascination comes out very clearly in the writings of Mungo Park and later in René Caillé's account of his journey to that town[38]. It is significant that Jackson's work, from which we have quoted and which contains much information about Morocco and letters demanding the conquest of North Africa, is entitled *An Account of Timbuctoo,* which no doubt attracted readers. In addition, if Jackson recommends a stay in Morocco, it is mainly in order to learn 'African Arabic' and the customs, dress and other information useful when travelling further south[39]. Jackson is perhaps an extreme example, but he helps us to see that interest in Barbary in the early Nineteenth Century was to some extent conditioned by awareness of it as part of the alluring African continent. Once the French had seized Algiers and begun the conquest of its territory, its African nature was firmly established, and the awareness of being in Africa is clearly visible in all colonial writers. The corollary was, on the one hand, as we shall see in Chapter 3, that the 'natives' were reduced to the level of savages and, on the other, that it was the Europeans' gateway for bringing civilisation to the rest of the continent. That this was their mission was by now undisputed.

Such unanimity should not blind us to the fact that, as I have already said, this 'African' image of Barbary was by no means undisputed in the Eighteenth Century. In addition to the persistent awareness of its Roman heritage, there is another facet of the region that we must take into account when investigating European attitudes, and that is its role as part of the Ottoman Empire (except, of course, for the Moroccan Empire). As we have already seen, this fact was rarely forgotten in dealings with the 'Turks' of Barbary. In a practical sense this meant, for example, that it was the British Levant Company that traded here, and that negotiations with the Regencies also had to involve the Sultan in Istanbul. However, by the late Seventeenth century, the increased powers of the rulers of the Regencies and their increasing independence from the Sultan's orders, particularly in their dealings with foreign powers, meant that the Europeans became aware of the difficulty of ensuring the enforcement in Barbary of any agreement made in Istanbul without negotiations directly with the government concerned on the spot. Thus they tended more and more to treat the Regencies as sovereign states and it was in consequence difficult to perceive them as just another part of the Ottoman Empire. Indeed, nearly all eighteenth-century observers speak of Algiers and Tunis as sovereign states independent of Constantinople, following the example of d'Argens who says specifically that Algiers can be considered as a free, self-governing Republic[40]. An exception is Venture de Paradis, who insists that nothing has changed and that the Sultan is still the supreme master in Barbary[41]. In addition, many observers are at some pains to point out that the rulers in Barbary are foreigners, generally referred to as Turks although, while all Levantines, many are of Greek, Armenian or other origin. There is also, we should not forget, unanimous agreement that they are the dregs of the Empire, frequently criminals who had come westwards to avoid punishment. There was thus a general awareness that these 'Turkish' rulers who paid lip-service to the Sultan but possessed a considerable degree of autonomy, were a foreign militia ruling a cowed and sullen population in an alien land, increasingly seen as African and in any case not Levantine. There are numerous descriptions of the Turks' way of life, cut off from the native population, which they treated very harshly. This peculiarity of the Regencies of Tunis, Tripoli and Algiers was not forgotten and made it difficult for Europeans to treat them as simply another part of the Ottoman Empire or even more as part of the Levant. They were considered by most Europeans to be independent states in Africa whose population was neither Turkish nor Levantine, even if it was not always seen as specifically African.

Despite this fact, the connection with the Ottoman Empire and, even more, Barbary's status as part of the Islamic world have meant that there is yet another way of considering the region, namely as part of the Orient. As a result, many contemporary critics have considered that Europeans in the pre-colonial period applied 'Oriental' stereotypes to the Maghreb. Thus Wadi Bouzar, in his interesting work *La Mouvance et la pause. Regards sur la société algérienne* seems to accept without question the idea that the Maghreb enters into the Orientalist patterns; he writes that the 'myth of the Maghreb' is part, in Western consciousness, of the larger 'myth of the Orient'[42]. This author also discusses at some length the point of view of Marx and Engels, explaining that their rather superficial and stereotyped grasp of the Algerian question 'passe par le canal oriental'[43]. In the latter case this is doubtless true, for in the Nineteenth Century there co-existed with the 'African' view of the Maghreb this 'Orientalist' view, however difficult it might appear at first sight to reconcile the two. For writers and artists (if not for soldiers or politicians) the Maghreb was, by its architecture, religion, language and customs part of the Orient and even 'Turkish'. In any catalogue of 'Orientalist' paintings we find a certain number dealing with North African subjects, of which perhaps the most famous is Delacroix's *Femmes d'Alger dans leurs appartements*. Here we see most of the classic Oriental characteristics: voluptuous luxury, seduction, drug-induced torpor. These characteristics are very different from the contemporary clichés associated with Africa, which were primitive barbarity and exotic horror. Similarly, nineteenth-century descriptions of the town of Algiers insist on its Oriental aspect; this is particularly important as Oriental imagery was particularly associated with its urban civilisation. Algiers becomes 'une de ces cités d'Orient qui dorment au soleil'[44], at least in expectation, even if it had become too 'French' in reality. Already in 1832 V.A. Hain, who argued forcefully for the colonisation of Algeria, spoke of the Oriental town that was rapidly becoming a European one[45].

But if these 'Orientalist' stereotypes are visible in the Nineteenth Century, was this the case in the Enlightenment, as Bouzar states? Before going into this question we should perhaps be clear as to exactly what is meant by the word 'Oriental', for the Orient has always been, as it still

is, rather a nebulous concept. It is a truism that has already been pointed
out by several critics, that the Orient only exists in opposition to the West
which considers itself as the centre of the world; it is a purely Western
creation[46]. In addition, its application is far from being fixed. On the
one hand — and this applies, I would think, more particularly to Britain
— it refers to the Far East, that is to India and the countries that in the
Eighteenth Century were involved in the East Indies trade. This was particularly so after the British occupation of India following 1757. The
word was therefore not necessarily synonymous with Islam or things
Moslem, or with the Turks, but referred as much to Chinoiserie and Indian fashions, whose vogue can be seen in the Royal Pavilion in Brigh-
ton. Indeed, the 'Oriental Renaissance' which occurred in the early Nineteenth Century concerned Indian philosophy, religion and literature
under the stimulus of scholars such as Jones[47]. In the *Encyclopédie* the
Orient is defined as the Far East, while the Turkish eastern Mediterranean and the Middle East are called the Levant. On the other hand it
is true that for centuries the 'East' that impinged the most on European
consciousness was precisely the Levant and the Islamic world in general,
although they were aware of China and its civilisation. Thus 'Oriental',
as in the *Bibliothèque oriental*, was frequently used to refer to things Islamic
and to the civilisations speaking Turkish, Arabic or Persian. It was this
Orient, as I have already said, which was felt as an enemy and against
which the Crusades had been launched. In addition, despite the Europeans' hostile attitude towards the Turks and Islam, this Orient was, like
the civilisations further East, recognised as being refined and as having
been so for longer than the West. It did not fail, as a result, to exercise
a certain attraction as is evident in Lady Mary Wortley Montagu's letters
from Constantinople. That it still had something to teach the West in the
Eighteenth Century was proved by her introduction into England of in-
noculation against smallpox, which she had learnt from the Turks. It was
to this Orient — shorn of its superiority but preserving its exotic seduction and now passivity — that the Maghreb was annexed by some
nineteenth-century writers.

In the Eighteenth Century, however, this is rather less apparent, as we
would expect from what I have said above of perceptions of its peculiar
status within the Turkish Empire, despite the fact that the inhabitants of
Barbary professed Islam. For one thing there was, I think we shall see,
an awareness of the simple geographical fact that the Maghreb was *not*
the East; indeed its very name means 'west' as is pointed out in
d'Herbelot's *Bibliothèque orientale*, in the article MAGHREB. It is included
in this Encyclopedia presumably insofar as it is part of the Ottoman Empire and an Islamic country, without any mention of the etymological

contradiction. It is instructive to compare different uses of the word 'Oriental' in the Eighteenth Century. D'Arvieux, who travelled widely in the Levant and knew, we are told, both Turkish and Arabic, does not hesitate to use the word to refer to the peoples he sees in Syria; he speaks, for example, of the 'vices of the Orientals', which concern sexual indulgence, to explain that the 'Arabs' are more restrained. The latter, who are the Bedouin, do however show the same jealousy as the Orientals in general. When he arrives in Barbary such epithets disappear and we find several indications that he no longer considers himself to be in the Orient. Following this reasoning, he distinguishes between the language of the Moors, which he calls 'arabe mauritanique', and 'l'arabe orientale'[48]. This is, I think, the attitude that mostly prevails during the Eighteenth Century and is shared by Mary Montagu; on her way home from Constantinople she stops off at Tunis and is very much aware that she has left the Orient and landed in Africa[49]. And the distinction that I have already mentioned between the Turkish rulers and the indigenous population emphasizes this difference. When, for example, Peyssonnel describes the inhabitants of Barbary, he sees no need to go into details concerning the 'Turks' who are the same as those in the Levant, whereas the native population is discussed at some length. In the main, with these authors, there is little attempt to convey an impression of Oriental exoticism, but rather a concern to describe a different way of life as clearly as possible; the 'myth of the Orient' is very little in evidence, mainly because most travellers are not aware of being in the Orient. There are, however one or two exceptions, particularly as the century progresses. Consider the following remark, made by Alexander Jardine in his *Letters from Barbary*, describing his visit to Morocco in 1771. In his second letter he discusses the 'difference between European and African manners' and writes, "We see Eastern manners here without going to the East. Every idea of change or improvement is excluded by their law and by their ignorance of their wants". He follows this remark by a reference to 'stupid Eastern governments, fed on despotism'[50]. Jardine's attitude is particularly interesting for, on the one hand, he points out that Barbary is not the Orient, as was generally recognised, while on the other he assimilates it to the Orient, not with the aim of making it more alluring but in order to condemn particularly 'Oriental' defects, namely unchanging passivity and despotism. Let us consider the second of these characteristics first.

The concept of 'Oriental despotism' was one which was widespread during the Enlightenment and is found in a wide range of writers, although it was given popularity by Montesquieu's use of the idea. It was abundantly illustrated with examples concerning the Chinese empire or, more frequently, the Ottoman Sultan, the very epitome, for the Eighteenth Century, of an oriental despot. What concerns us here is the fact that the governments of the Barbary states very seldom figure as examples of Oriental despotisms. We find a single reference in Montesquieu's *Esprit des Lois*, concerning the fact that in Algiers people hide their wealth in the ground for fear of confiscation by the government (this example is taken from Laugier de Tassy)[51]. Even Morocco, which was after all an Empire, only figures in passing[52], as it does in the *Encyclopédie* article DESPOTISME, written by Jaucourt. Morocco is also the only example of 'Oriental' despotism in Barbary mentioned in Helvétius's *L'Esprit*, and again only in passing[53]; otherwise for this author the furthest west that the Orient extends is apparently Egypt. In Adam Ferguson's *Essay on the History of Civil Society*, a reference is made to Algiers, together with Constantinople, but it is an example of the anarchy ensuing from revolts against the ruler fomented by men who 'pretend to act on a foot of equality'[54]. It is this reputation for frequent revolutions (also mentioned by Voltaire in *Candide* with reference to Morocco[55]) which particularly struck contemporaries writing about Barbary, and it led to comparisons with ancient Rome in decline rather than with Oriental despotisms. The parallel is made by Shaw[56] and by d'Argens, who compares the government of the 'African states' to that of Rome under Caligula, Nero or the Diocletians, on account both of the cruelty of the sovereigns and the insolence and turbulence of the soldiers[57]. The same comparison with Rome occurs in Montesquieu's *Considérations sur la Grandeur et la Décadence des Romains,* in a passage for which the author is taken to task by Gibbon, who calls it an 'ingenious though somewhat fanciful description'; he considers that the government of Algiers cannot, as Montesquieu claimed, be called an aristocracy as it is a military government which 'floats between the extremes of absolute monarchy and wild democracy'. He proposes a juster comparison with the Mamelukes in Egypt[58]. Another comparison made, for example, by La Condamine was that between the Dey of Algiers and the Venetian Doge[59]. As we can see, to eighteenth-century observers, the Barbary states were not obvious examples of Oriental despotisms, however much criticism of their functioning we find. When we do find the adjective 'despotic' used by writers on Barbary, it is not particularly associated with Oriental characteristics; this is the case of Ockley, for example, writing about the government of the Moroccan Empire, or Peyssonnel discussing that of the Algiers Regency[60]. I shall discuss in much greater detail in Chapter 3 below the question of European perceptions of the governments of the Barbary states; my aim here is simply to see how far they coincided with the 'myth of the Orient'.

When we come to Venture de Paradis, nevertheless, we do observe a subtle yet decisive change in attitude. Venture, a scholar of Arabic, Turkish and other eastern languages, was also a diplomat and interpreter and as I have already said, can be seen as a representative of the 'Orientalist' school. His notes on Barbary, left among his manuscripts and first published a century later, show great knowledge of the Barbary states, their governments and customs, but also reveal a certain contempt for the object of study. He seems to consider their inhabitants, with a few notable exceptions, as ignorant and uncongenial. His attitude is particularly revealed in his annotations to Raynal's 'mémoires' on Barbary, conserved in the latter's manuscripts in the Bibliothèque nationale in Paris[61]. It is already clear from his own notes on Barbary that he considers the government of Algiers to be 'essentiellement vicieuse'[62]; but in his remarks for Raynal we can see that this is closely linked with his view of this country as Oriental. For example, Raynal, following many other commentators including Laugier de Tassy and Poiret, refers to the government of Algiers as republican; Venture refuses to accept this term for "on ne doit jamais s'en servir lorsqu'il est question d'un gouvernement oriental. Le chef est despote tant qu'il est en place". The same remark reappears later when Venture writes that the 'Orientaux' have never had a republican form of government and that there is always the despotic rule of a single man; thus Algiers is no more of a republic than is Egypt. Raynal did not follow Venture's injunction that the word should never be used and left 'republic' in the text[63]. Venture is here clearly appealing to the concept of Oriental despotism and for him Algiers is despotic *because* it is Oriental. I should, however, point out that the same attitude is not in evidence when it comes to the Tunisian government towards which he, like most other western commentators, is more indulgent. Here Venture uses the word 'republic' several times, although this usage alternates with that of the word 'kingdom', and he speaks of the Bey of Tunis as ascending the throne[64]. There is undoubtedly some confusion on his part and even here we can find indications that the idea of Oriental despotism is not far away; for example, when speaking of the Bey's minister and brother-in-law 'Mustapha Cogea', a Georgian slave, he writes, "Il est rare de voir, je ne dis pas dans les pays despotiques de l'Orient, mais même chez les peuples les plus civilisés, un homme plus sage, plus régulier dans ses moeurs ..."[65]. From which we can only conclude that Tunis too, despite his comparative praise for its unexpected virtues, was finally in Venture's eyes an Oriental despotism. It is difficult to ascertain how far Venture de Paradis's attitude should be taken as typical, even among those who, at the beginning of the Nineteenth Century emphasize the Barbary governments' depotism, for they rarely deduce this characteristic from their 'Oriental' nature, as does Venture, but rather from the evidence of their behaviour. Of course they were not in general, like Venture, professional orientalists.

Before drawing any conclusions, let us look quickly at the other characteristic associated with Orientals, which was present in Jardine's remark, namely the unchanging nature of their society. This belief refers to a set of characteristics that we have already noted; Orientals are considered to be passive, voluptuous and lazy and consequently sunk in unchanging ignorance. How far do we find such descriptions applied to the inhabitants of Barbary? Here again there would appear to be little specific awareness, in descriptions of the ignorance that Westerners see as reigning in Barbary, that this is a particularly *Oriental* characteristic, except insofar as it is on occasion, as we have seen, associated with the Islamic religion[66]. Rehbinder reports that, according to Venture de Paradis, the inhabitants of Algiers are ignorant not only of arts, manufactures, sciences, medicine and so on, but even of the Arabic language which, he says, is only mastered by one Moorish cadi[67]. In this writer we do find some of the clichés associated with Orientals, particularly when referring to the Turks of Algiers; he describes their laziness and passivity, ignorance and 'Sinnliche Wollust', although it is true that he also ascribes such defects to southern Europeans[68]. This makes me wonder whether he considers these to be particularly Oriental characteristics or whether he is merely expressing the Northerner's contempt for the effete Southerners, be they European, Asiatic or African. In addition, as I have said, Rehbinder is describing the Turkish militia and rulers who were, unlike the indigenous population, Orientals and were perceived as such, and hence as foreigners. But he does describe the buildings in the towns as Oriental[69]. There is also a trace of Oriental stereotypes in Poiret's letters, for in his description of the plague that I have already mentioned he ascribes the ravages made by this disease to the ignorance of the Orientals who do not take the precautions observed by the 'nations éclairées'; however from the context it is possible to infer that for Poiret this is merely another way of referring to the Moslems[70]. In some other authors we find descriptions of the inhabitants of Barbary that flatly contradict 'Oriental' stereotypes. They are frequently, for example, shown to be hard-working and sober; thus Laugier de Tassy, despite references to the 'dissolution des moeurs' informs us that the respected citizens of Algiers live in a simple, frugal, hard-working manner, an opinion that he repeats several times[71]. It is expressed also by Peyssonnel, at least as far as concerns the Turks and the 'Andalusian Moors'[72].

It is clear, then, that there is far from being unanimity on this subject.

The references to Oriental stereotypes or utilisation of the 'myth of the Orient', while present, are far from predominant in eighteenth-century writers. Instead there appears to be, as I have said, a general awareness of geographical realities. The clear exception of Venture de Paradis is instructive, for here we have a man who was an Oriental scholar and a diplomat. How far does he prefigure nineteenth-century opinions? If we return to the colonial propagandist Hain, whose remark concerning the town of Algiers we have already quoted, we notice that he uses the adjective 'Oriental' to describe the refined, sensual life of the rich Moors. This example entitles us to ask whether the reference to 'Oriental' clichés was not perhaps (except in the case of Venture — the exception that confirms the rule?) the result of ignorance of Barbary. This was the case of the nineteenth-century Romantics; Lucas and Vatin describe the disappointment of Eugène Fromentin or Théophile Gautier who arrived in Algiers in the mid-Century looking for oriental exoticism or, as Duvignaud puts it, on their 'voyage en Orient'[73], only to find a town (Algiers) which had become French and a poverty-stricken countryside. They therefore fled southwards, where the exoticism was different and equally false[74].

This reference to the Romantics brings us back to the painters already mentioned and to Delacroix's *Femmes d'Alger dans leurs appartements*. For the traits associated with Orientals, namely passivity and sensuality, were precisely those which were also associated with women. Hence the connection between the Orient and femininity, and the peculiar fascination exercised by 'Oriental' or Moslem women on the minds of European men. All the accounts of Barbary under discussion were written by men, who brought to their descriptions their own male point of view; for this reason their reactions to the women of Barbary, to whose world they were doubly alien, are particularly revealing concerning the stereotypes present in their writings. As they were excluded from the women's world, with which it was impossible to have any direct contact, it is not surprising to find the same details repeated from one author to another, and a reiteration of the same clichés and obsessions. The most obvious stereotype concerning Oriental women, and the women of the Ottoman Empire in particular, is that of the harem or 'seraglio', given great popularity in the Eighteenth Century by Montesquieu's *Lettres persanes*. The fascination it exercised (reappearing in works by Voltaire and Diderot as well as a score of other authors) is too well known to need further elaboration. But how far is this obsession at work in writings about Barbary? The answer would seem to be that it is there but in an indirect form, apart from romanticised accounts such as Thomas Pellow's *The History of the Long Captivity and Adventures [...]*, concerning Morocco[75]. By this statement I mean that we find frequent references to the seclusion of women, often in connection with criticisms of the Moslem religion, and of their subordination to men, which is frequently said to reduce them to the status of slaves[76]. Polygamy is often mentioned as well, again in the context of the religion, and there is frequent interest in descriptions of marriage-customs, often with quite far-fetched details. But most frequently writers on Barbary are forced to admit that the Oriental cliché par excellence − the harem − is sadly absent. While remarking on the existence of polygamy, they elaborate but little on the subject and observers such as Vallière, Rehbinder, Jackson or even Rozet in 1833 concede that it is little practised in towns and that 'seraglios' are extremely rare[77]. Rehbinder claims that polygamy is more frequent among the peasants, but this is hardly in keeping with the traditional image of the harem![78] It is interesting to observe that d'Argens, who is not in general favourably inclined towards the Barbary Regencies and is particularly hostile on the subject of their religion, insists on the liberty of women in North Africa and particularly in Algiers, compared to those in the Levant. He goes into some details, as is his wont on such subjects, concerning their tendency to 'galanterie' and explains that they have ample opportunity, given their husbands' long absences at sea, to indulge in their vices[79]. This opinion as to the liberty of Algerine women (which is not found in accounts by d'Argens's contemporaries) is echoed some time later by Rehbinder[80]. One aspect of Moorish women's 'galanterie' which is found, for example in Poiret's letters, is their taste for Christians and frequent affairs with European slaves, despite the dangers involved[81]. D'Argens recounts tales of such intrigues, which we should not take too seriously in view of his penchant for titillating stories which attracted readers. He thus exploits here the 'harem' myth of Oriental women made lascivious by their seclusion, for he explains their behaviour by a desire to react against their slavery. He is not apparently disturbed by the contradiction between this presentation of the facts and what he also said about their liberty. There is thus, behind his apparent refusal of the Oriental stereotype (for he had contrasted these women with the Levantines) the exploitation of this very cliché in order to appeal to his readers' prurience.

Among the writings of more reliable observers, there are remarks on the different status of women in the towns and the countryside; thus according to Peyssonnel the peasant women are freer and not veiled[82]. But as Shaw, Poiret and Rehbinder observe, they pay for this comparative freedom by hard work while the men take their ease[83]. But whether they enjoy some degree of liberty or are kept in complete seclusion, women are always presented as being the victims of men, to whom they are totally subordinated. This condemnation of the subjection of women, which was in fact a condemnation of Islamic society, reflects of course the Christian prejudices we saw in the first part of this book, but also the attitude of the eighteenth-century intellectual towards women. They were not considered as the equals of men but rather as companions to lighten men's idle moments and provide refinement and pleasant company. Given this viewpoint, it is inevitable that these European men would find little to attract them in Barbary, or in Islamic society in general, where the male and female worlds were totally separate. Interestingly enough, Mary Wortley Montagu, who saw the life of the upper-class women in Constantinople from the inside, is much less hostile. Typical of the attitude of the Western male is that shown by Poiret who, in his letter on women, condemns in particular the cruelty of husbands in Barbary and their lack of tenderness or consideration, even going as far as to affirm that they prefer their mare[84]. Few other writers go as far as the 'Rousseauist' Poiret, who describes these women as objects of pity or alternatively, in the case of the peasant women, with horror. His presentation of the latter contrasts with that of Shaw who had remarked on their beauty[85]. What we find, then, is a condemnation of the servile status of women in Islamic society rather than the fantasized 'Oriental' stereotype, which only surfaces briefly, as in d'Argens's sentimental stories. It is however amusing to observe the stereotype at work in the mind of the French Vice-consul Vallière; although he reports that polygamy is non-existent in Algiers, he gives an evocative description of women taking the evening air on the terraces in a half-naked and alluring state (which he can hardly have seen himself!). He describes in pathetic terms the domestic slavery of the women, but also their penchant for Christian slaves, and he makes some suggestive remarks concerning their behaviour in the Turkish baths[86]. We see here the eternal fascination held by the closed world of the women (despite awareness that there are no harems), which encouraged foreigners to let their imagination run riot, and which is an essential element of Western images of the Orient. It is surely not a coincidence that it is present in an observer who displays none of the Enlightenment's open-mindedness towards North Africa. For a similar tendency can be seen in the attitude of the Italian Pananti; his hostility towards Algiers likewise finds expression in this domain and we see the Oriental myth of the harem becoming an element of his argument for the European conquest of Barbary. He writes:

> Masters of Northern Africa, the harem walls must fall and suffer the miserable inmates to regain their natural rights in society, rendering the most beautiful part of creation what it should be, the happiness and consolation of mankind[87].

In such an argument we can see a large number of contradictory prejudices, concerning the existence of harems in North Africa and the role of women in society in general. An echo of the same obsession is found shortly after the French conquest, in a work by an anonymous writer refuting Hamdan's *Le Miroir*, to which I have already referred; here the author speaks of the Moors as 'amollis par la vie des harems'[88]. Such attitudes can be contrasted with the contemporaneous ones of James Grey Jackson, who considers women to be less confined than had generally been said although still at the mercy of their (monogamous) husbands, and even more William Shaler, for whom the women of Algiers are slaves not to their husbands but to custom[89]. Even Paul Raynal in 1830, who insists on the reclusion of Algerian women, informs his reader that in this town polygamy is very rare, although he claims that it is quite common among the 'Moors' in the countryside[90]. But by the time we come to Carette, in the 1840s, we find a contrast made between the liberty of the Kabyle women and the subjection of those in 'les villes musulmanes' who are, as it were, non-persons, buried alive in veils which are compared to shrouds[91]. What, though, are we to make of P. Raynal's decription of a marriage feast which he claims to have observed from his terrace? When the bride noticed him watching she brought her husband and, according to him, kissed him 'avec fureur' in order to provoke the Christian observer[92]. It is difficult to know how much credit to give to this story, but it is at least evidence of the persistence of erotic fantasies concerning the lascivious nature of 'Oriental' women and their application to Barbary. There is no doubt that they were present throughout the colonial era, as can be seen from a recently-published collection of early twentieth-century French postcards depicting Algerian women[93]. In general, eighteenth-century accounts of women in Barbary oscillate between fascination for their reputation for 'libertinage' and supposed passion for Christians, and contempt for their ignorance or pity for their servile status, between curiosity concerning the secluded beauties of the towns and horror for the miserable 'African' creatures of the countryside. In this domain, in which real knowledge or possibility of observation was extremely rare, hearsay and prejudice were the rule. It enables us to see that 'Oriental' stereotypes, here as elsewhere, although not entirely absent in the Eighteenth Century, are far from predominating and more often than not are seen to be contradicted by the evidence. They emerge more clearly at the beginning of the next Century, at least in connection with the towns, while the countryside tends to be more assimilated to African stereotypes.

This confirms the general impression we have received of the coexistence of disparate and even conflicting perceptions of Barbary's true character. On the one hand it is European, as is 'proven' by the evidence of ruins and history; but this does not really serve, until the end of the Century, as a justification for its occupation by European powers. The Mediterranean is not yet a European lake, for the Turks were still a force to be reckoned with and Europe's attention was still turned westwards. European nostalgia for the Christian past of North Africa, never extinguished, comes gradually to the fore, to be voiced for example in l'abbé Raynal's famous call for its conquest. The renewed interest in the Maghreb, which eventually culminated in the French expedition, is clearly voiced by Hegel in his *Lectures on the Philosophy of History*, contemporaneous with the French seizure of Algiers. Describing the coast of Africa North of the Sahara, which he even calls 'European Africa', he says that it is,

> A magnificent territory, in which Carthage once lay — the site of the modern Morocco, Algiers, Tunis and Tripoli. This part was to be — *must* be attached to Europe: the French have lately made a successful effort in this direction: like Hither-Asia, it looks Europe-wards. Here in their turn have Carthaginians, Romans and Byzantines, Mussulmans, Arabians had their abode and the interests of Europe have always striven to get a footing in it[94].

Here are the arguments that were to be reiterated by French colonial writers up to the present day. But at the same time, European expansionist aims were served by other conceptions of the Maghreb, which equally came to the fore during the same period. However contradictory it might appear, the inverse conception of Barbary, as an integral part of the African continent, grew concomitantly and justified the same end. For 'African' as we have seen meant primitive and barbarian, ripe for exploration and civilisation by Europeans. However difficult it might be to reconcile the accounts of travellers with the image of Africa as unknown and uncharted, peopled by 'black savages', this conception of the Maghreb was reinforced by commercial interest and became dominant after the French occupation of part of the region. All that was known of its civilisation or (to quote Shaler) its 'unafrican' characteristics, was forgotten, and this image was reconciled with the 'European' one, particularly in the early Nineteenth Century, by accusing the Moslems (or Turks, or Arabs) of having reduced, by their ignorance and despotism, this fine region to a state of ruin. The Turks were generally seen as aliens to be expelled, and Oriental visions of Barbary were confined to this ruling class and their government; they rarely concerned the ordinary inhabitants of North Africa. Oriental stereotypes only seem to have gained a hold on writers and artists in the Nineteenth Century and were not in evidence in the writings of soldiers or other officials, who were in no doubt that they were coming to the wilds of Africa. But whether passively

Oriental or savagely African, Barbary was in the Nineteenth Century tamed and conquered, reduced to an entity that no longer inspired fear in European hearts. The Moslem rulers were reduced to a passing, alien phenomenon, and the Christians could see themselves as simply continuing the tradition of North African history, interrupted momentarily by the 'barbarians'.

CHAPTER TWO

RACE

The problem of location, discussed in the last chapter, concerned to a great extent the land and its history; indeed, if it was seen as European, the contemporary inhabitants became either invisible or invaders to be expelled. But we have also seen, in connection with these diverging assessments of Barbary as a place, a corresponding disagreement as to its inhabitants. On the one hand, the image connected with Africa in European minds was that of 'black savages' which did not fit descriptions of the 'Moors' or Turks living in Barbary; on the other, as we have just seen, the women of the towns were perceived very differently from those in the countryside or in the mountains. It is this question of European perceptions of the inhabitants of Barbary that I propose to discuss in this chapter. It is complex, but also vital in view of the Enlightenment's particular preoccupation with the study of the human race. The main interest in study of foreign societies and customs was in order to further understanding of Man in his different manifestations, and the principal way of classifying the different parts of the world was according to their inhabitants. This classification falls into two main parts, namely that according to 'race'[1] and that according to social development; or, in other words, Man as a physical being and Man as a social being. In this chapter I shall deal with the first of these, reserving the second for Chapter 3.

In order to understand the issues involved here, we must first of all see briefly the background to the question of racial classification in the Eighteenth Century. It was during this century that the formal differentiation of the varieties or races of mankind was made, based essentially on the criterion of supposed biological differences as seen in varying physical appearance. It was one of the consequences of the new awareness of man as a physical being and part of the animal world, an awareness which began to develop during the Seventeenth Century, partly as a result of the revival of Epicurean philosophy[2]. The radical step in this process was the denial of an immaterial and immortal soul to distinguish man from the animals; the human being became simply a more perfectly constituted animal whose intellect was the result of his physical make-up and determined by the organisation of his body, and particularly of his brain.

Though the new attitude was in part stimulated by Descartes's writings, it also involved a questioning of the Cartesian distinction between mind and matter, for a more dynamic conception of the latter, to include the properties of motion and even thought. The more extreme forms of materialism to be found in writers from Hobbes to La Mettrie, Diderot, d'Holbach or Helvétius were widely rejected; it is nevertheless, in my opinion, true to say that the assumption that man was an essentially material being and determined ultimately by his physical organisation and/or environment came to underlie much of the thinking about his nature and place in the natural order[3]. Although most thinkers claimed to believe in the existence of an immortal soul and to follow the teachings of the Christian church, in practice they tended more and more to put such beliefs to one side and to treat human beings as if they were purely material entities and part of the animal world. Consequently, like the rest of the animal world, they could be classified according to the different varieties that had been observed in the different regions of the globe. The pioneer of such classifications of the natural world was Linnaeus with his botanical system. As a consequence of these developments Buffon, in his huge *Histoire naturelle* included man, as a matter of course, in the natural world; in his essay 'Sur les variétés de l'espèce humaine', from which Diderot took his *Encyclopédie* article HUMAINE, ESPECE, he gives a survey of the different human types, their customs and habits. He distinguishes these different varieties mainly according to their skin colour, but also notes other physical and moral characteristics. He insists on the unity of the human race, but assumes as a matter of course the superiority of the European nations. Thus he is concerned to show that the white variety is the original one and that changes in colour or 'degenerations' from this original perfection have come about due to the effects mainly of the climate but also of food or way of life. In this way were created the less perfect races, ranging through different degrees of 'difformity' to the black Africans[4]. The relative importance of climate, to which Buffon accorded the prime role, was a subject of debate throughout the century, with arguments for and against, using the examples of black Africans transported to temperate zones; whether or not their children became white would, it was thought, provide evidence as to the influence of climate. This question of the colour of the Africans and the reason for their apparent radical difference from the rest of the human race was a subject of perpetual interest. A considerable number of scientific works were published concerning the origin of their skin colour[5]. There were even those, such as Lord Kames or Hume in the notorious note in his essay 'Of National Characters' — to say nothing of racist writers like Long, the proslavery propagandist — who concluded that the negroes

were of a totally different and inferior race that was nearer to the apes
than to Man[6]. For these writers, 'racial' differences were not simply the
result of accidents such as climate or way of life but much more fundamental. Of course these arguments concerning the relative influence
of climate, way of life and 'moral' factors on the one hand, and inherent,
physically-determined characteristics on the other, was part of a wider
debate concerning the factors influencing human nature. The most
famous, though by no means the first, proponent of the influence of
climate on both human character and social organisation was Montesquieu, while among the materialists who explained human conduct by
determinisms beyond his control, there was a sharp division between
Helvétius — who insisted on 'moral' factors, in particular education —,
and those who, like La Mettrie and Diderot, paid much more attention
to his inherent physical organisation. As far as the question of race rather
than individual characteristics was concerned, Buffon's climatic theory
exercised a preponderant influence on scientific investigations into
human varieties. But he himself did not attempt a rigid classification of
races, being content to describe the different peoples, physical
characteristics, way of life and customs, and including some dubious
anecdotes culled from travellers' tales. In his account, the peoples of
North Africa, living to the south of the ideal temperate zone, home of the
perfect white races, had consequently degenerated slightly from this
original perfection and are described as 'swarthy'; the same description
is repeated by Diderot in his *Encyclopédie* article[7]. This is also J.B.
Robinet's opinion in his *Considérations philosophiques de la gradation naturelle
des formes de l'être*, for he includes the Arabs, Persians, Egyptians and
Moors among those who, living to the south of the most temperate zone,
are well-proportioned and handsome, but browner than the Europeans,
although he does say that Moorish women are very white, "d'un teint de
lys et de roses, d'une taille grande et dégagée'[8].

The haphazard descriptions of Buffon, mixing as they did cultural and
physical characteristics (not to mention fantastic details) were inadequate
from a scientific point of view and soon led to more systematic racial
classifications, of which the most influential well into the Nineteenth
Century was that of the German Blumenbach, published in the second
half of the Eighteenth Century[9]. Although he too insisted on the unity
of the human race, he was more concerned than his predecessors to
divide it into subgroups according to purely physical characteristics. The
main ones were skin colour and, following the Dutchman Peter Camper,
skull shape[10]. Like Buffon, he explained the different varieties by
degeneration from an original prototype, and among the reasons that he
gave for this degeneration, the main one was the climate. The influence

of the climate on the degeneration of the human race became more pronounced in later editions of his work as Blumenbach perhaps realised the dangers of polygenecist arguments that the Negroes were of a totally different, and inferior, origin from the rest of mankind; for such arguments could find apparent confirmation in purely physical — and hence inherent and unchanging — determinations of racial differences. Blumenbach's desire to argue against polygenecism can be seen from the very title of his work, *On the Unity of the Human Race*. But, like Buffon, although Blumenbach and his followers insisted on the common origin of all mankind, they nevertheless believed in a clear hierarchy of 'races', with the whites at the top and the Negroes at the bottom. One may infer, though, that in view of the influence of climate and 'moral' factors, racial differences are not fixed and unchanging; indeed, Blumenbach remarks frequently on the difficulty of drawing clear demarcation lines between the different varieties, which shade imperceptibly into one another. Such subtleties tended to be forgotten by later users of his classificatory system. But in what does his system consist? For Blumenbach there are five main varieties or races, distinguished according to characteristics such as skull shape, hair and of course skin colour. These varieties are: Caucasian, Mongol, Negro, American and Malay (the last two intermediate between the first three main groups). They shade into one another but are confined to certain regions of the globe; it is the geographical location which in the last resort seems to determine their classification in one group or another. Thus, if we look for the North Africans, whom Buffon described as swarthy, we find that the only place we can fit them in is in the class of Caucasians or whites, for the intermediate races are either the Americans or the Malaysians, both geographically circumscribed. It is impossible to describe them as Mongol, and they are clearly very different from the black Africans as they live in a more temperate zone. As a result, together with the inhabitants of Western Asia (which includes the Arabs), they are admitted into the favoured category of the whites. It may be that, with the shading off from one group into another, they are often close to the blacks who are palest, such as the Mandingos or others[11]; but for all that, they are indisputably part of the finest race, the original humans, from whom the other varieties have degenerated. It is perhaps possible to see here the lingering influence of religious beliefs, with the Biblical story of the Garden of Eden as the cradle of humanity, but whatever the reason, it is perfectly clear that in this highly influential system of racial classification, the inhabitants of Barbary and all the Arabs are assimilated to the European variety of mankind. They appear, we might say, to have gone up in the world since Buffon and the *Encyclopédie* article, where the emphasis was on their swarthy skin. The importance of this racial classification resides in the value judgements associated with it from its original formulation, which had a long and tenacious existence. The classification codified a hierarchy of peoples throughout the world, and both reflected and influenced the way in which they were seen by Europeans. It is in this context quite significant to see that the peoples of Barbary could, in the Eighteenth Century, be put in the same category as the Europeans without apparently shocking anyone. Indeed, such a conception was not new but was rather, as it were, consecrated by custom, for already Leo Africanus had called Barbary the most noble part of Africa, inhabited by the white race[12].

If we turn to the works of those who wrote about the Maghreb in the Eighteenth Century, we find traces of the same attitude in remarks to the effect that the inhabitants of the region are not black but simply sunburnt; the fact that they are born white can be seen in the complexions of the secluded women[13]. Rehbinder in fact echoes Blumenbach when he writes that the town-dwelling Moors belong to the superior, most beautiful white race[14]. Otherwise the question of the racial classification of these people is not an important matter for speculation in the sense that, apart from these isolated remarks there is no serious discussion of the physical characteristics that would consign the inhabitants to a particular racial group. In other words, it is rare to find, in the Eighteenth Century, specifically racist remarks about the North Africans[15]. This will become very clear if we look, in comparison, at what was written about their black neighbours to the south. The difference in attitude is particularly flagrant in the case of Gibbon who, as we have seen, shows a certain amount of sympathy towards the Arabs in general. Concerning the 'Moors', whom he refers to as barbarians, he shows contempt but no more; when it comes, however, to the "unknown and uninteresting tribes of Africa" who "differed only in their colour from the ordinary appearance of the human species", he considers them to be too ignorant to be dangerous. Indeed,

> They appear incapable of forming any extensive plans of government or conquest; and the obvious inferiority of their mental faculties has been discovered and abused by the nations of the temperate zone[16].

Although he continues by condemning the slave trade and refers to the *Histoire des Deux Indes*, it is clear that his attitude to the black Africans is not merely that they are ignorant barbarians, but that they are constitutionally incapable of any further progress. His judgement is based on their supposedly natural inferiority. This attitude towards the Africans was widespread even before it was enshrined in racial classifications and was, as we have seen, held even by those who insisted on the common origin of mankind. Those who believed in the totally separate origin of Negroes went even further, assimilating them to the apes. The same restriction of racist attitudes to blacks lies behind Peyssonnel's division of the population of Barbary into three classes, of which the highest, or Turkish race has fine 'white blood', while the lowest is that with the greatest mix of negro blood[17]. Here we can see the existence of uninterrupted racial prejudice concerning the superiority of the whites over the blacks, which the Enlightenment did very little to combat, but instead codified in the racial classifications that we have seen. But Peyssonnel's undoubtedly racist judgement concerns 'blackness' and not the 'Moors' or 'Arabs' as such. It confirms, I think, what I have said concerning perceptions of the North Africans in the Eighteenth Century; to the extent that they were perceived as whites and hence different from the blacks to the South, they were not considered as inherently inferior.

It has been suggested that a racist attitude towards the North Africans emerges before the middle of the century, in particular with Thomas Shaw[18]. The remark by this author that is particularly incriminated is that made in the introduction to his *Travels*, about the 'Wild Arabs', who are "all of them the same and have all the like inclinations (whenever a proper opportunity or temptation offers itself) or robbing, stripping and murthering, not strangers only, but also one another"[19]. It should first of all be pointed out that the supposedly larcenous tendencies of the Arabs were noted by several writers, including Gibbon, who explains it by the way of life and geographical conditions in which they live and which make them consider all strangers as enemies. It does not prevent him from praising their bravery and warlike virtues[20]. It is true that such remarks were part of the racist panoply of colonialist writers in the Nineteenth Century, but here it is made in a very different context. It is also true that Shaw shows his fear of these turbulent peoples, for whom he has little sympathy, but their tendency to rapine is a cultural and not a racial characteristic and does not imply a judgement as to their supposed inferiority. It should, I hope, be clear from what I have said above about eighteenth-century perceptions of racial differences, and value judgements based on racial classifications, that this remark by Shaw does not express a *racist* judgement but rather distaste for a certain way of life and fear of warlike peoples; this latter detail is noted by Gibbon, who writes at one point, "But Shaw had seen these savages with distant terror"[21]. As for Shaw's comment that they are 'all of them the same', it was not made in the sense of later racists, but instead to express the contemporary belief, found in many authors, that all the nomadic Arabs lived in the same way and were the same from the Arabian desert to Africa; no one group could be singled out as 'wilder' than the others. The difference will become clearer if we compare Shaw's attitude to the openly racist ones that are to be found creeping in towards the end of the century, during a period that coincides with the development of polygenecist arguments designed to demonstrate the hopeless inferiority of the Negroes. Particularly virulent were the partisans of the West Indian planters who felt themselves to be threatened by the anti-slavery campaigners. The coincidence of these two developments is perhaps not fortuitous. In the work on Algiers written by Pananti, we find the following description of the Moors, whom he contrasts extremely unfavourably with the mountain and desert dwellers of Barbary, and even with the Negroes; he writes that "there is something harsh and ominous in their physiognomy, extremely repulsive to the European". Their sobriety, praised by earlier commentators, is rendered thus: "Their countenance is never enlivened by a noble thought or a generous sentiment"; "theirs is the smile of death". And their constancy under suffering is not stoicism but the "cold ferocity of a savage". They are perfidious, debauched, avaricious and so on[22]. Such an attitude can be qualified as racist, although Pananti does admit the possibility of improvement if they were governed by Christians who would convert "those who are now scarcely superior to the brute creation" "into good men and industrious citizens"[23]. It is, however, no more than a possibility which he considers to be rather remote in view of the Moors' 'fanaticism'. His condemnation is therefore sweeping; as we can see, it applies not simply to their way of life but, more generally, to their very nature which arouses in this author instinctive loathing. It is for this reason that we can, I believe, call Pananti a racist, which distinguishes him from the majority of eighteenth-century writers on Barbary. This racism is expressed in terms of instinctive revulsion and is not given a scientific justification which would, at the time, have been difficult to find. The only earlier traces of a similar attitude can perhaps be discerned creeping into works dating from the end of the century. Venture de Paradis's manuscripts are a case in point; concerning the population of Barbary, he writes, in a remark that bears some resemblance to those of Pananti: "rien de plus grossier, de plus barbare, de plus approchant la brute que la populace de la Barbarie"; or he compares the character of the Algerines to that of children whose reactions are excessive and who cannot distinguish between an individual and the government he represents[24]. Again, in his notes for Raynal, he insists that there are no 'gens délicats' among the Arabs and Moors, both men and women[25]. For Venture, then, the inhabitants of Barbary, as a whole, are apparently included in his condemnation of everything 'Oriental' and they are considered not as individuals (with the exception of some of the ministers), but as an undifferentiated mass. Here again, I think we can say that Venture is a representative of a new attitude which distinguishes him from a man of the Enlightenment such as Raynal, who did not take account of such remarks[26]. But can we qualify it as racist? This epithet can, I think, be given to a rather worrying reaction on the part of the abbé Poiret, the 'Rousseauiste', whose disillusion with the North Africans perhaps led him to excesses. I am referring to his remark concerning the 'loi du sang' according to which, if a 'Moor' killed a Christian, he should pay 300 piastres (which he usually, according to Poiret, neglected to do), while if a Christian killed a 'Moor' in any circumstances, he was forced to pay 500 piastres. Poiret exclaims, "Voilà donc le sang maure, ce sang impur et féroce, évalué plus de la moitié plus que celui des chrétiens"[27]. The aim of this remark was to condemn the debasement of the French merchants at La Calle, but it reveals an unpleasant attitude towards the Moors, with distinctly racist overtones, for the latter's 'impure and ferocious blood' is apparently inferior even to that of the degraded and despicable Christian merchants. Poiret was writing at the same time as Venture de Paradis, and his reaction is another sign of a change in attitude towards the end of the century, when criticism of the Barbaresques' behaviour seems to turn into contempt for the whole North African 'race'.

The direction in which such contempt could lead can be seen from the pamphlet written by V.A. Hain, member of the Société coloniale de l'Etat d'Alger, entitled *A la Nation. Sur Alger* and published just after the conquest. Hain explains that it is ridiculous to think of civilising the inhabitants of the conquered territory, for they are incapable of any improvement; they must be cleared off the land to make way for French colonists. The expressions of contempt for these ferocious, degraded and miserable inhabitants pile up; their inferiority to the Europeans is proven, but they refuse to admit it and vow an implacable hatred towards the conquerors, which they hide under an impenetrable mask. But beneath their perfidious smile lies the desire to torture the French and tear them limb from limb. His racist diatribe leads him to say that "tout Arabe est né bourreau, bourreau par essence, bourreau par vocation"; they delight, according to Hain, in causing suffering[28]. Such excesses, which can only be explained in terms of psychoanalysis, are 'substantiated' by the story of an innocent young French girl who had supposedly been cruelly assassinated by the Kabyles, an event which is depicted in a melodramatic fashion on the frontispiece of the pamphlet. Hain is perhaps an extreme and pathological case, but such attitudes run through colonialist writings and had a tenacious existence after their officialisation by those who wrote about the 'indigenous races' after the colonisation of Algeria[29].

Given such developments, it would have been difficult to continue to consider the North Africans as part of the superior Caucasian race, and indeed we find indications that their demotion had begun some time before 1830. In the work by J.J. Virey entitled *Histoire naturelle du genre humain* published in 1802, there is, despite the dedication to Buffon, a racist utilisation of Blumenbach's classification of the human race; the Celts are exalted as the most perfect species, while the Negroes are compared to the apes, and the 'savages', his lowest category, are quite simply counted as part of the ape family. In Virey's work, the classification has become even more explicitly a hierarchy of the races according to their progress towards perfection, although the author admits that the order is not eternally fixed and may vary with time. In this system, which follows Blumenbach's five-part division, the Turks, Persians and ancient Egyptians are now part of the second race, called 'esclavonnes et mongoles', while the third, corresponding apparently to the Malays in the German's classification, now includes the 'hordes arabes', the Moors and the Barbaresques, as well as the Tartars[30]. The inhabitants of Barbary have been demoted in racial terms, and in terms of their progress towards civilisation. They appear, for Virey, to have little hope of improvement despite his concession that the classification may alter, for he does not consider that the climate always plays a crucial role. For him, intelligence is related to the size of the brain, measured by skull shape and thus to inherent, physically-determined characteristics. We could also mention the work by Bory de Saint-Vincent, *L'Homme. Essai zoologique sur le genre humain*, which provides a much more complex system of classification, with fifteen main racial types; here the Arabs occupy the second place after the 'Japetic' or European race which is, of course, the most perfect. Despite certain intellectual qualities, the Arabs' bilious and sanguin temperament, which makes them miserly, leads to brigandage. Hence their tendency to thieving, attributed to them by European observers, as we have seen, becomes now a racially-determined characteristic[31].

There is indubitably during the early years of the Nineteenth Century a set of developments concerning racial theories that all point in the same direction. On the one hand, given the increase in anti-slavery propaganda, prosegregationists such as Long evolved more elaborate theories as to the inferiority of the Negroes[32], and on the other, support for such views came from 'scientific' evidence based mainly on skull shapes, considered to be an indelible racial characteristic which conferred inferior mental faculties on the non-European races. This tendency was particularly marked in France and championed by scientists such as Cuvier who 'demonstrated' that the Negro was closer to the ape than to the European[33]. At the same time there is evidence that the peoples of Barbary came gradually to be considered as inferior not only in civilisation and culture but also in supposedly racially determined intellectual capacities. Evidence of this belief can be found both in scientific works and in descriptions by visitors and, again, more in French than in English writers. That the French were more inclined to racist arguments was the opinion of J.C. Prichard, who argued strongly, in works such as *Researches into the Physical History of Man*[34], for the unity of the human race against writers such as Bory de Saint-Vincent. Prichard tends to distinguish between different human groups on criteria of language rather than physical characteristics. Thus he discusses the Berbers of North Africa, using evidence taken from the works of Shaw, Venture de Paradis or Jackson, essentially in terms of their language[35]. Likewise, English writers on Barbary tend, in the early Nineteenth Century, to criticise the population, not in racist terms but on the grounds of their customs, government and so on. For Americans this is less evident; a remark by Shaler is extremely interesting in this connection, despite his balanced judgements that we have already seen. When discussing the advantages of conquering North Africa and of establishing European colonies of settlement, he lists the various advantages presented by the Regency of Algiers in particular and adds the 'moral advantage' of its smallness of population; he explains that, as a result, the natives could intermarry with the colonists 'without dishonour to, or deterioration of the pure blood of Europe', and he goes on to say,

> To the generality of Europeans, this remark may appear trivial but a citizen of the United States, accustomed to contemplate his own country, unfortunately encumbered with a mass of black population which cannot be thus disposed of, will feel its force and importance.[36]

The racism of this remark is too obvious to need further elaboration, and it shows that the North Africans were considered by Shaler to be, like the other Africans, of an inferior racial stock; hence no doubt his belief that they could only be civilised by European occupation. But he does nevertheless consider that they can be 'easily led into' civilisation "through a system of government less repugnant in its principles and practice, than that under which they live"[37]. This indicates that even for Shaler 'moral' factors play a role in determining the character and degree of evolution of different peoples. Indeed, what we note about writers on Barbary during this period is that there is practically no appeal to 'scientific' theories of racial differences, but rather to 'instinctive' and emotional feelings.

Attempts at explaining the apparently inferior civilisation of the Barbary states turned more frequently in the early Nineteenth Century, as they did in the Eighteenth Century, to sociological rather than racial explanations; in other words, to come back to the division I mentioned at the beginning of this chapter, moral factors were preferred to physical ones when considering the forces determining human development. These moral factors were essentially the government, religion and social organisation, while the physical factors were on the one hand climate and on the other, physical organisation. Climate was also conceded an indirect influence, through the form of government which, following Montesquieu, was seen to be to some extent determined by it. But, while physical organisation was seized upon as a determining factor by racial theorists, as we have seen, it plays but little role in eighteenth-century speculation on the North Africans; this fact once more differentiates works on Barbary from what was written about Sub-Saharan Africa. Instead, as a few examples will show, writers prefer to explain the ignorance and lack of advancement that they saw in terms that were not racial but sociological. Here is Shaw, for example, describing the ignorance and lack of learning in Barbary:

> The roving and unsettle life of the *Arabs*, and the perpetual grievances the *Moors* meet with from the *Turks*, will not permit either of them to enjoy that Liberty, Quiet and Security which have at all Times given Birth and Encouragement to Learning.[38]

Likewise d'Argens explains the frequent revolutions in the Barbary states, not by any innate tendency towards bloodshed, but by the defects of the governments, and insists that in the same situation a Frenchman or a German would behave in the same way[39]. And in 1770 the Russian Kokovtsov believes that if the Barbaresques are pirates it is not because they are naturally ferocious but because of their tyrannical governments that push them to it[40]. Even Vallière, who has nothing but contempt for the natives of Algeria, implies that their vices come from the tyranny from which they suffer, although his condemnation does also have racial overtones[41]. Leyden, in 1799, considers that despotism leads to 'ferocity and voluptuousness of character' as well as apathy, meanness and vice[42]. He explains the unchanging character of the Moors by the spirit of their laws, institutions, customs and manners rather than by physical causes. We find therefore in such writers, despite their hostility towards the North Africans, something of the spirit of the abbé Raynal who insisted on the degrading effects of despotism; the call for the invasion of Barbary, published in the *Histoire des Deux Indes* and reproduced in his manuscripts, is justified by the need to save the inhabitants from Turkish tyranny, under which they can never progress. His sentiment was echoed by Rehbinder who admits the Moors' corrupt character, but likewise attributes it to the Turks' despotic treatment of them[43]. This German follower of the Enlightenment includes, at the end of his work on Algiers, a discussion of the influence of climate and geographical situation on the character of peoples and on their form of government, in the course of which he appeals to Herder, de Pauw and Boulanger. He accepts a certain influence of the climate but believes that it should not be overestimated; at the same time he criticises those who have gone to the opposite extreme and denied all role to the climate. Here he quotes Helvétius as the main representative of such extremists. His own opinion is exemplified in the same section, when he describes the effect of a hot climate as leading to 'Trägheit, Gemächtlichkeit, herrschende Sinnlichkeit', which he considers to be the main characteristics of the Algerians; he adds that these tendencies are amplified by their education and religious beliefs[44].

It is this general acceptance of theories concerning the role of social and 'moral' factors, even when combined with the influence of the climate, which apparently hindered the appearance of fully-blown racial explanations for what was seen to be the degraded character of the North Africans during the Eighteenth Century. A truly racial contempt, for which 'scientific' explanations were gradually found, was felt towards the black Africans, but inasmuch as the peoples north of the Sahara were not considered to be black, they were excluded from this contempt. Racial denigration of the North Africans begins to appear towards the end of the Eighteenth Century; it coincides with perceptions of them as no longer forming part of the white race and with the exacerbation of polygenecist arguments. The connection between these developments is not, however, completely clear, as racist remarks concerning the inhabitants of Barbary tend, in the early Nineteenth Century, to be purely emotional and do not appeal to scientific evidence. For example, we find no reference to arguments concerning skull shapes, of the type found in Cuvier's works. For the moment, all we can do is note the coincidence and the fact that all of these developments are symptoms of the general change in outlook concerning North Africa that occured during this period. Before attempting an explanation, we shall have to discuss other aspects of this change in outlook. First, however, there is an aspect of the racial question that I have so far glossed over, but which is an essential part of the puzzle; I touched upon it above when I quoted Peyssonnel's division of the population of Barbary into three classes according to their racial mixture. For Peyssonnel's attempt to classify this population is just one example of the different ways of approaching the evident lack of homogeneity of the North Africans, a question which we must now go into in some detail.

The way in which the 'Moors' fitted into the general system of racial classification and of explanations of national characteristics is only one aspect of European perceptions of them, which is a much more complex subjet. For all writers agreed that the population of Barbary was far from homogeneous. I have already mentioned the distinction made between the Turkish or Levantine ruling group and the 'African' natives; but this distinction was not the only one made. The popular view today is that the population of North Africa is divided into two main groups, the Arabs and the Berbers; the acceptance of this two-fold division by non-specialist writers is reflected in remarks such as that made by J.B. Wolf in his book *The Barbary Coast*, where he writes that "Père Dan was one of the first Europeans to recognize the difference between Arabs and Berbers (Moors)"[45]. Insistence on a simple two-fold division of the population leads this historian into a certain amount of confusion in his apparently unhesitating identification of the Moors and the Berbers, which is to misinterpret what was written during the Eighteenth Century. Before going any further into this tangled skein, I should emphasize here that I have no intention of trying to sort out the rights and wrongs of different interpretations of the composition of the North African population; this is an extremely sensitive and politically-charged field which I am not at all competent to discuss. My aim is simply to try to understand the perceptions of this population that existed during the Eighteenth Century and the way in which these perceptions changed with the colonisation of part of North Africa after 1830. This is, in itself, no easy task for, to quote Shaler, 'everything relating to these countries is very loosely fixed'[46]. The problem concerns essentially the indigenous population as there was little disagreement possible concerning the Turks, Christians or Jews, although the Jews present a slightly different problem which I shall deal with separately at the end. As for these native inhabitants, there are various combinations of names used to distinguish the different groups among them; those that we find most commonly used are Moors, Arabs, Bedouins, Berbers and, for Algeria, Kabyles. Some authors, such as Rehbinder, mention the Negroes, but in the main little attention is paid to this group as it apparently presented no particular interest for most observers. The complicating factors concerning attempts to describe the population is that the groups designated by these names vary from author to author and we even find a writer like M. Noah in 1819 claiming that most of these groups were not in fact indigenous[47]. More recent specialists, writing during the colonial era, do not usually seem to be aware of the existence of a problem. Thus M. Canard, who edited Kokovtsov's journal in the *Revue africaine*, notes that the term 'Bedouin' or 'Arab' was used by eighteenth-century writers to refer to all country-dwellers, in opposition to 'Moors' which designated townspeople[48]; he refers the reader to a note by Monchicourt in an earlier article in the same *Revue africaine*. When we turn to this latter note, concerning a sixteenth-century Italian account of Barbary, we find that while Monchicourt agrees that 'Arabs' designates 'les musulmans des campagnes' or Bedouins, he gives the term 'Moors' as referring to the 'indigènes' in general and only sometimes also to the 'musulmans des villes et bourgades' — which is not quite the same thing[49]. Furthermore, in the very text he is editing, we find later on the information that the country around Algiers is inhabited by the 'Moors', with the explanation 'c'est à dire des Arabes sous des tentes'[50]. Apparently here 'Moors' means the same thing as 'Arabs' or 'Bedouins' instead of being contrasted with them. It would appear that these historians have rather over-simplified earlier usage. J. Cuoq, more recently, in a note to his edition of Venture de Paradis's texts on Algiers and Tunis, gives the social stratification in the Eighteenth Century as follows: below the Turks and Coloughlis (children of Turks and native women) come the 'Moors' or Arab population of the towns, then the 'Arab' population of the countryside, whether fellahs or nomads and then the Berbers, the last two categories being designated as 'Bedouins'. At the bottom come the Jews[51]. As we shall see, however, eighteenth-century usage among Europeans was not as clear-cut and unproblematic as this.

If we turn to what was written in the Eighteenth Century, we find a remark by Venture de Paradis that may throw some light on the matter. This author corrects Raynal's manuscript concerning the latter's use of the word 'Moor', explaining that this term is only used by the Europeans and never by the inhabitants of Barbary themselves, to refer to all the 'Arabs'; instead Venture explains that they should be distinguished according to whether they live in the town or in tents. It would appear from this remark that for this specialist the terms 'Arab' and 'Moor' in fact designate the same group among the population[52]. Confirmation of this loose European usage of the word 'Moors' can be found in the *Encyclopédie* article HUMAINE, ESPECE or in Chénier's *Recherches historiques sur les Maures*, where it simply designates the inhabitants of 'Mauritania'[53]. But Venture does himself use the word 'Moors' on occasion and, in his replies to Raynal's questions on Tunisia, distinguishes this group — which he prefers to call the Arabs in the towns and villages — from the 'Arabs', or as he prefers, the Bedouins living in tents[54]. Here then the word 'Moors', although still, for Venture, improper, designates only a part of the 'Arab' population. It is evident that popular usage was far from standardised. But what of those who, in the Eighteenth Century, tried to give a coherent account of Barbary? It would perhaps be useful at this point to give some idea of the different systems of classification that I have found; in order to avoid a fastidious enumeration of all the descriptions to be found, I shall only indicate the most common or significant terminologies and those to be found in the most important works on Barbary.

In the account of d'Arvieux's travels that was published in the early Eighteenth Century, the whole of the indigenous population of North Africa is referred to as 'Moors', whether they live in the town or the countryside. This author also mentions the 'Morisque' town-dwellers, descendants of the Moors who had been expelled from Spain and Portugal. He makes a distinction between the true Arabs, originally from the Middle East, who are nomadic Bedouins, and the Moors whom the former regard with contempt as they have given up their ancestors' way of life to settle on the land or in the towns. Otherwise he says very little about the Moors, preferring to praise the way of life of the Bedouins or 'Arabs'. As he does not describe the countryside or the mountains in Barbary, he has no occasion to go into details concerning their inhabitants as he had concerning the Arabs in the Middle East. Once, when speaking of the country around Tunis, he mentions the 'Arabs' who are apparently Bedouins, but this is all[55]. There is a greater attempt at classification in Peyssonnel's account of his journey in Barbary. As I have already mentioned, he divides the population into three classes: the Turks from the Levant, the well-off town-dwellers, and the Bedouins or Arab peasants. This third group is also referred to as the 'Maures de la campagne' or 'Bedouins maures'; he thus apparently uses the terms 'Bedouins', 'Arabs' and 'Moorish peasants' as synonymous. The town-dwellers are also referred to as 'Moors', whence the need to distinguish between town and country Moors. Like d'Arvieux, Peyssonnel treats the Andalusian Moors as a class apart, considerably superior to the indigenous Moors. Unfortunately, his use of these different terms is far from clear, for he also distinguishes between Arabs and Moors in the countryside[56]. In addition, there is a difference in his perception of the Regencies of Tunis and Algiers, for in Tunis he mentions only the 'Spanish Moors' of the towns and the 'Bedouin Arabs' of the countryside, whether in the plains or the mountains. This usage is later extended to Algeria, where the peoples of the Auress mountains and Kabylie are described as Arabs although perceived as being different from the other Arabs. He also says that the 'Arabes kabyles' or Berbers are perhaps descended from the Saracens and are thus different from the 'Arabes du pays'[57]. Could we say that in general the term 'Moors' is used by Peyssonnel for the town-dwellers and the word 'Arabs' for all of the rest? This is in the main true, but it does not prevent him from distinguishing the 'Arabes maures' in the towns from the 'Arabes bédouins' in the countryside. His awareness of the difference between townspeople and countryfolk is clear, but his terminology is hardly so; furthermore, his distinction between sedentary inhabitants and nomads is clear neither in his terminology nor in his description. Finally, the word 'Kabyles' is used for the mountain 'Arabs' of the whole region from Algiers to Collo, but the word Berber is not used[58]. If we turn to Shaw, who used Peyssonnel's notes to some extent, we again find the words 'Arab', 'Moor' and 'Bedoween'; he appears to distinguish the Moors from the Arabs, the latter term being used on the whole as a synonym for the country-dwellers and often for the Bedouin. These Bedouin, described as those living in the plains in tents, are carefully distinguished from the Kabyles, who live in houses in the mountains and whom Shaw considers to be the ancient Africans; they are said to have retreated to the mountains to flee the invaders, from whom the present Arabs are descended. This distinction between the Kabyles and the Bedouin is much clearer in Shaw's work than in earlier descriptions and is substantiated by examples of their language, which he considers to be very different from Arabic or Hebrew[59]. In comparison to his clear definition of the Kabyles, his use of the word 'Arab' is more confused, although the word 'Moor' seems to refer consistently to the townspeople. We should also mention Shaw's description of the blond-haired Auressians, whom he considers to be descended from the Vandals, an affirmation that was repeated by Gibbon, Bruce, Shaler and even some present-day writers; but Shaw insisted that this theory only applied to the inhabitants of the 'Jibell Auress' who are different from the 'other Kabyles'[60].

Laugier de Tassy makes a more systematic attempt to distinguish the different groups among the population, which are, according to him: the original inhabitants, the Moors and the Arabs, as well, of course, as the Jews, Turks and Christians. He says nothing about the original inhabitants, beyond the fact that they were white and were originally called Berbers; they were pushed into the mountains by the different waves of invaders and also invaded Spain after the arrival of the Arabs from the East. Those Moors now living in the plains are, for Laugier, the miserable descendants of the original Berbers, while the town-dwellers, a separate group, are the descendants of those who fled from Spain. As for the Arabs, they are the offspring of the conquerors from the East who were dispossessed by the Turks and fled to the mountains and the deserts where they live in liberty. Laugier criticises the majority of authors, who have confused the Arabs with the Moors; the latter is, according to him, the name improperly given by the Turks to all those living in the countryside (and not in the towns)[61]. Thus Laugier is at great pains to distinguish not only the inhabitants of town and country, but also the Arabs and Moors, who are for him of totally different origins, although both live in the countryside. 'Arabs' seems for this author to designate the Bedouins, a term which is absent from his work. However, he too falls into the habit on occasion of using the term 'Moors' to refer to the whole of the indigenous population. Despite this inconsistency, his attempt to clarify the complex question of the composition of the population of Barbary is praiseworthy and it is greatly superior to the usage to be found in the much later letters written by the abbé Poiret. This traveller does attempt, in his first letter, to throw some light on the question, explaining in a footnote that the inhabitants of Barbary go by several different names; but unfortunately the punctuation makes this note difficult to interpret. Apparently those living on the coast are called Moors, while the nomads in the interior are 'Arabes bédouins' or Berbers; the farmers and pastors he calls 'Cabaïls'[62]. Despite this attempt at definition, Poiret uses the terms 'Arab' and 'Moor' indiscriminately to refer to the mass of the indigenous population, changing from one word to another in the middle of a description. For example, in his Sixth Letter, he talks of looking for traces of the ancient Numidians among the mountain 'Arabs' and continues by praising the physiognomy of the 'Moors'. After this he describes the costume of the 'Moors', concluding by writing that this costume is particularly found among the 'Arabes errants des montagnes et du désert'[63]. In view of his complete lack of precision, it is difficult to find a pattern in his usage, although the word 'Arabs' is most often used when he insists on a description of wild or roving peoples. The word 'Cabaïl', after his initial attempt at definition, is not used again. With Poiret, then, confusion appears to have reached its height, and it is interesting to observe the same confusion in his contemporary, and for a while fellow-traveller, Desfontaines. In his *Fragments*, Desfontaines attempts no classification of the inhabitants or even definition of the terms he uses, which are imprecise. We find the inhabitants of the region around Sfax in the Tunis Regency called Arabs; the mountain tribes of the Algiers Regency are called in one place 'Kabyles' and two pages later 'Arabes des montagnes', which term is also used for the mountain-dwellers in the west of this Regency[64]. The term 'Arabs' is the one most frequently used to refer to the inhabitants of Barbary in general, rather than 'Moors'. On the contrary, Vallière, whose description of the population lacks any real understanding, prefers the term 'Moors'; he uses this word to refer to the town or country dwellers and those who cultivate the land. The others he calls 'Cabaye' or highlanders, but he believes that they live in tents and are sometimes found in the plains, from which we infer that they also include the Bedouin[65].

It is hardly surprising that Raynal, who relied on second-hand accounts, was confused. Venture de Paradis tried to clarify the situation for him in his reply to Raynal's third question concerning Tunis; here, as we have seen, Venture makes a fundamental distinction between what the Europeans called the Moors and what he calls 'les Arabes habitant les

villes et les villages' on the one hand, and the 'Arabs', or those he terms
Bedouin or Arabs living in tents, some of whom at least he considers to
be the descendants of the ancient Numidians. The mountain-dwellers
come under the first heading of 'habitants mixtes', for they are not
descended from the original African inhabitants. He further explains in
a note that the highlanders in Morocco are called the 'Schulouh', those
in Algeria 'Cabaïls' and those in Tunis — who are the most docile and
least independent — Arabs, but that they are all the result of a mixture
of Carthaginians, Romans, Vandals and Greeks, together with the last
of the Arab conquerors. He bases this affirmation on a study of their
language which is similar to that spoken in the Sahara and is very different from Arabic[66]. Thus he distinguishes these Berbers from the
nomadic Arabs, although he apparently considers some of the non-
sedentary Tunisian tribes to be of Berber origin. On the whole, Venture
attempts to distinguish the inhabitants of Barbary according to, on the
one hand, whether they live under a roof or in tents and, on the other,
their origin and language. The confusion appears to come from the fact
that these categories overlap in different ways; thus, for example, he explains that the small Arab tribes are sedentarised, although they still live
in tents and thus enter the category of Bedouin. Certain peasants, like
those in the mountains, are classed as Moors because they live in houses
rather than tents. It is clear that the opposition made by other writers between town and country is for Venture de Paradis incorrect[67]. But
despite these explanations, the abbé Raynal stuck to some extent to the
more usual classification made by European writers, distinguishing between the Moors or inhabitants of the towns, the Berbers or highlanders,
and the Arabs, subdivided according to whether they are migrants or
semi-sedentary, with a third class of Arabs in the Sahara[68]. Put like this
it is much less clear than Venture's distinction between those who live in
houses and those who live in tents.

If we turn to Rehbinder's comprehensive work on Algiers, which includes a review of his predecessors' descriptions, we find that, following
popular usage, he frequently calls all the indigenous population 'Moors';
nevertheless he insists that this population is subdivided into Moors,
Kabyles and tribes of Arabic origin. The sub-group which he calls
'Moors' is not however homogeneous, as those living in the towns are different from those living in the country, but he has little respect for any
of them, apart from the small group of better-off townspeople. He considers these Moors to be the descendants of the original inhabitants of
North Africa, some of whom went to the Iberian Peninsula and whose
later offspring returned to mix with those who had remained behind. The
'Moorish mountain-dwellers' or Berbers, whom he also calls Kabyles, are

also in his opinion descendants of the oldest inhabitants; thanks to their mountain retreat they have retained their ancient simplicity and independence[69]. As for the Arabs, whom he considers to be the remnants of the conquering tribes and essentially the same as the inhabitants of Arabia (in which he was simply following a generally held opinion), they are different from the Moors; this can be seen from their speech and the fact that they live in tents in the desert. He admits however that some of them have been assimilated by the Kabyles and Moors, a fact which led Poiret to confuse them with the Kabyles[70]. Rehbinder's classification thus attempts to take account of the different groups' specific characteristics, and he attempts to divide them according to their way of life, language and place of residence. Although sub-dividing more than Venture, he follows the latter's insistence on the separateness of the Arabs, as defined by the fact that they live in tents. (We should not forget that he met Venture in Algiers, as he himself says[71].) Thus when he adds further remarks on their way of life, he describes those Arabs who live on the land but in tents as being distinct from the Moorish tribes including the Kabyles[72]. It is clear that for this author the Moors are not simply townspeople but, again, house-dwellers of a totally different origin from the Arabs, irrespective of whether they live in the mountains or in the plains. Rehbinder's division is therefore essentially two-fold, despite his initial statement, for it is evident that for him the Kabyles or Berbers are of Moorish origin.

For James Grey Jackson, writing not about the Regencies but about the Empire of Morocco, or 'West Barbary', the division of the inhabitants into groups is similar, but these groups encompass slightly different things. The Moors, who are townspeople, are considered to be the descendants of those who fled from Spain and are thus not the original inhabitants; these are the 'Berebbers' living in the mountains in tents. The latter are distinguished from the 'Shelluhs' who live in the Atlas mountains in walled habitations and some of whom are reputedly descended from the Portuguese. Their language, Amazirk, is different from that of the 'Berebbers', whose speech is considered to be probably a dialect of the ancient Carthaginian. The Arabs, who are nomads and live in tents, are from the Sahara and are occasionally driven North by famine; note also that he writes, "The term Kabyle applies to all cultivators of land and to those who rear the cattle flocks"[73], which could create a certain amount of confusion. Jackson's definitions, although not amounting to a thorough-going system of classification, are nevertheless based on the criteria of habitation, speech and origin. Again, those who live in tents are distinguished from those who live in houses, and the word 'Arabs' seems to denote the Bedouin.

To return to the Regencies, Shaler in 1826 attempts to classify the
population of Algiers in his turn; he seems unaware of earlier attempts,
apart from the one contained in Shaw's *Travels*, although he also mentions Bruce who himself relied heavily on Shaw. Shaler too says that the
word 'Moor' is "a generic term, designating all the inhabitants of Morocco and Barbary", but in fact he uses it, like others, to refer to the townspeople. They are (apart of course from the Turks) according to him a
mixture of ancient Africans, Arabs and emigrants from Spain; he distinguishes them from the Arabs, who live in tents in the plains and keep
cattle and are, as always, the same as the Arabs of Asia. He mentions
also as distinct groups the Biscris and the 'Mozabis', who speak the same
dialect as the Barbary tribes and are probably descended from the
original inhabitants. He is most interested in the Kabyles or 'Berebers'
who live in the mountains, are white and are descended from the ancient
Numidians; he also however repeats Shaw's theory that they are a remnant of the Vandals, perhaps mixed with indigenous tribes, as they speak
the same language which he calls, following Shaw, Showiah. Finally, he
distinguishes the 'Touariks', also Berbers and speaking the Berber
language[74]. Here we see that, like Shaw, Shaler defines the different
groups among the population mainly according to their language. For
him, the Moors are of mixed descent and are only town-dwellers; there
appear to be no fixed inhabitants in the plains for this author, a perception which is very interesting in view of future development, as we shall
see below. Equally interesting is the fact that he considers the Moors,
despite their mixed origins, to have a distinct national character and to
be capable of the 'highest degree of civilisation'[75].

One hesitates, after such attempts at some sort of scientific classification of the inhabitants of Barbary, to turn to Pananti, whose incipient
racism has already been mentioned. But his work is interesting, partly
as a contrast to Shaler's, which it preceded, and partly to show that the
preferences of the French conquerors after 1830 were not the only ones
possible. This Italian finds two main groups among the population (apart
from the Negroes, and the habitual groups of evidently foreign origin),
namely the Moors and Bedouin Arabs. 'Moor' is a term that apparently
covers all of the indigenous population, including Shaw's fair-haired
descendants of the Vandals and what he calls the Berberi or Berrebers,
the descendants of the original inhabitants mixed with the various invaders, who go by the name of 'Schulla' in Morocco, 'Towaricks' in the
Sahara and 'Kabiles' or 'Cubail' in Algeria, the latter being the poorest
and filthiest[76]. In contrast to these different Moorish peoples — towards
whom he manifests the racist contempt that we have already seen above
— he presents the Bedouin Arabs as noble, generous, laborious, tolerant

and so on, living a simple pastoral life which distinguishes the 'wandering Arabs' in tents from the sedentary population. The inhabitants of the fixed villages, whose origin is not clear, are more miserable and less humanised and generous than the nomadic Bedouin[77]. As we can see, Pananti's classification resembles his contemporaries' in so far as he distinguishes the Bedouin, but his description is characterised less by a desire to inform his readers about these peoples than by an obsession with the denigration of the Moors. To this end, he was willing to exalt the Arabs, even claiming that the tranquillity of their pastoral life predisposes them to a study of the arts and sciences[78]. This image of the 'Noble Bedouin' — which I shall come back to in the next chapter — was not to be taken up by the colonial writers who adopted a different version of the 'noble savage', namely the Kabyle. But something of the same attitude can be seen in Noah's *Travels*, which were published about the same time as Pananti's work and which generally show considerable ignorance concerning the population of Barbary. Noah considers this population to be composed of a mixture of different peoples with very few indigenous inhabitants; thus for him all the Moors are originally from Spain. The few original inhabitants are the Berbers, 'a savage people', descended from the Carthaginians, Romans, Numidians and Saracens, who live in both houses and tents, cultivate the land and own flocks. They are distinguished from the Bedouin Arabs, pastors living in tents, who conform to Pananti's description[79]. Compared to the previous writers we have seen, Noah is in fact surprisingly unobservant, or it may simply be that he did not have much opportunity to visit the countryside. But we are even more surprised to find Paul Raynal, in 1830, broaching the subject of the different inhabitants of Algeria as if it were totally new. Amongst the mixture of peoples constituting the population, he distinguishes, apart of course from the Turks, Coloughlis and Jews, the Arabs who dress like the Turks and Coloughlis, and the 'Cabails', Bedouin or peasants. He also speaks of the Moors in both the countryside and the towns; this term perhaps covers, for him as for others, the native population in general[80]. We are again in presence of the old confusion, as if attempts at clarification had never been made. This account indicates the degree of ignorance of many of those who came in 1830, and their belief that they were explorers in uncharted territory, or, as James Grey Jackson wrote some years earlier, "There are more books written on Barbary than on any other country and yet there is no country with which we are so little acquainted"[81]. P. Raynal's description also shows that the distinctions between the inhabitants which came to be regarded as evident in the Nineteenth Century were less so to the casual observer.

Despite such ignorance in the Nineteenth Century, it is clear from the

survey that I have given that there was in the Eighteenth Century a suc-
cession of attempts to elaborate a precise and detailed classification of the
North African population, and a corresponding greater awareness of
what distinguished its composite groups one from another. The different
criteria of language, habitat, customs and ethnic origin were combined
to make some coherent sense of the bewildering diversity of peoples that
confronted European visitors and of the different names given to them.
A general consensus emerges finally in the late Eighteenth Century, after
a period of great confusion, that there is a distinction to be made between
the 'tribes' descended from the Arab invaders — usually called Bedouin
— and the descendants of the original African inhabitants, whether they
be called Berbers or Moors. The Europeans seem unable to rid
themselves of the obsession with the 'Saracen' invaders who brought
Islam and drove out the Christians. An awareness of the nomadic, or
rather semi-nomadic way of life of the Bedouin or tent-dwellers and their
apparent similarity with the inhabitants of Arabia, meant that they were
usually considered to be of a different origin from the other inhabitants
of Barbary and this belief was further backed up by linguistic evidence.
It was thus in the Eighteenth Century a generally accepted fact that the
same race occupied the whole desert area from Arabia to the Atlantic[82].
This belief was superimposed with varying degrees of coherence on the
interpretations which saw the essential dichotomy as being between town
and countryside, in view of the very different way of life to be found in
each. Perceptions of the difference could take surprising forms, as for example in the article BARBARE (RESQUE) to be found in the *Dictionnaire de
Trévoux* in 1732, where the inhabitants of the countryside are described
as 'laborieux, doux, libéraux', while those in the towns are considered to
be 'fiers, avares, vindicatifs et de mauvaise foi'. There is a general agreement on calling the townspeople who were neither Turks, Coloughlis,
Jews nor Christians, the Moors, but precisely what this term meant remained unclear, as Shaler confirms. Were they town-dwellers of mixed
origin, were they the native inhabitants, were they the same people as the
sedentary peasants? Different authors give different answers to these
questions. The specificity of the highlanders is also generally observed,
but whether or not they are fundamentally different from the plains
people is again disputed. Their different language aroused considerable
interest, and the difficulties of establishing contact with them led to much
speculation, such as the long-running belief concerning the Vandal
origin of the fairest, confined by Shaw to the Auress Mountains, but extended by others to apply to all mountain-dwellers. The very term
'Kabyle' did not yet have a fixed application. Thus, even after all these
attempts at rational classification, Campbell could still exclaim in 1834,

"one is confused here with the variety of names applied to the natives"[83].

By the Nineteenth Century there tends to be a greater insistence, when distinguishing between different groups among the population, on origin rather than way of life. This can be seen in the remarks made by Captain Rozet at the beginning of the French occupation of Algeria. He too distinguishes two main groupings, the first being that of the oldest inhabitants, descendants of the original peoples and the 'soldiers of Hercules'; they are subdivided into the Moors, living in the towns who have intermarried with the different invaders, and the Berbers, also called 'Kbaïl', descendants of the Numidians, living in the mountains. The latter live either in cabins or in tents and their language is the 'chovia'. The other main group of the population is comprised of the Arabs, descendants of the conquerors, who live in tents and are nomadic; according to Rozet, however, they cultivate the land as well as raising flocks. The main difference, we can see, between these peoples is not so much their way of life or habitation, or even appearance, as their origin, location and — for the Berbers — language. Rozet's description is not otherwise radically different from his predecessors', especially in his depiction of the 'Moors', who are unlike the warlike tribes outside the towns and villages, and the most numerous class of the population[84]. However he ignores the dichotomy between tent and house, and between pastors and farmers, instead seeing the two as mixed together. These Moors are the people who, according to Shaler, were capable of reaching a high degree of civilisation. Although few others were willing to go as far as this, there was a general consensus of opinion concerning the town-dwelling Moors, considered to have preserved their urban civilisation, despite their degraded situation under Turkish despotism. It is, in consequence, hardly surprising that, in accordance with the desire to present Barbary as an uncharted and savage African territory, these urban Moors gradually faded from the Europeans' consciousness. Hain in 1832 gives us a foretaste of this process: forced to admit that the Moors present a civilisation of a certain degree of refinement and that they are capable of being 'civilised', he reassures his readers with the remark that they only make up one-thirtieth of the population of the Algiers Regency and that their number has rapidly diminished with the conquest. As a result, with the probable emigration of the few who remain, there will soon be none left[85]. This assessment is rather surprising in view of Rozet's contemporaneous assertion, already mentioned, that the Moors are the largest group among the indigenous population. Having conveniently disposed of the Moors, Hain is left with the Arabs and the Kabyles, neither of whom can be civilised, in his opinion. Carette, in 1848, also considers that the Arabs and Berbers make up the mass of the population, while the Moors or townsfolk only constitute less than 10,000 individuals of indeterminate origin, mainly the offspring of renegades. They constitute therefore a sort of bastard group, definable only by being neither Arabs, Berbers, Coloughli, Turks, Jews nor Negroes[86]. The transformation of the Moors is thus complete and they can vanish from the scene to leave the stage free for the confrontation between Arabs and Kabyles, with the coloniser favouring the latter; the French did not follow the preferences of a writer like Pananti who, as we have seen opted for the Arabs[87]. In Carette's writings, dating from the mid-1840s, we can see the elaboration of the 'mythe kabyle', which has been discussed at some length by historians such as Ch.R. Ageron or Lucas and Vatin[88]. Essentially this was the belief that the Kabyles, descendants of the ancient African inhabitants, and perhaps also Nordic invaders or the early Christians, were a proud, industrious peasant people, cultivating the land and possessing some form of democratic institutions; they were as a result the natural allies of the French. On the contrary the Arabs, shiftless and thieving descendants of the invaders, were lazy and untrustworthy. Developed in the 1840s, this myth grew in strength throughout the Nineteenth Century and still persists in certain quarters today.

If we compare it with what went before, it would appear at first sight that little in eighteenth-century perceptions of Barbary prepares the reader for such a development. The Bedouin Arabs struck observers on account of their difference from the rest of the population, and though they were perceived as irremediably addicted to brigandage, the mountain peoples were, if anything, considered to be even wilder and certainly more miserable and degraded. There was frequently, as we have seen, more appreciation of the Arabs than of the highland Berbers and even, as we shall see in the next chapter, signs of the beginning of a myth of the 'noble Bedouin' on the lines of the 'noble savage'. It was this role that was to some extent taken over in the following century by the Kabyles. Nevertheless we can perceive a certain continuity of the colonial theory with the eighteenth-century perception of the dichotomy between the inhabitants of town and country; we have seen that in the *Dictionnaire de Trévoux* the latter were praised to the detriment of the former. This was transformed by Venture de Paradis into the opposition between those who live in houses and those who live in tents. For Venture, it was the Moors who lived under roofs, whether in town or village, plain or mountain, and this difference in housing corresponded for him to a difference in origin, which marked off the two groups one from the other. His interpretation was also in line with the general tendency we have observed among serious eighteenth-century observers to distinguish the native inhabitants of Barbary on the one hand from the invaders on the other.

The nineteenth-century theorists developed this distinction in a particular direction: the Arabs or Bedouin (the invaders), exclusively pastors, became the nomadic plains-dwellers, while the Kabyles were the mountain-dwellers who cultivated the land. This implies, as has been pointed out by Yves Lacoste, that the only peoples in the plains were the wandering Arab pastors and that all the Berber farmers lived in the mountains; this thesis was to reach its high point, as he shows, with E.F. Gautier[89]. The result was that the plains were emptied of their indigenous inhabitants and the land was thus free to be cultivated by the French settlers. Thus, in addition to dispossessing the native peasants, the colonial rulers denied that they had ever existed. Such a belief is nowhere apparent in the eighteenth-century texts; on the contrary, there are descriptions of farms in the Mitijah as elsewhere. Indeed, even Jardine made a distinction between the mountain Berbers and the Moors living in the plains, and insisted that there were very few of the old Arabian race living in Africa, although he concedes that there are possibly some in the interior. Interestingly enough, he also considers that the Berbers are descended from the conquerors and that there remain none of the original African inhabitants who, he considers were probably Negroes[90]. Whatever the aim of such an analysis, it nevertheless amounts to an admission of the existence of sedentary inhabitants in the plain. The nineteenth-century classificatory scheme is new and its usefulness, in denying the existence of indigenous farmers in the plains, is evident.

The process I have described concerning the transformation of the inhabitants of Barbary is parallel to the one discussed in the previous chapter according to which Barbary became the 'wilds of Africa'. Again the urban civilisation vanishes and the inhabitants are reduced to inferior beings, incapable of exploiting the land; the only inhabitants of the lowlands, apart from the Turkish oppressors, become the remnants of the Arab invaders who therefore have no right to the land, which they do not even cultivate, being nomadic pastors. In the mountains are the primitive but virtuous farmers, usually considered to be the original African inhabitants (with the addition of some vigorous Nordic blood) who can be civilised by the French. Hence the country was open to colonisation, cultivation and civilisation by the conquerors. In this process the term 'Arab' whose connotations had fluctuated under the pens of different eighteenth-century writers, went back to its earlier meaning of a wild and uncivilised people living by rapine and terror. It was against this image that some writers in the Enlightenment had tried to react, but subsequent usage succeed in fixing the derogatory stereotype that is not eradicated even today. It is difficult to deny that this stereotype of the

wicked Arab and the good Kabyle was a deliberate creation, for by the
time that it took clear shape, in the 1840s, a certain number of serious
studies of Algeria had been undertaken and the works of pre-colonial
writers had been rediscovered, edited and frequently translated[91]. But
these works were only used to reinforce the new presentation of reality.
For example, one of the marks of the different origins of the Arabs and
Kabyles was seen to be their different languages. This fact had, as we
have seen, been discussed throughout the previous century, with much
speculation as to the origin of the Berber language. But eighteenth-
century writers were much more prudent in their conclusions; thus
Shaw, while devoting some space to the difference in language, remarks
on the danger of drawing positive conclusions in view of the changes that
had occured over time with the different invaders. He seems to consider
that those living in the plains, both nomads and sedentary farmers, had
lost their original language by adopting that of the conquerors, but that
they were of the same origin as the Kabyle highlanders who had been
able to preserve their language in their mountain strongholds[92]. But he
is nevertheless doubtless partly responsible for the myth of the fair-
haired, blue-eyed Kabyles, as his remarks concerning the possible Vandal origin of the Auressians were extended to concern all the Eastern
highlanders. Already in Shaler's work, published in 1826, the distinction
made by Shaw between the inhabitants of the 'Jibel Auress' and the others
is rather blurred, as the American insists on the 'whiteness' of the
Kabyles[93]. Around 1830, then, the myth was beginning to take shape
but was not yet evident to all. Rozet insists on the gentle manners of the
Moors and describes the Berbers as indeed brave and warlike but as very
swarthy with black hair; they are also, he says, very cruel, a characteristic
that is reflected in their expressions[94]. Campbell, slightly later, seems
rather mystified by descriptions of fair-complexioned Kabyle tribes of
Vandal origin, saying that he had never seen any with light hair or
eyes[95]. But by 1847, in Daumas and Fabar's book on *La Grande Kabylie*,
the white Kabyles (as opposed to the swarthy Arabs of course), with blue
eyes and red hair, 'en partie germain d'origine', was an accepted truth,
as was the implacable hatred between Arabs and Berbers[96]. The persistence of this belief can be seen from a book published in 1966 on the
American-Algerian war of the late Eighteenth Century; its author writes
of the blond-haired, blue-eyed Kabyles 'who bore then . . . and still bear
today, such strong signs of Vandal blood'[97].

Charles-Robert Ageron, who discusses the Kabyle myth, describes its
elaboration between 1840 and 1857 and considers that it was deliberately
reinforced between 1860 and 1870 for political and propaganda purposes
and that it was triumphant after 1870[98]. An important aspect of its

development in the Nineteenth Century was an insistence on the racial difference between the two component parts of the native Algerian population; we have seen the emergence of this belief at the end of the previous century. The fact that the term adopted for the uncongenial mass of the lowland population was 'Arab', while the word 'Moor' all but disappeared is evidence of a desire not only to deny the existence of sedentary farmers in the plains but also to depreciate their inhabitants. This may seem in contradiction with the fact that, as Venture de Paradis explained, the term 'Moor' was the one in use among the Europeans. But perhaps his own insistence on the word 'Arab' was part of the same process. For the connotations of this word or of its alternative, Bedouin, were, on the one hand of cruelty, ferocity and brigandage, and on the other, of social inferiority; they were considered to be at a primitive, pastoral level of civilisation, whereas the urban Moors' comparative refinement could not be denied. (It is significant that the word remained in use for such things as 'café maure' or 'bain maure'.) Thus, during the agitated period leading up to the 1830 expedition, the Marseille newspaper *Le Sémaphore*, which was particularly in favour of an attack on Algiers, recounted the misadventures of a French crew washed up on the Barbary shore; it describes the heroic struggles of the sailors against the 'Bedouin' and later calls for revenge against these 'cannibals' who had massacred French sailors[99]. Such remarks betray a deliberate desire to denigrate the Barbaresques, coupled with a total disregard for accuracy. There was also the advantage that the 'Bedouin' were considered to be invaders whereas the Moors could be considered to have more right to the country. The emotional charge of such terms can still be seen in 1930 when Ibos wrote in his biography of Cavaignac that the latter carefully looked for traces of Roman civilisation in Algeria "afin d'exhumer les vestiges qui demontraient aux Bédouins les droits antérieurs des Européens à la possession du pays"[100]. Apart from asserting the anterior right of the French over the Moslem invaders, this statement demonstrates clearly the force of racial contempt conveyed by the word 'Bedouin'. With this goes contempt for peoples at a lower level of civilisation. It is to this question that I shall turn in the next chapter, but first I propose to deal briefly with the particular question of the Jews and their position in North African society.

THE JEWS

There is one class of the North African population which I have hitherto ignored, as it presents no problems of classification and everyone is agreed as to its specificity. I would however like to discuss the Jews briefly here as they do give rise to disagreement of a different sort. It is frequently said that they were the most miserable and harshly treated portion of society, being forced to live in 'ghettos' and wear distinctive clothes; they were in addition punished severely for the slightest misdeed. It is true that visitors to Barbary painted a pretty bleak picture of their condition and the way in which the Turks treated them, in keeping with d'Arvieux's remark that of all the subjects of the Turkish Sultan, the Jews were the poorest and the worst treated[101]. This opinion is echoed over a century later by Shaler who claims that they are 'one of the least fortunate remnants of Israel remaining'[102]. La Condamine, in 1731, describes the punishments reserved for this community, which are crueller than those meted out to the 'Moors', and he considers them to be in such a state of oppression and such an object of contempt that he wonders how they can remain[103]. The same opinion is expressed by Laugier de Tassy who says that they are miserable, oppressed and despised by all the other inhabitants; they are however free to worship in their synagogues[104]. He here introduces a distinction that it is important to underline: Laugier writes that they are considered as Moors — who were, by all accounts, very cruelly treated by the Turks — and thus that their condition is not unique. Their closeness to the Moors is also pointed out by Poiret, Shaler and Rehbinder[105]. Secondly, Laugier distinguishes the indigenous Jews, very numerous, from the Italian *Judeos francos*, who controlled the foreign trade of Algiers and who were very rich; these Jews, mostly from Leghorn, were treated in the same way as the other European merchants and were under the protection of the French consul[106]. It is amusing to note that he calls the latter group 'Christian Jews' and the indigenous group 'Moorish Jews'. The differences between these two groups — perceived by other visitors besides Laugier — should make us hesitate before drawing conclusions as to the status of the Jews in the Barbary Regencies. The contempt for the Jews that is described by European visitors does not appear to be based on religious or 'racial' discrimination, for the foreign Jews were not concerned; indeed they apparently enjoyed the trust of the Turkish rulers. The reasons for this contempt appear instead to be social; the 'Moorish Jews' were on the lowest rung of the social ladder and were despised as such. It is, furthermore, apparent that the Turks' contempt for them was shared by the Europeans. Laugier openly despises the miserable native Jewish tradesmen and condemns their 'basses pratiques'[107]; Peyssonnel writes that the 'Moors' who come into the towns from the countryside are corrupted by contact with the Jews, 'dont le caractère est assez connu'[108]; Vallière considers them to be equally 'avilis' and vice-ridden wherever they are found and only worthy of contempt[109], while Jackson considers the Jews in Morocco to be 'scandalously deficient' in the Moors' 'natural desire of cleanliness'[110]. Likewise, Rehbinder describes them as ignorant, superstitious, fanatical and untrustworthy[111]. After the French conquest of Algiers, Rozet insists that the condition of the Jews was worse than that of the rest of the population, although all suffered from Turkish despotism, and he claims that they have been liberated by the French; despite these claims, however, he has little respect for them, considering that here, as elsewhere, they are given to trade and are 'd'une avarice sordide'[112]. Campbell confirms this French hostility towards the Jews and claims, for his part, that they are more honest than the other natives; and although he too says that they were oppressed by the Turks, he insists that they enjoyed a financial predominance that they have lost with the arrival of the French[113]. These examples show clearly that European accounts of the condition of the Jews in Barbary are also coloured by their own anti-Jewish prejudice. In addition it is interesting, after their accounts, which appear to confirm the impression given by M. Eisenbeth's study of the persecuted condition of the Jews[114], to turn to the opinion of Mordecai Noah. As I have already said, this American Jew visited the Barbary states as U.S. consul in Tunis in 1813—15; his commission was eventually revoked by Monroe on the grounds, according to him, of his religion[115]. He insists that the Jewish communities in Barbary are in the power of 'barbarians' and 'assassins' and hopes that 'some civilised power' will take over these states and relieve them. But despite all this, he finds no evidence of cruel treatment, although much of 'indignity and insult'. It is also interesting to note that unlike the Christian observers, he explains that the 'Mohammedan' faith is not hostile to the Jewish religion because of many similarities, and he condemns the ignorance and prejudice of previous travellers who have misrepresented this community. Attempting to prove that his brethren are not the miserable beggars of other accounts, he explains that they are the principal merchants and hold practically the monopoly of trade; they keep the Bey of Tunis's jewels, and are treasurers, secretaries and especially interpreters. (This privileged position can be likewise inferred from some other works; according to Venture de Paradis, for example, the consul for the Italian state of Ragusa in Algiers was 'un juif du pays'[116].) According to Noah, the Jews are also the most learned citizens, being the only ones to master science, medicine and the arts. Thus many are immensely wealthy and, he claims, their oppression is 'in great measure imaginary'[117]. This conclusion is surprising in view of the opposing consensus of opinion and in view of Noah's own hostility towards the Barbary governments. Indeed Noah seems at great pains to contradict the impression given by other writers, which he attributes to their own anti-Jewish feelings. We are forced to give credit to his account; after all, even

Pananti, who describes the insults and humiliations they receive at the hands of the Barbarians, also points out their influence and wealth. Perfidiously, he quotes them as saying, "we suffer a great deal, but then what money we make" — a dig at them for their sordid lack of dignity and supposed avarice[118].

I do not wish to discuss the rights and wrongs of the question nor to pronounce a judgement on the condition of the Jews in Barbary. It is I think safe to say that European comments on the subject reflect mainly their own hostility towards this community on the one hand, and on the other their desire to show up the barbarity and despotism of the Turkish rulers in Barbary, by denouncing their treatment of the Jews as well as of the Moors. It is also important to point out that attitudes to the Jews expressed on both sides do not reflect a *racial* prejudice in the sense in which we have used this term above. This question is the subject of some controversy, and much has been written about the Enlightenment's supposed anti-semitism. But in eighteenth-century European thought, the Jews do not at all figure in racial classifications; instead, as we see here, most writers see them as an integral part of the community in which they live, despite the fact that they constitute a clearly recognisable group within that community. Thus Rehbinder explains that the Jews, despite their distinctive features (in particular their noses) adopt the manners and customs of the countries in which they live[119]. We have also seen the distinction made in Barbary between, in Laugier's words the 'Christian Jews' and the 'Moorish Jews'. The undeniable hostility towards them expressed by most Europeans is, I believe, essentially a continuation of deeply-ingrained Christian prejudices inspired by religion. It should not be forgotten that this religiously-inspired prejudice did not exist in Moslem societies. It would thus be a mistake to view the comments we have seen through twentieth-century eyes, and to forget that the colonial French writers had every reason to insist on the sufferings of the Jews at the hands of the Moslem authorities who preceded them, in order to provide further proof of their beneficial rule. All of this is not to claim that the Jews in the Barbary Regencies lived in enviable conditions, but simply to point out the dangers of over-hasty interpretations of the texts concerning them.

CHAPTER THREE

SOCIETY AND GOVERNMENT

The degree of civilisation of the peoples of Barbary is a question that I have so far touched upon here and there; we saw in the previous chapter that by the Nineteenth Century it was a tenet of faith that they were primitive Africans to whom the Europeans must bring enlightenment. But it should be evident to those who have followed me thus far that such an opinion would not have been easily accepted by a Laugier de Tassy or even a d'Argens. What had happened? Basically, a drastic simplification of a complex set of judgments and analyses concerning the social and political development of nations, combined with a new way of looking at Barbary as a whole. Let us take the first of these developments to begin with. There is little doubt that eighteenth-century Europeans considered themselves to have reached the highest level of social development, that of 'polite' nations enjoying a refined civilisation characterised by a stable government, sensible laws which were generally respected (whatever disagreement there might be as to the exact nature of the government or the wisdom of particular laws), and the development of commerce and the arts. This awareness gave rise to different sorts of speculation concerning the bases of this social organisation and its development, growth and possible decline. The usefulness of the study of alien societies and their different degrees of civilisation lay in the attempt to understand the past as well as possible future development of the Europeans' own society. Believing in general in one universal process of the rise and decline of civilisations, with fixed laws, European thinkers considered that primitive societies presented them with a living image of their own past, while those in decline could serve as an equally living lesson in possible future developments and hence as a warning. It would be a mistake to consider that the Enlightenment believed in a simple dichotomy between civilised Europe and the primitive rest of the world, which was a more common belief in the following century; Lucas and Vatin are thus slightly misleading when they refer to an 'opposition mécaniste' between two possible states of civilisation in the Eighteenth as well as the Nineteenth Century[1].

One should not forget that, however much evidence was drawn from travellers' accounts of foreign lands to support it, the Enlightenment's model of social development was a theoretical, *a priori* construction, which could not always be easily reconciled with the facts. To begin with, the postulate of a state of nature existing prior to all forms of society was an entirely imaginary creation, based not on observation of any known country but instead on the negation of the important attributes of contemporary polite nations. Thus, for Hobbes as for Locke after him, it was characterised essentially by the lack of government, laws and justice. It is significant that Hobbes gave no real example of a known region where life was 'solitary, poor, nasty, brutish and short', beyond a vague reference to the tribes of America, who were in fact living in organised nations and not in a state of nature[2]. He prefers to insist, as does Locke after him, on the relations existing between sovereigns of independent states, who have no superior authority to arbitrate between them[3]. Despite the completely abstract quality of this state of nature, which was criticised for this very reason by Hume[4], there was a willingness to believe in its existence. When, with Rousseau, it came to be seen no longer as a real or potential state of war but as an ideal golden age which had been corrupted by civilisation, the search for, and idealisation of, peoples living in this way developed and the myth of the noble savage flowered. He was first thought to have been found in America where, as we have seen, Hobbes thought men lived in the state of nature; the American 'savages' were for a while viewed with admiration rather than contempt. But disillusion rapidly set in, with the spread of European colonisation and the resulting degradation of the Americans or their attempts at armed resistance to the outsiders. The discovery of the South Seas, and particularly of Tahiti, in the second half of the Eighteenth Century gave new life to the myth which was used by Diderot to attack Christianity, although it is not clear how far he really believed in the superiority of 'natural man'[5].

If the savage living in the state of nature was elusive, it was evident that there were several degrees between the pristine simplicity of natural man and the civilisation of polite nations. The different degrees of progress towards the highest state of evolution were defined by the existence of various characteristics, the most important of which concerned the presence of private property and the mode of subsistence. To simplify somewhat, we can say that there were considered to be three main stages in social development, namely the savage, the barbarian and the civilised. Montesquieu distinguished between the savage and the barbarian states on the criterion of their means of subsistence. Thus the savages are small nations living separately by hunting; when they join together to become pastors, they reach the level of 'barbares', the examples being the

Tartars and the Arabs[6]. The definition given by de Jaucourt in his *Encyclopédie* article SAUVAGES, however, blurs the distinction somewhat, for he says that they are "peuples barbares qui vivent sans loi, sans police, sans religion et qui n'ont point d'habitation fixe". In this latter definition, the savages appear to be very close to the state of nature, while in Montesquieu's they are considered to be organised into nations and have thus developed beyond this state. The question remains rather confused, but we can say that in the main they are thought to be near to the natural condition rather than still in it. Behind the distinction between savage and barbarian lies, in the main, the question of the existence of private property. It is the appearance of property that marks the transition from the savage to the barbarian state. This is more evident in Montesquieu's definition than in Jaucourt's, for flocks constitute property, although it also lies behind the formulation in the *Encyclopédie*, for it is property that creates the need for laws and government. For Rousseau, following Locke, it is clearly the absence of private property in the savage state that distinguishes it from that of the barbarians[7]. And if we turn to Ferguson's *Essay on the History of Civil Society* (1767), one of the most important eighteenth-century works on the question, we find that the savage state is personified by the hunters of North America whose 'natural indolence' prevents them from developing private property[8]. These rude nations are distinguished from those who have, by their industry, instituted property which they wish to bequeath to their children. Their industry is agricultural and the form it takes depends on the climate; the barbarians may be nomadic pastors like the Scythes or the Tartars, or farmers cultivating the land in a single place, but their stage of social development is similar, and the introduction of property has led to the development of government, usually constituted of chieftains. Notice the influence of the climate on the form of subsistence, although Ferguson abandons the distinction, found in some writers such as Adam Smith, between the pastoral and farming states of civilisation. As for 'polished' nations they are also, hardly surprisingly in an eighteenth-century British writer, seen as commercial nations. Finally Ferguson discusses the decay of civilisations, which tend to decline through corruption and lose their commerce. Such is the case of the Oriental despotisms, for a variety of reasons which it is not necessary to go into here; as the different degrees of civilisation give rise to different forms of government, the declining, generally Oriental, nations, have of course despotic governments[9]. This is obviously rather a simplified outline of the different authors' analyses, but it is sufficient for the main point that I wish to make here, namely that societies were seen by eighteenth-century thinkers, whatever their differences on individual points, as progressing through different stages before arriving at the polished state of their own, enlightened society. Among the 'rude' nations there were important differences to be made, as Rousseau insists in his *First Discourse*, between the savage state with no private property or social organisation and barbarian societies in which there is a beginning of social organisation due to the institution of property. The savage state can be compared, in this view of things, to the state of nature which is no longer Locke's purely theoretical construction. Given these distinctions, it was possible for those who criticised the corruption of civilisation to admire the simple savage state in which man was supposed to live in accordance with the promptings of Nature and his own basic needs; but it was much less easy to find virtues in the way of life of the barbarians.

If we turn from these general theoretical considerations to see what was written about Barbary, we find that there is a problem in relation to the classification of the North African societies. We find, first of all, that in the examples given of the different stages of human development they are totally absent. Savage nations tended to be represented by the North Americans, barbarous ones by the Sythes, Tartars or ancient Gauls, with an occasional mention of the Arabs of Arabia, and decaying states by the Eastern Empires. Barbary does not seem to have a place in these discussions. But if there is no trace of it in theoretical writings, what trace is there of these theoretical discussions in writings about Barbary? Here too we come up against a problem. It is clear from what we have already seen that eighteenth-century writers on North Africa were describing states with an organised government and institutions, an army, a navy and foreign commerce, although the state of learning is hardly considered to be flourishing. These characteristics were enough to exclude the Regencies from the categories of savage and even of barbarian nations; but were they enough for them to be counted as 'polite nations'? We have already seen that several writers were at some pains to point out that the name 'Barbary' did not necessarily denote that its inhabitants were barbarians; but at the same time they all insisted on the ignorance of these same inhabitants, the insolence of the rulers and their cruelty and despotism, which made even apologists like Laugier de Tassy hesitate. He is forced to admit, despite his attempts to counter Christian prejudices, that the Barbaresques are 'fort grossiers et fort ignorants'. His only counter-argument is that the Europeans' education makes them more shocked by such behaviour than they need be, and that there is *some* good in these peoples[10]. As a defence it is, we must admit, a little weak. He also writes that the character of the inhabitants of the kingdom of Algiers is marked by a general moral dissolution, overweening pride and brutality towards foreigners, none of which is very flattering[11]. Should we then take seriously d'Arvieux's qualification of the Algerines at least as 'barbares'[12]? But there is, on the other hand, Laugier's somewhat contradictory remark that the majority of the population is composed of people who are 'fort humains et gouvernés par des lois'[13]. I think we could say that the Regency of Algiers, like the other Barbary states, floats somewhere, in the eyes of Europeans, between barbarism and civilisation. The latter is found, for example, among some of the rich 'Moors' living in the towns, with their sumptuous country villas just outside, and in certain aspects of the government and the administration. Concerning the latter, travellers particularly admire the prompt justice that is dispensed, with a minimum of fuss, by the Dey of Algiers, as is observed by Shaw, Peyssonnel and even La Condamine, whose brief visit to Algiers inspired mainly hostility; nevertheless he is astonished not only by the prompt and severe administration of justice but also by the efficient police which ensures that one is more in security here in one's home than one would be in a Christian country, and need have no fear of theft[14]. In the same vein, Venture de Paradis, half a century later, seems to consider that the court of the Tunisian Bey is very civilised, although his general attitude to Barbary as a whole can be seen from his accompanying remark that it is, in consequence, untypical of Barbary[15]. But, at the same time, the way of life and condition of the ordinary people in the countryside are generally viewed with pity, although it should be remembered that the peasants in many 'civilised' European countries, including France, were no better off. This fact is mentioned by the Russian officer Kokovtsov who expresses considerable sympathy for the inhabitants of Barbary; he insists that they are not barbarians, a term which, he explains, implies a ferocious, cruel people with no laws. On the contrary, the North Africans are gentle and hospitable. If they are pirates, it is because of their despotic governments; in fact, according to him, if anyone deserves the name of barbarians, it is the ruling class and not the ordinary people[16]. In a similar vein, Rehbinder reminds the reader that the Moors had an ancient civilisation which flourished in Spain and Portugal while Europe was sunk in barbarism and ignorance[17]. This confusion as to the correct assessment to be made of North African society, created by the contradictions visible in Barbary, can be summed up in Peyssonnel's reaction to the government of Algiers; behind his discussion of the form of government, his comments can be seen to deal with the country in a more general way.

> J'y ai vu un ordre assez beau et des lois si justes et équitables que je ne sais comment les exposer en contredisant l'opinion commune que nous avons de ce gouvernement. En meme temps, j'ai aperçu tant de choses infâmes, la malice des hommes à corrompre si fort les idées des législateurs; il s'y est introduit tant d'abus et tant de coutumes y sont contradictoires, qu'il est très difficile de les exposer nettement et de les rendre croyables[18].

(I found quite a good order and laws so just and fair that I do not know how to describe them while contradicting the common opinion that we have of this government. At the same time I saw so many infamous things and men's ingenuity to corrupt to such an extent the legislators' ideas; so many abuses have been introduced and so many customs go against them that it is very difficult to expose them clearly and in a credible manner.)

He admits that the ordinary reader would probably consider the Algerian Turks to be faithless, lawless, lacking in good sense, inhuman, barbaric, cruel and 'sans politesse'— all of which adds up to a description of a barbarian rather than civilised people — but he himself has been surprised to find that the state is well governed and 'leur politique si belle'. It is also interesting to note that he considers the Andalusian Moors to be more civilised than the other inhabitants[19].

One way of dealing with these contradictions was to consider the Barbary states as the remnant of a past civilisation which had reached its high point in Moorish Spain and had subsequently declined, lapsing into despotism and barbarity. This is the main thrust of Voltaire's discussion of Barbary in the *Essai sur les Moeurs*[20] and is the idea that runs through Raynal's remarks on North Africa, whose rich and enlightened past he praises and contrasts with its present degradation, brought about by the tyranny of its different governments. Now he sees nothing but leaders without principles, tribunals without understanding, priests without morals, merchants without honour and workers without pride in their work[21]. Despotism and decline go hand in hand; the remarks concerning the despotism reigning here, increasingly frequent towards the end of the century as we have seen, seem to confirm the view that Barbary was the home of a civilisation in decline. This was considered particularly apt in view of the fact that those exercising the despotism were Turks, the emanation of a declining empire. But despite this fact, it is interesting to note that the connection between decline, despotism and the Orient was not necessarily made; thus Raynal, while insisting on the decline of Barbary and the despotism reigning there, prefers to consider it as part of Africa as we have seen. And Venture de Paradis holds an opposing point of view; for despite his insistence on the despotism of the governments of the Barbary Regencies and his description of them as Oriental, he seems to consider that these countries have not yet attained the level of civilised nations. We have already seen his description of the Tunisian court and the untypical signs of civilisation that he discerns there; the point of view from which he judges such signs is made clearer by a remark at the end of his account of the trade between Tunis and Europe. This trade is increasing with the rising prosperity of the state and his conclusion is that if Algiers ceased to exist, Tunis and Tripoli would rapidly become 'des peuples policés', for these towns already contain the principles of civilisation and a greater number of educated people than else-where[22]. From this it would appear that they are not declining states, but emerging civilisations gradually progressing out of the state of bar-barism in which, we presume, Algiers is still floundering. Such an assess-ment is in line with the contempt we have already noted in Venture's ac-count of the Regency of Algiers. Venture de Paradis represents, I be-lieve, with all his contradictions, the trend of the later Eighteenth Cen-tury. The Barbary nations are gradually refused the benefit of the doubt and classified, with growing assurance, as barbarians. This is certainly the opinion of Venture's contemporary, the vice-consul Vallière who shares all the prejudices of the European diplomats. As we have already seen, the ordinary people are likewise reduced to a level comparable to that of the brutes. Confirmation of this attitude is found in the abbé Poiret's letters; despite his initial 'Rousseauism', his disillusionment with what he sees leads him to exclaim that he has never so much appreciated the advantages of living in 'une nation policée' as since he has been stay-ing among 'un peuple barbare'[23].

But there persists a disagreement as to whether Barbary was con-sidered to be in a state of decline (which was Voltaire's and Raynal's opi-nion) or as not yet having emerged from the barbaric state (the opinion, at least in part, of Venture), although whichever thesis was favoured, the resulting condemnation was identical. Hence both Jardine in 1788 and Leyden in 1799 speak of 'rude nations in Barbary'; but while the latter seems to consider that they have not yet roused themselves from their lethargy, the former believes that they have degenerated from a more civilised state. He explains that the North Africans are different from peoples still living in a savage state who retain a primitive energy, for they are weaker and more abject, and incapable of reviving by their own efforts. Considering that "there must be a great resemblance between the rude nations of all ages and countries", he compares the people of Moroc-co to those seen by Xenophon in the East[24]. This opinion is echoed by Pananti shortly afterwards, when he writes that "from a high state of civilisation, the Moors have fallen into a barbarism, worse than they were probably ever in before. They are like an old wine, of which nothing is left but the dregs". And like Jardine he makes the comparison between them and 'mere savages', but Pananti arrives at the opposite conclusion: "the latter are ferocious and inhuman; while the former, though un-cultivated, retain some degree of mildness". They are consequently more capable of being civilised by an outside force than are true savages[25]. Whatever the differences in the argument, the corollary is the same, namely the need for civilisation by the Europeans. Shaler's attitude is slightly different. He does not apparently share the blanket condemnation of these last authors for the peoples of Barbary, nor even for their governments, and he writes, "There is probably no city in the world were there is a more vigilant police, where fewer cognizable crimes are committed, or where there is better security for persons and property than in Algiers". But despite such apparent signs of civilisation, mentioned also by several of his predecessors, the Algerians are not, in Shaler's eyes, really civilised. They are merely on the verge of civilisation: "I think there can be no doubt that these peoples stand on the very brink of civilisation and might be easily led to it through a system of government less repugnant to improvement in its principles, than that under which they live". Starting from opposing premisses, Shaler then ends up at the same conclusion as a Pananti, which is that the Barbaresques can only be civilised by the Europeans. They are hereby thrust back willy nilly into a primitive stage of development, from which they can only be rescued by nations at a higher level of civilisation, for, "in the pride of barbarism and ignorance" they "despise the arts, the sciences, the improvements of civilised society"[27]. By the time of the French conquest of Algiers, it had become an accepted truth that its inhabitants were barbarians at best and, at worst, savages. Campbell, the Scotsman, is consequently at some pains to point out that the Algerians are not, as vulgar prejudice would have it, 'savage and unsocial', but are on the contrary capable of one day becoming 'a literary, scientific and highly refined people'[28]. The 'vulgar error' was held by colonial propagandists such as Hain who, as we have seen above, considered the mass of the Algerian population to be savages who were incapable of any form of civilisation and must be removed to make way for the French. For this campaigner for the colonisation of the Algerian territory, its people have reaced the level (and are promised the fate of) the American Indians.

Those who in the Eighteenth Century believed, on the contrary, in the possibility that the North Africans could progress towards a truly civilised state, insisted on the importance of commerce, a factor generally considered to lead towards 'politeness'. Thus Desfontaines, writing of Bône (Annaba), considered that the trading activities of the French African Company had greatly contributed towards civilising the 'Moors' of the region; Kokovtsov repeats this remark, applying it to the militia rather than the ordinary inhabitants of Bône[29]. The same idea is present throughout Raynal's observations on Barbary and, with the same logic, Rehbinder writes that as long as the inhabitants of the Algiers Regency are prevented from engaging in trade freely with foreign nations, this country will be unable to progress from its present primitive state which keeps it behind Europe in science and culture. In addition, he contrasts the state of Algiers with that of Tunis which had developed its trade rather than piracy[30]. Tott too, in his brief remarks on Tunis, insists on the civilising effect of commerce and industry, which form the basis of this state's riches and creates 'une sorte d'affabilité', which distinguishes its inhabitants from those of the other 'Nations Barbaresques'. Shaler likewise remarks on the civilising effects of commerce[31]. It was a corollary of such a belief in the civilising effect of trade and in the existence of trading activity as an indication of civilisation, that the Barbary states, inasmuch as they did engage in trade to some extent (a fact attested by the detailed descriptions of Raynal, Venture, Rehbinder and others), could not be considered as totally barbarian. But to the extent that their governments were seen to favour piracy and to hinder commerce, in the same way as their despotism hindered improvements in science and caused the decline of agriculture, they were barbarian. Shaler writes of the fertile Mitijah plain near Algiers that "through the silent operation of the barbarous despotism of the Algerine government, [it] has become a perfect desert, without inhabitants or culture"[32]. Whether this description is accurate or not, it reflects the author's belief in the barbarity of the government and its evil consequences. True civilisation could only come about by a transfer of responsibility into the hands of Christian nations who would favour agriculture, industry and commerce and thus civilise the region. Shaler's belief that this 'primitive' nation was incapable of progressing by its own unaided efforts is in line with the racism that we have already seen expressed by this author. As such opinions gained ground, so the emphasis was put on the nefarious effects of the existing governments due to their interference in trade, and on the possibilities for agriculture and trade that were wasted by their preference for piracy. As we shall see, this was a criticism that was particularly directed towards the Algerian government.

But if the Barbary states in general, and Algiers in particular, had in European eyes — after some hesitations and despite contradictions — sunk by 1830 to the level of rude rather than polite (or semi-polite) nations, what of the different groups of inhabitants who made up their population? After all, everyone was agreed that the Turkish rulers who were the particular object of this chorus of condemnation, were distinct from the mass of the native inhabitants. If the Turks were, by common agreement, the dregs of the Ottoman Empire, perhaps the indigenous population was different. Kokovtsov, after all, considered that unlike their rulers they were not at all barbarian but honest, simple and hospitable; but positive as this judgement is, it is hardly the equivalent of considering them to be civilised. The only inhabitants who apparently approach the norm of civilised peoples are the rich urban Moors or, for some writers such as Peyssonnel, the Andalusian Moors[33]. Even Hain in 1832 admits that they possess a certain degree of refinement, although for him it is limited to their material standard of living[34]. And this is the same group whom Shaler considers to be on the brink of civilisation. It is no doubt for this reason that their very existence was denied soon after 1830. Having subtracted these groups, we are left with the rest of the population, that is to say the mass of the inhabitants of the interior, whether living in the plains or the mountains, in tents or in cabins, and whether called Moors, Arabs, Bedouin or Berbers. Whatever the qualities that might or might not be accorded to them, no-one was willing to call them civilised. An exception is an ironic remark by Gibbon, referring to Shaw's description of their contemporary way of life, as opposed to their condition at the time of the Vandals; 'How civilized are these modern savages', he exclaims, describing their bountiful provisions when compared to those of their ancestors[35]. Eye-witnesses, on the contrary, usually remark on the Moors' poverty, ignorance, misery, and the bad treatment they receive at the hands of the Turkish soldiers. Their ferocity is also a constant theme, for travellers only felt in security on the roads when accompanied by a strong contingent of Turkish military. The attitude of many visitors is summed up by Gibbon's remark concerning Shaw's attitude towards the 'roving tribes of Barbary, of Arabian or Moorish descent', namely that "Shaw had seen these savages with distant terror"[36]. Desfontaines's attitude, too, is typical: his only interest in the inhabitants of Barbary seems to concern the danger they represent for the foreign traveller and the extent to which they have been tamed by the Turkish authorities. In the latter case they inspired no longer terror, but pity and even contempt.

We are drawn to the conclusion that the mass of the population appeared to most European observers to be little more than savages, to use Gibbon's oft-repeated epithet. But to classify them definitively as such created a certain number of theoretical problems, in view of the strict definition of the term that we have seen above; savages were peoples living in isolated bands as hunters, with only a very rudimentary social organisation. Despite the rather loose usage of the word 'savage', no-one really claimed that this was an acurate description of the Moors and the Arabs. It was evident from the descriptions given of their way of life that they had reached at least the stage of development at which there was private property and agricultural activity, for they engaged either in sedentary cultivation of the land or in nomadic pastoral pursuits. Thus we find frequent comparisons between the way of life of the North Africans and that of the Biblical Patriarchs; such a parallel is made in Shaw's *Travels* and in the *Histoire des Deux Indes* which compares the 'Arabs' to the 'Patriarchs of Moses or the heroes of Homer'[37]. They are, to quote Jardine, in a 'shepherd state of society'[38] which, while being a 'rude' stage of civilisation, does not make them savages but rather barbarians. Rehbinder, too, while considering the inhabitants of Barbary to be primitive peoples with the simple manners of an early stage of civilisation, compares their way of life to that of the Patriarchs[39]. This does not prevent him from insisting on their contentment with their lot and lack of desire for change. These characteristics, coupled with his reference to Poiret, give us a clue as to what is behind his remarks; Rehbinder, as a man of the Enlightenment, has in mind in this passage, contained in an appendix to his book, contemporary discussions concerning primitive peoples. Like Diderot, in a certain number of his works which betray an affinity with J.J. Rousseau, this author is reviving the question of whether primitive peoples are happier than civilised ones. He points out that these primitive peoples consider themselves to be happier, for they do not have civilised man's artificial needs[40]. He is thereby drawing the peoples of Barbary into the discussion, pursued throughout the second half of the Eighteenth Century, as to the respective merits of the state of Nature (and the states approaching it) and the civilised state. In this context, the true nature of these populations tends to be obscured and they become, for the purposes of comparison, savages, so that on occasion they are glorified as 'noble savages'. Such a view of them could only be based on distortion of the facts or on ignorance of their true nature. The latter is the case of Poiret, the follower of Rousseau, who went to Barbary with the firm intention of finding noble savages, as he himself explains. He arrived with the belief that the closer man was to Nature, the better he must be; he saw the 'Arabs' as being like the Patriarchs of Antiquity, freed of the artificial need for luxury and possessing the qualities of simplicity, hospitality and honesty, which are the qualities to be found in 'l'homme de la Nature'. He is rapidly disillusioned, finding that these savages, far from being noble, are riddled with vice and corruption; their savage nature expresses itself in ferocity and cruelty rather than in simplicity and directness. A trace of his original attitude nevertheless subsists in his Preface, where he still claims that, though ignorant, the Bedouin are free and that they are therefore happy; but his revised opinion can be seen in his description of them as "des hordes errantes, livrées à toute la dépravation d'une nature avilie et d'un coeur insensible à l'aiguillon de l'amour-propre et de la gloire"[41]. As for the 'Moors' in the mountains, they are true savages, and he quotes a memoir concerning them written by the French Company's agent at Collo, a certain M. Hugues; the list of epithets with which Hugues gratifies them leaves little room for any positive qualities, and elsewhere Poiret himself even suspects them of being cannibals![42]. During the same period, another

Frenchman there in an official capacity, the vice-consul Vallière, echoes the same opinion of the highlanders, whom he calls 'Cabayes'. He writes that they are little different from the brutes and even that they 's'allie[nt] souvent avec lui'[43]. For Poiret, as for these French officials, the North Africans, or at least a large number of them, have become truly ignoble savages, with no redeeming feature. But Poiret does find one exception, in the persons of two devoted 'Arab' brothers living in rural peace and tranquillity with their families and flocks in a valley near La Calle. His Rousseauistic description of his visits to them, complete with 'herborisation' shows that, despite all his discouragement, his ideal has not totally vanished[44].

Indeed, Poiret's disillusionment did not bring the hunt for the noble savage in Barbary to an end; on the contrary, it seems to have gained in intensity towards the end of the century. Broadly speaking, there were two candidates for the role of the noble savage, the wandering Bedouin and the mountain Berber. The first of these was generally the more popular choice, beginning with the Philosophes. D'Argens is one of the first to see the North African 'Arabs' in this way, in his description of the tribes whom his Jewish traveller finds camping in the ruins near Tripoli. He praises their morals, their simple food, their hospitality and contempt for riches, concluding with the reflection that if they were not quite so lazy, they could be considered as 'de véritables Philosophes', for they despise useless riches and limit their desires to what is strictly necessary[45]. These stoical philosophers present many of the characteristics of the noble savage, an idea developed in Diderot's article BÉDOUIN in the *Encyclopédie*. In this short article, after a succinct description of their way of life, said to be the same from Arabia to North Africa, with details taken from d'Herbelot's *Bibliothèque orientale* and d'Arvieux's travels (amongst others), Diderot concludes by remarking that they have neither doctors nor lawyers and therefore follow the laws of natural justice and suffer from no diseases apart from old age. These two attributes place the Bedouin firmly in the category of the noble savage, as can be easily seen from a comparison with Rousseau's *First Discourse*, Diderot's own *Supplément au voyage de Bougainville* and his reflections on the differences between the savage and the civilised man in the *Histoire des Deux Indes*; for in all of these discussions, great importance is given to the fact that peoples living in a state of nature follow the laws of Nature and suffer no illnesses[46]. Diderot's application of these criteria to the Bedouin was perhaps influenced by d'Arvieux, who wrote that thanks to their simple way of life, the Arabs were exempt from one of the most unpleasant consequences of original sin, namely doctors and their medicines[47]. Whatever the reason, there is no doubt that Diderot is tempted, at least briefly, to see the Bedouin as an example of the noble savage, before he found a more convincing model in the Tahitians[48].

Other descriptions of Bedouin in Arabia contain similar praise. Their freedom had already been remarked upon by Montesquieu who compared them favourably, from his point of view, to the Tartars despite the fact that they have the same mode of subsistence[49]. More relevant perhaps is the description of the Arabs that I have already mentioned, to be found in the *Histoire des Deux Indes*, which refers to their simple, noble manner, dictated by Nature[50]. And even more, Volney's *Voyage en Egypte et en Syrie* which contains a long passage devoted to the 'Arabes bédouins' of Syria, who are said to be the same as those living in the Barbary states. They live according to the simple mode of life of their ancestors and have preserved their virtues of hospitality, generosity and morality; in addition, their religion is closer to Deism than to Islam. Although Volney considers that their form of government and possession of property raise them above the level of mere savages, he nevertheless compares them advantageously to the savages of America who, he says, they resemble in many ways[51]. Rehbinder finds the same characteristics among the 'Arabs' of the Sahara; he quotes Herder's remarks on their simplicity, love of freedom, contempt for riches, sense of honour and hospitality, and he too believes that this description applies to all the Arabs from the Euphrates to Senegal[52]. Jackson describes the 'Bedouins or primitive Arabs' of West Barbary in the same way. He gives a flattering description of their 'simple patriarchal hospitality', which compares favourably with the 'dissipation and pleasure of civilised life', whose luxury he criticises. The Bedouin, temperate, sober and benevolent, 'do good to men', and on the whole he seems to consider their behaviour to be better than that of the Christians, who consequently have little hope of converting them[53]. Traces of the same attitude are to be found in Pananti's praise for the Bedouin Arabs, even if, as we have seen, his aim is essentially to condemn the Moors by comparison. For him they still possess their 'pristine simplicity of manners and customs' and have kept their 'ancient manner' and 'primitive mode of living', dating from the days of Job; in addition, they possess the virtues of strength and independence, and can be compared to the heroes of Homer, Ossian and Fingal. None of this is true of the sedentary villagers[54]. Following him, Noah describes the Bedouin Arab as 'a child of nature divested of the dross of luxury or the refinements of wit', and possessing numerous moral qualities[55]. We thus find a respectable number of champions, from all shades of opinion, of the Bedouin's moral qualities, inherent in their simple mode of life and their supposed closeness to nature. The tenacity of such a conception can be seen in the fact that in 1835 La

Rochefoucauld-Liancourt felt the need to deny the supposed greater happiness of the 'Arabs', in order to demonstrate the need to civilise Algeria[56]. But it should not be forgotten that such an idealisation rests on a simple dichotomy between civilised and non-civilised, for the Bedouin could not be considered to be a savage in the true sense of the term, having reached the pastoral and therefore barbarian stage of development, as Volney remarks. Thus, despite the fact that the qualities ascribed to the Bedouin by Diderot conform exactly to those attributed to noble savages, they could finally not really be a serious contender for this title; they tended instead to be considered as representing the simplicity of the way of life of the Biblical Patriarchs. Rather than emphasizing their closeness to Nature, this conception of them underlined their unchanging nature and their refusal of progress. They thereby became simply 'primitive' and a sort of living museum-piece rather than children of Nature.

The other candidates, the mountain Berbers, are frequently described as 'savages' but in the Eighteenth Century this was not usually intended as praise. It is interesting to see that the American Noah, at the beginning of the following century, whose positive description of the Bedouin we have just seen, compares the Berbers to 'our Indians', the difference being that the Indians have always been savages whereas the Berbers are a 'savage people descended from a civilized community'; this is the first time we have met such a category, for civilisations which have degenerated are usually described as 'rude' or perhaps 'barbarian'[57]. Here, however, the comparison with the Americans leaves no room for doubt that they are really considered to be savages. Much earlier, Peyssonnel had described the 'Kabyles' as 'bêtes féroces' or 'espèces de sauvages', not a surprising attitude in view of the fact that they were, in their mountain fastnesses, independent of the Turks whom they did not hesitate to attack in order to defend their liberty[58]. Hence the general opinion concerning them was that they were fierce and cruel. Bruce in the 1770s, writing of the inhabitants of the Auress Mountains, whom he calls 'Kabyles', also calls them savages[59]. Indeed, they apparently corresponded much more closely to the eighteenth-century idea of savages, being seen as ferocious and untamed and, according to some Europeans, living in wild bands and acknowledging no government. Despite the general fear they aroused, they were promoted by some writers to the dignity of noble savages, which is essentially the way they were considered by the colonial promoters of the 'Kabyle myth' that I mentioned in the last chapter. Ageron considers Raynal to be the originator of this myth (although we should point out that their supposed Vandal origin which, he claims, is an essential part of it, was found long before

Raynal)[60]. In fact, if Raynal is indeed the author of all the passages in question, his attitude evolves; in *L'Histoire des Deux Indes*, preference is given, as we have seen, to the Bedouin, while in Raynal's posthumously published text, 'La Barbarie en general', the 'Arabs' tend to be seen as lazy, ignorant and superstitious. In contrast, the Berbers are here represented as 'hommes agrestes et féroces' but as lovers of liberty who are living examples of the character of 'le monde naissant'[61]. Such a change in attitude can hardly be attributed to the influence of Venture de Paradis who shows in the main nothing but contempt for the miserable highlanders or 'Cabaïls'; he nevertheless considers them to occupy a position somewhere between 'les hordes sauvages' and civilised nations; for him they are characterised essentially by their ferocity and their perpetual warfare. He has rather less hostility for the Bedouin, admitting their love of liberty, created by their desert habitat[62]. As for the other authors writing during the same period, Poiret expresses the most extreme contempt for the highlanders, while Rehbinder's account of them is more measured; although he too insists on their ignorance and ferocity, he remarks on their love of liberty, which has led them to resist despotism by staying in the mountains where they preserve a simple and independent way of live. But they are not for him radically different from the other country people, who have likewise remained true to the same simple and unchanging way of life which is for them preferable to the advantages of civilisation[63]. Pananti, too is willing to associate them with his praise for the Bedouin, although to a lesser degree; he writes that the inhabitants of the Atlas mountains are superior to the 'Moors' and that these mountains are the 'refuge of the patriotic and high-minded sons of liberty'[64]. Such praise for the Berbers is less clearly associated with the myth of the noble savage than is the admiration that we have seen expressed for the Bedouin; it is also less generally shared, there being many writers who saw nothing good in these miserable savages. The Arab therefore remained a more likely candidate for the role of the good native.

It is undeniable however that in these descriptions of the highlanders we can discern some of the seeds of the later myth of the Kabyles (although it is important to notice that these descriptions were not confined to those living in the regions to be called 'Kabylie' by the French); the most noticeable characteristic accorded to them by eighteenth-century writers was their love of liberty, an important ingredient of the myth. Nor should we forget their supposed Vandal origin, mentioned as we have seen by Shaw and, following him, Bruce, but not present in the majority of descriptions. Such an origin does not make the highlanders any less savage but it seems, for Shaler, to account for what he calls their

'unafrican moral qualities'; this American also insists on their different
physical appearance, their 'lively social manners' and ingenious
disposition[65]. All of this explains why he considers them to be the most
interesting inhabitants of Barbary, but it does not make them, for all
that, any more apt for civilisation. The corollary of a belief in their Nordic origin was, for the conquerors of Algeria after 1830, that the Kabyles
were closer in origin to the French and were as a result their natural
allies. This belief could also be comforted by the fact, brought out in all
colonial descriptions, that these highlanders had resisted all the suc-
cessive waves of conquerors and had stubbornly refused to submit to the
Turks. It was as a result believed that if the French respected their love
of liberty, they would be welcomed by the Kabyles as their liberators
from the Turkish and 'Arabic' oppressors. This seemed all the more obvious to those who denied that the Kabyles were really Moslem. But
despite the existence of these elements, which could contribute to the
French image of the Kabyles, there was, around 1830, no unanimous
preference for this group of the population over the other inhabitants of
the Algiers Regency. Campbell, in 1834, prefers the Moors who, he says,
are physically more attractive and have a fairer complexion and more
dignified manners. The Kabyles, he insists, dress like the Arabs and,
apart from a few tribes, are 'brown complexioned and black-haired'. He
therefore compares their way of life to that of the Arabs, whom they
resemble, and he even considers their language, although different from
Arabic, to be a 'cognate tongue'[66]. Campbell, it is true, was a Scot who
had no reason to share the preferences of the French conquerors, but we
can also point to the opinion expressed in the same year by the
anonymous author of an article in the *Observateur des Tribunaux* attacking
Hamdan's *Miroir*. This author criticises in particular the Moor's description of the 'Kabails' as timid and inoffensive and willing to submit to the
French; on the contrary, they are for this Frenchman warlike thieves and
the enemies of the French as of the Turks before them. Instead, it is the
inhabitants of the plains who are the natural allies of the French
nation[67]. As we can see, it was far from being a self-evident truth that
the Kabyles were the virtuous farmers of colonial myth, and before the
1840s appreciations of the highlanders remained contradictory. Some
observers considered all the natives to be equally savage. This is the opinion expressed by Hain who saw no difference between 'Arabs' and
Kabyles and considered them as all equally incapable of civilisation and
worthy of extermination[68]. Bory de Saint-Vincent in his report for the
War Ministry in 1838, expresses equal contempt for all the inhabitants
of Algeria whom he seems to consider, without discrimination, as
savages:

Les indigènes, de quelque race ou nuance de croyance qu'ils appartiennent ont les Européens en antipathie; ne faisant aucun cas de nos arts, n'ayant pas nos besoins habituels, méprisant notre civilisation.[69]

(The natives, to whatever race or nuance of belief they belong, have an antipathy for the Europeans; taking no account of our arts, having none of our habitual needs, despising our civilisation.)

No 'natural allies' of the French here!

But it is noteworthy that even in the writings of those who elaborated the 'Kabyle myth' in the 1840s, there appears to be no perceptible difference in the level of civilisation of Arabs and Berbers, which would enable an observer to say that one is more or less savage than another. The Arabs tend to be pastors and the Berbers cultivators, but the Berbers are also artisans. At the same time the Arab, despite his apparent laziness which differentiates him from the Kabyle, is better dressed and, for Carette, more sociable and given to meditation, poetry and even 'intellectual culture'[70]. The factor of civilisation that is considered to distinguish them is their degree of 'subservience' to Islam; while the Arabs are represented as fanatical Moslems, the Kabyles are seen as nominal believers only, whose customs differ from those of the Koran and whose religious practice is perfunctory. The Berbers' lack of religious enthusiasm was one of the elements mentioned by Peyssonnel in his description of the inhabitants of the Auress Mountains; they are brave, independent and different from the 'other Arabs' in that "ils ont le sang blanc, de grands cheveux et sont bien faits". Their language is different and although outwardly Mohametans, they have in fact no religion[71]. Rozet makes a similar remark, saying that although the Berbers living near the plains have adopted Islam through contact with the Arabs, the majority of the highlanders have no religion at all, only revering their 'marabouts'[72]. Daumas and Fabar, in the 1840s, carry this process of de-islamicisation to its limit, writing that if one scratches the Moslem exterior, the Christian essence appears, symbolised by the cross which figures in their facial tattoos[73]. The Kabyles are thus not only Nordic in origin, but even originally Christians forcibly converted to Islam. Such a claim is nowhere to be found in earlier writings, the authors being content, at the most, to observe the lack of enthusiasm for Islam found among these people. In this connection, we observe that those who, in the Eighteenth Century, had presented an idealised vision of the noble Bedouin had likewise felt the need to insist on their purely nominal attachment to the Moslem religion, although here of course their aim was different. Volney in particular depicts the Bedouin almost as Deists, for each individual, according to him, follows his own conscience and they

have neither priests nor temples, nor do they have 'une culte regu-
lière'[74]. The Islamic religion is, we can see, a persistent obstacle for
Europeans in their search for primitive, virtuous peoples. For Volney, in
the tradition of the Enlightenment, as for Gibbon before him, natural
virtue precluded any organised religion, while for nineteenth-century
Frenchmen, it implied a trace of Christianity.

The identification of the Arabs as fanatical Moslems marked them out
as the implacable enemies of the French, and hence of the Kabyles once
the latter had become France's natural allies. Christian stereotypes concerning Islam and Islamic peoples reappeared in force in the Nineteenth
Century, particularly the belief in the stupid immutability of all Islamic
peoples. Hain, in 1832, uses the same terms to describe the Bedouin
Arabs as had many before him, insisting on their unchanging way of life,
similar to that of the Patriarchs; but while for Raynal, and even Poiret,
this was a cause for approval, in Hain's eyes it is a criticism, as it was
to some extent for Shaw a century earlier[75]. We are left, after attempts
at rehabilitation and even at idealisation of the Bedouin way of life, with
a negative stereotype of North African 'Arabs', henceforth seen as lazy,
untrustworthy and fanatical. Even their supposed liberty, an essential
part of positive appreciations of them, is reduced to more realistic proportions; Carette, for example, explains that they are not true nomads
but move in a strictly prescribed and unvarying pattern[76]. So much for
their untrammelled freedom! The result of this denigration was that
Engels was able to write in 1848, in an article in *The Northern Star*, that
the French victory over the Emir Abd el Kader was finally a good thing
for the progress of civilisation, as the Bedouin are barbarous thieves
preying on the sedentary populations, whose supposed noble liberty can
only appear admirable from a distance[77]. The myth of the noble
Bedouin, a son of Nature, lingered on among some romantic lovers of
the desert and is not totally dead today, but it served no useful purpose
for the French in North Africa after 1830. For them, the Arabs became
merely a barbarian people who refused civilisation and deserved only
contempt. The inhabitants of Algeria are thus reduced to manageable
proportions. With the Turks expelled and the Moors ignored, the French
were left with primitive peoples in the mountains and deserts. The
former, virtuous, industrious and racially acceptable are to be (in theory)
civilised by the conquerors who will raise them from their ignorance and
savagery, while the latter, sunk in immemorial barbarian savagery and
ignorance, are to be combatted. Rozet sees the main obstacles to the
civilisation of North Africa to reside in the savage and barbarian customs
of the population and in their religious fanaticism (which the French have
insufficiently respected), as well as in the mountain strongholds which
protect the recalcitrant[78]. As religious fanaticism came to be seen as the

exclusive appendage of the 'Arabs', so the latter became the greater enemy. But whether friendly or hostile, all the natives were at the same primitive level of civilisation. The earlier distinctions between savage and
barbarian are no longer important, all those who are not civilised being
considered as equally primitive. There is no question of their state being
preferable to that of civilised man; the good savage is now the one who
is friendly towards the new rulers. Barbary has become truly barbarian.

* * *

I have in the course of the foregoing discussions had several occasions
to mention perceptions of the different governments of the Barbary
states, particularly in connection with accusations of despotism made
against the 'Turkish' rulers. It would, however, be a mistake to conclude
that the Regencies were classed definitively as despotisms and that there
was no doubt as to their nature. This applies particularly to the governments of Tunis and Algiers for Morocco, once again, was a case apart,
being ruled, in Gibbon's words, by a "barbarian we condescend to style
the Emperor of Morocco"[79]; he was, as an emperor, automatically considered to be a despot. Concerning Tunis and, even more, Algiers however, we find throughout the Eighteenth Century conflicting accounts of
their governments. We have already seen that most European observers
treated them as independent states despite their nominal subservience to
the Turkish Sultan, and that this belief was contested by Venture de
Paradis who was particularly well-informed. He insists, in his manuscript corrections to Raynal's 'Mémoires' on Barbary that the Sultan
still has 'droits réels' over the Barbary states and that in Algiers, nothing
has changed since the advent of the Deys in 1671; contrary to what is
asserted by Raynal, following earlier writers, Algiers has not become
independent[80]. Again, in answer to Raynal's question concerning the
relations existing between the European powers and Tunis, he explains
that the apparent independence of the Regencies was only a trick on the
part of the Turkish Sultan, so that he could pretend to be powerless to
stop the pirates, whereas in fact he remained 'le maître absolu'. In fact,
according to Venture, the more dangerous the pirates, the more power
is exercised by the Sultan; thus he has least power in Tripoli and most
in Algiers[81].

But despite such vehemence, all commentators, even including Venture himself, describe the workings of these states as if they were independent. There is, however, far from being agreement as to the nature
and form of their governments. The Barbary Regencies seem to present

great problems of interpretation, in this field as in others, for Europeans; they saw the immense power of the ruler, but at the same time they were aware of the prerogatives of the Turkish militia, represented in the Divan, who elected the head of state. Thus foreigners had difficulties in interpreting what they saw. In order to understand the problem clearly, it would perhaps be useful to discuss, at the outset, the different forms of classification of governments at this period, for certain labels have particular meanings, and usages change somewhat as the century progresses. The classic definitions took account, of course, of the source of power, that is to say, whether power rested with the mass, with a few or with a single man; but these basic distinctions allowed for variations in definition. In Aristotle's theory, the first category corresponded to the republic, which could degenerate into democracy, the second was aristocracy whose degenerate form was oligarchy and the third monarchy, degenerating into despotism. The threefold division into democracy, aristocracy and monarchy remained the norm, but the divisions popularised by Montesquieu in his extremely influential *Esprit des Lois*, published in 1748, were slightly different. Montesquieu's first category was the republican form of government, but he subdivided it into democracy, in which the power lies with the people, and an aristocracy in which it is held by only some of the people; the other two categories were monarchy, in which a single person rules according to established laws, and despotism, in which one man rules without laws, according to his own whims[82]. This last category was essentially that of Oriental empires and was determined to a large extent by the climate. As for democracies, the only examples that Montesquieu gave, and hence with which this form was closely linked, were the Greek and Roman republics. As the principle on which they were based was considered to be virtue, we can see immediately the difficulty involved when attempting to characterise the Barbary states as democracies. The same problem did not necessarily arise with the other form of republic, namely aristocracy, of which the main example given by Montesquieu was the city-state of Venice; this is particularly interesting for our present purpose as at least one writer makes the comparison between the ruler in the Barbary states and the Doge of Venice[83].

The main problem involved in deciding which appellation to attach to the Barbary states was that of ascertaining where the power in fact lay — with the militia or with the head of state. The word most frequently used to describe the Regencies of Tunis and Algiers is 'republic', which denotes that the power lies with the people or their representatives. Voltaire is particularly insistent that Tripoli, Tunis and Algiers are republics because the Dey or Bey is elected by the militia[84]. But at the same time many authors use the word 'kingdom', which means that power lies with one man. Indeed for the *Encyclopédie* both Algiers and Tunis are undisputably kingdoms, although it points out, with reference to the Dey of Algiers, that his power is not absolute, as he can be disowned by the militia[85]. This explains why most observers are more circumspect. D'Arvieux, for example, explains that Tunis is a republic which is called a kingdom, adding 'like Poland', and he later describes Algiers in the same way[86]. To complicate matters further, despite his own apparent belief that these states are republics, he explains that the Dey of Algiers does exactly what he wants. D'Argens calls the Dey of Algiers a king, but at the same time he describes this Regency as a republic, which he compares to Rome under Caligula and Nero, insisting that the power of the Dey is limited by that of the Divan[87]. What particularly impresses visitors is the fact that the Dey can be overthrown by a plot and a new one elected by the militia. Thus the main characteristic for them — of Algiers at least — is its penchant for bloody revolution. It is this characteristic that makes Ferguson, who follows Montesquieu's theories, consider Algiers to be a democracy which is corrupted in its essence, being guided by self-interest instead of virtue. He writes:

> At Constantinople or Algiers, it is a miserable spectacle when men pretend to act on a foot of equality; they only mean to shake off the restraints of government and to seize as much as they can of that spoil, which, in ordinary times, is ingrossed by the master they serve.[88]

Although he refers to Montesquieu as the source of his theory of government, he does not agree with his predecessor in this particular case, for Montesquieu had written in his *Considérations sur les causes de la grandeur des Romains et de leur décadence* that the government of Algiers was an aristocracy like the declining Roman Empire, which was the opinion not only of d'Argens but also of Shaw[89]. His opinion is based on the power of the militia to depose the sovereign; a military government is thus more republican than monarchical. Gibbon, as we have already seen, disagrees violently with this opinion, writing,

> Can the epithet of *Aristocracy* be applied with any propriety to the government of Algiers? Every military government floats between the extremes of absolute monarchy and wild democracy.[90]

Montesquieu seems finally to have come round to the first of these alternatives and to have decided that the government of Algiers was despotic, to judge by a passing remark concerning the fact that its inhabitants need to bury their wealth to protect it from seizure by the government; this detail was drawn from the work on Algiers by Laugier de Tassy[91]. This latter author, who is willing to excuse much of what he sees in Algiers, has apparently little sympathy for its government and those who compose the ruling élite. His tentative conclusion concerning the form of this government is that it is monarchical rather than democratic, despite the militia's 'vast power', because the Dey exercises the sovereignty exclusively. At the same time, he insists on the Dey's vulnerability to plots and revolution and his uncertain control of the throne, which makes him act like a despot. Thus Laugier writes 'le Dey n'est que l'esclave des esclaves'[92]. Le Roy, in 1750, attempts to defend the government of Algiers and the order reigning in its administration, even admiring 'tant de lumières et de science dans l'art du gouvernement', but he admits that it has certain despotic characteristics, such as its treatment of the Jews, Moors and Christians (that is, the majority of its subjects!), who are slaves rather than citizens. He too compares it, as a military government, to that of Rome and finally admits that it is at once a despotism, a monarchy and an aristocracy, in other words, partaking of all three of Montesquieu's categories; this mixture has led to the habit of calling it either a kingdom or a republic indiscriminately[93]. Such prudence contrasts with, but explains in part, the contradictory, if peremptory, affirmations of other writers. As for Tunis, its government was more frequently seen as a monarchy, due to its hereditary principle which differentiated it from Algiers. Peyssonnel, for example, calls the Bey of Tunis a king, unlike the Dey of Algiers, who has a king's powers but who is elected[94]. Poiret sees fewer problems, for he qualifies Algiers as a republic and Tunis as a monarchy; however, this clear-cut distinction does not prevent him from referring later on to Algiers as a kingdom[95].

At the end of the century, the German Rehbinder reviews the different writings concerning the Algiers government and emphasizes the confusion reigning among European observers. As he points out, most of them had considered Algiers to be a republic, up to and including the author of the *Histoire des Deux Indes*; this is also the case for the diplomatic writings on Algiers. In passing, he takes Poiret to task for the confusion that we have just seen. His own conclusion is that this state was originally a republic, or rather that its constitution was 'aristocratisch-republicanisch', but that it has gradually become more monarchical. In fact, the power of the Dey has, according to him, increased so much that, while the Divan is consulted *pro forma*, if any of its members disagrees with the Dey he is removed. The régime has therefore become 'monarchisch-despotisch', despite the election of the Dey[96]. Again, when discussing the government's monopoly of trade which hinders commercial development, Rehbinder remarks that this is an inevitable result of despotism, and the stronger the despotism, the more stringent the monopoly. Here, significantly, he compares Algiers with Siam, an

'Oriental despotism'[97]. Is this perhaps the influence of Venture de Paradis and his belief that Algiers is an example of such a régime? Or is it simply the case that by this period such had become the generally accepted opinion concerning Algiers? As for Venture himself, despite his opposition to Raynal's use of the word 'republic' to describe Algiers and his insistence on its Oriental, and hence despotic, nature, there are signs of a certain confusion in his attitude as well. In his discussion of the government of the Tunis Regency, he contrasts it with Algiers, the only Regency that had not changed its form of government, and calls the latter a republic[98]. Nevertheless, despite this remark, which may only be a slip, his hostility towards the Algiers régime is constant; he considers its constitution to be 'essentiellement vicieuse' as it makes the Dey absolute enough to exercise his despotism over his individual subjects while at the some time making him dependent on the soldiers in matters concerning the general good of the state. Tunis, on the other hand, he views with much more indulgence, considering it to be a hereditary monarchy[99]. This is also Pananti's opinion; the Italian insists on the despotism of the Algiers government which he describes as a 'species of military republic', combining the worst features of different systems. Tunis, in contrast, is 'monarchical and hereditary' although, "like all the Turkish states, subject to incessant and violent revolutions"[100]. Likewise, Noah describes the government of Algiers as being different from those of Tunis and Tripoli (which are still arbitrary nevertheless) in that it is a military despotism subject to frequent revolutions, with the result that the throne is "founded on blood and maintained by the scimitar"[101]. Notice that in these last two descriptions of the Algiers government, seen essentially as a military one, the terms 'republic' and 'despotism' are apparently equivalent and the exact meaning of the former is not immediately clear. Algiers is considered to be ruled by the militia, who exercise a sort of collective despotism, rather than being subject to the despotism of a single man. What is important here is less the definition of a particular type of régime than the condemnation of its oppressive — or rather 'despotic' — rule. This was already the main impression given by Vallière's *Mémoire* in 1781, for the French vice-consul was less concerned to classify the country than to give a description of its workings to his own government[102].

Shaler, an astute observer, combines these different descriptions. He begins by affirming that "a Dey of Algiers, while alive, is the most despotic and implicitly obeyed monarch on earth", and he goes on to describe the government of Algiers as unique in modern history in that 'a handful of barbarian adventures' — who are foreigners — govern it in an arbitrary manner. He thus calls it an 'encampment of barbarians' rather than an established government and even, with little accuracy, an

'absurd empire'. The nearest he comes to a description rather than a condemnation is the statement that it is,

> a government established by strangers on the right of conquest, democratic
> as to the conquerors, aristocratic as to the natives; extremely rigorous in its
> general character and generally impartial in its administration of
> justice.[103]

By the time the French landed in Algiers in 1830, there was even more
reason to present the government they had overthrown in the worst possible light. Thus Rozet shows little restraint, describing it as excessively
despotic and the Dey as a 'despote sanguinaire'; he exercised arbitrarily
the right of life or death over his subjects until he was inevitably assassinated during one of the numerous revolts by the army, 'une soldatesque
indisciplinée', during which 'le sang coulait à grands flots'[104]. Excessive
as this description is, we can see that it is merely an extension of attitudes
which recur throughout the Eighteenth Century, despite attempts to view
Barbary in a more favourable light. The differences of definition that we
have seen cover a general consensus of hostility, and few later writers
would disagree with Shaw's opinion, put in the mouth of 'Ali Bashaw, a
late Dey', "The Algerines are a company of rogues and I am their
Captain"[105].

But Shaw, while condemning the government of Algiers for its despotism, also explains that the 'Arabs' or Bedouin have kept their own
customs and laws. Thus he explains that a 'Dowar' or village is like a little
principality, presided by a particular family, although power is not necessarily passed on from father to son. His definition of this patriarchal
government is rather vague, for he writes, "Notwithstanding the despotic
power which is lodged in this person, all Grievances and disputes are
accomodated in as amicable manner as possible", and are judged by
the village as a whole. These rulers of the Douars are not, therefore, for
him simply despots[106]. This is not at all the opinion of Peyssonnel, who
was in Barbary at the same time as Shaw and whose notes Shaw drew
on; Peyssonnel considers that the rulers of the 'Arabs' treat their peoples
harshly and rule them despotically, maintaining their authority by
assassination and crime. Thus he contrasts their way of life with that of
the Kabyles or 'mountain Arabs' who have, according to him, neither
chiefs nor rulers and live not in nations but in total liberty and independence[107]. This way of life, which marks them off from the 'other
Arabs', also brands them as savages. Here again we find in Peyssonnel's
writings elements of the nineteenth-century Berber myth, one of whose
facets was the belief that their traditional institutions were uniquely
democratic, unlike the patriarchal slavery of the 'Arabs'. Something
of the same idea, although less specific, is found in one or two other

eighteenth-century visitors; Kokovtsov, although he does not specifically mention their form of government, discusses the highlanders around Bône, believing that they are 'Arabs' who have fled from the Turkish yoke to live in their former independent state. Their courage and liberty encourage, he says, the coastal peoples to see them as their possible future liberators from the Turks[108]. Such an attitude could lead to a belief in their preservation of free, democratic institutions that the French exploited. This belief also had a respectable ancestry, being already present in d'Arvieux's writings on Barbary; here the 'Moors' around Bougie (Bejaia, in Kabylie) are described as enemies of the Turks and hence not opposed to a landing by the Christians if the latter treated them well and respected their freedom[109]. This is all, nevertheless, rather vague and concerns more the highlanders' refusal of Turkish rule and their love of freedom, than their supposedly democratic institutions. Venture de Paradis insists on the independence and liberty of the highlanders in both the Algiers and Tunis Regencies, but nowhere does he mention a different social organisation or form of government, limiting himself to a remark concerning the 'Cabailis' of Flissa, to the effect that they have their own 'chaïks'[110]. It is not until we come to Shaler — whose interest in the Kabyles we have already had occasion to observe — that the question of their form of self-government begins to take on some importance. Shaler qualifies it as 'a mixture of aristocracy and democracy' and although he considers it to be inefficient, this trait can only serve to mark it off still further from the rigorous despotism apparently ruling elsewhere[111]. Thus the form of democracy, or 'moeurs republicaines', described by Daumas and Fabar in what they saw as a 'Suisse sauvage' was not completely their own invention[112]; but this theory was developed systematically from the 1840s onwards so that a love of democracy was considered to form an integral part of the Kabyles' character. This trait marked them off from the 'Arabs' and supposedly made them more accessible to civilisation by the French. Here again we find that a characteristic — love of freedom — originally considered to be typical of the Arabs, or Bedouin, was now transferred to the Berber highlanders. It was pushed even further in their case than it had been before; for the Bedouin's social organisation had always been described as patriarchal, however benign. In the case of the Kabyles, on the contrary, belief in their distinctively republican institutions came to be a tenet of faith; the corollary of this belief was that the other inhabitants of Algeria — the Arabs — were seen to be the apathetic victims of despotism. This view of things contrasts not only with previous praise for the Bedouin but also with the point of view generally expressed by eighteenth-century visitors who brought out the opposition of the great mass of the population to Turkish despotism. There are frequent references to the dangers of travelling in the Algerian countryside without a strong escort for fear of attacks by tribes in revolt against the Algiers government. Those 'Moors' who were not protected by either the mountains or the desert suffered the depradations of the Turkish troops, which is why, as several authors explain, they camp away from the frequented routes; they hoped thereby to escape from the obligation of giving hospitality to the soldiers. As for the inhabitants of the towns, whether Moors, Jews or Christians, they were all at the mercy of the militia, described, as we have seen, as the dregs of the Ottoman Empire.

Thus the native population was viewed either with pity or with fear, and when it came to discussions of the political organisation of these states, attention was concentrated on the Turkish rulers. Whatever the disagreement concerning the precise label to give their government, there was absolutely no dispute as to the despotism and oppression with which they ruled those among the North African population over whom they had power. It should thus be understood that the discussions as to whether the governments of the Barbary Regencies were republics, monarchies, despotisms or whatever only concerned the question of the division of power within the ruling foreign-born élite, who alone made up the Divan and from whom the ruler was recruited. In such discussions, the native population, of whatever social class, origin or religion, was treated as a non-existent quantity. But at the same time, it is precisely because of awareness of the peculiar status of the militia that observers found such difficulty in classifying these governments. This comes out particularly clearly in Shaler's analysis of the distinction between the rights of the militia and the slave-like condition of the mass of the population. It was indeed a growing insistence on this chasm separating the Turks from the rest of the population, and on the foreignness of the rulers that provided a justification for conquest, as the Europeans pointed to the need to liberate this oppressed majority. At the same time and in the same perspective, the Barbary governments — and particularly that of Algiers — were with increasing assurance described as despotic. Here, as in the other fields that we have been considering, the nuances vanished; positive appreciations of the Barbary governments were forgotten, so that the rulers could even be qualified as 'African potentates'. The Barbary states, their inhabitants and their governments were reduced to the most primitive and simplified level as the Enlightenment's attempts (however unsatisfactory) at doing justice to the complex reality they observed gave way before the growing demand for conquest. In addition, it is no coincidence that the particular object of this rising chorus of denigration was the Algiers Regency. In the last part of this book we shall discuss the pressure for conquest that built up in the early years of the Nineteenth Century, resulting in the 1830 expedition, and as an essential prelude to the question, we shall have a closer look at this particular antagonism towards Algiers and the reasons for it.

PART THREE

TOWARDS THE CONQUEST

Throughout the Eighteenth Century there was much greater hostility among Europeans towards the Algiers Regency than towards the other Barbary states, as a glance at almost any text will reveal. So much so that it is difficult to decide whether writers on Barbary were reflecting their own personal impressions or simply adopting current prejudices and interpreting what they saw in the light of their expectations. Take for example d'Arvieux's *Mémoires*, published in the early Eighteenth Century, although his visit dates from the middle of the Seventeenth: the impression that his reader receives of the Tunis Regency, which he visits first, is quite favourable. D'Arvieux is well received by the rulers, establishes friendly relations with certain among them and despite obvious criticisms of the state and some aspects of its workings, comes away with a positive attitude towards the country as a whole[1]. But when he arrives in Algiers, his attitude is hostile from the outset. He insists from the beginning on the arrogance of the Dey and regrets that the Algerians' insolence had not received its due punishment from the French king[2]. The contrast is striking between this antagonism and his earlier willingness to understand the Tunisians' point of view. Indeed, in Tunis he had constantly criticised his fellow-negotiator's unthinking hostility and arrogance which, according to him, almost wrecked the negotiations. The impression we receive is not simply that what he saw in Algiers displeased him, but rather that he had arrived there expecting to be unfavourably impressed and to find a nest of insolent pirates. Thus the Algerine Turks are the 'excrements' of the Ottoman Empire and are characterised only by brigandage and disorder. His conclusion on leaving Algiers is typical:

> Voilà à peu près ce que je pouvais dire de ce mauvais Pays, qui n'est peuplé que de la lie des Provinces de l'Empire ottoman, et qu'on peut regarder, sans craindre de se tromper, comme la plus indigne canaille qui soit en Afrique, et comme une tanière de voleurs dont je ne me repentirai jamais d'être sorti[3].

> (This is more or less what I could say about this unpleasant country, which is only peopled by the dregs of the provinces of the Ottoman Empire, and which we can consider without fear of error as the most unworthy rabble in Africa and as a lair of thieves, which I shall never regret having left.)

Peyssonnel seems to share this opinion, although he expresses it with rather less vehemence. He makes frequent comparisons between the Regencies of Algiers and Tunis, which are all to the latter's advantage. Thus, for example, the roads are safer in the countryside depending on Tunis, while in the Algerian provinces there is constant danger from wild beats, brigands and dissident 'Arabs'; these Arabs are much more miserable and badly treated, with the result that they are more 'méchants'. But it is interesting to see that he praises the Algiers government in a way that he does not do for that of Tunis; perhaps he is here influenced by Laugier's pleas for understanding, for he refers to the latter's work[4]. Shaw shows the same preference for Tunis, making similar remarks, not surprisingly perhaps, as he used Peyssonnel's notes; but in addition he is very hostile to the Algiers government, as we have already seen[5]. Half a century later, Poiret shows a preference for the hereditary monarchy of Tunis over the tumultuous Algerine 'republic', frequently shaken by revolt and bloodshed[6], while Bruce considers that the inhabitants of Tunis are more civilised and its government milder than those of Algiers[7]. It would be fastidious to quote every author who expresses a similar preference, which is omnipresent up to the conquest of Algiers, the town called by Noah 'the sink of iniquity and the curse of humanity'[8].

It is more interesting to consider the reasons for this special antagonism towards Algiers, which finally led to its occupation by the French. The most obvious reason can be summed up in a single word: corsairs (or as they were more often termed, pirates). I have not so far had occasion to go into this subject in detail, beyond a few passing references, but these references have been enough to show that it is of capital importance for an understanding of European attitudes towards Barbary in general, and Algiers in particular. The first image that came to mind at the mere mention of these states was that of bloodthirsty pirates attacking Christian shipping: the Barbary pirates were part of European folklore[9]. It is this picture that we find, for example, in Voltaire's *Candide*[10]. But we should be very careful when dealing with this phenomenon, for modern attitudes towards piracy are not those of even the Eighteenth Century, and the question of the Barbary corsairs in particular has been distorted by colonial justifications for the conquest of Algiers. Firstly, as has frequently been observed, piracy was by no means an activity confined to the Barbary states; the earlier plundering activities of the English seadogs are well-known and, still in the Eighteenth Century, the Maltese knights of Saint John carried on rigorously similar activities on the Christian side. We have seen that this fact was pointed out by authors such as Voltaire or d'Argens. The question of the European nations' hostility towards the Barbary corsairs and a discussion of how far their condemnation is justified are to be found in Fisher's book *Barbary Legend*[11]; although this work has been criticised for its indulgence towards the corsairs, it nevertheless provides a welcome counter to the traditional vituperation from European historians. Other historians have also recently attempted to provide a more balanced view of the question[12]. But as my aim here is not to go into the rights and wrongs of the matter, as I am instead trying to understand the development of eighteenth-century opinions, I shall simply refer the reader to the more recent remarks of Fernand Braudel. Comparing the problems of the Barbary states, and particularly Algiers, with those of Sweden under Gustavus Adolphus, both countries being excluded from the mainstream of European commerce, he observes that the only way for Algiers to react against European hegemony was to resort to 'piracy'[13]. Note that Braudel too refers mainly to Algiers although she was not the only one of these states to indulge in piracy. Why then if she was not unique did she constitute a focus of attention and attract so much hostility? If we look again at the *Mémoires* of d'Arvieux — who, after all, went to Tunis, as to Algiers, precisely to arrange for the liberation of Christians captured by corsairs — we find that the apparent reason for his greater hostility towards the Algerines is their insolence. But the Tunisians had shown themselves to be just as proud, which had almost led to catastrophe when, according to this work, the chevalier du Moulin attempted to browbeat them. On this occasion d'Arvieux explains that the Tunisians fear no-one and should be treated with respect and deference. As a result he is successful in Tunis. But he is unwilling to show the same diplomacy or understanding in Algiers, remarking that the money spent on ransoming the captives would be better employed in fitting out a fleet to defeat these 'écumeurs de mer'[14]. One can only assume that this greater hostility towards Algiers, based on pre-existing prejudices, was due not only to their piratical activities (in which case it should apply equally to Tunis) but also to their greater strength, which made them behave in a more 'insolent' manner. As a result, the Christian nations who signed treaties with the Barbary states to protect their shipping were forced to pay higher sums to Algiers than to the other Regencies; in general Algiers seems to have made higher demands and to have been less willing to compromise. The hatred felt for the pirates in general was aggravated in the case of Algiers by the greater fear they inspired, the higher tributes that were paid to them and the humiliations that they imposed. Many observers mention the lack of consideration accorded to the representatives of European powers by the Algiers Deys; one has only to read Vallière's *Mémoire* to find examples of the way they were treated. And towards the end of the Eighteenth Century we can see, from the comparison made by Venture de Paradis between the conditions imposed by the Tunisians and those imposed by the Algerians in their dealings with foreign powers, that the greater aversion for Algiers was hardly avoidable[15].

But the writers we are concerned with were not in the main diplomats and did not, in general, visit or write about Barbary in the context of diplomatic negotiations. Despite this greater independence, their descriptions reflect the greater hostility towards Algiers. It is evident in all aspects of their accounts, from the form of the government — considered to be less despotic and anarchic in Tunis —, to the condition of the inhabitants. D'Argens, who reflects the prejudices of contemporary visitors, on whose accounts he relies to a large extent, considers the 'Moors' in Tunis to be less miserable than their counterparts in Algiers, while Kokovtsov describes the Algerine militia as more brutal and insolent than those of both Tunis and Tripoli[16]. In view of the latter's short stay and his limited opportunities for observation, his remarks must also reflect the general opinion; as he himself says, his account owes a lot to conversations with the British Consul on the spot. While such official observers may have been particularly influenced by the greater power of Algiers and the greater threat she presented for European navies, more 'philosophic' writers were probably also influenced by another aspect of the question of piracy which, again, made Algiers more objectionable. We find in the Eighteenth Century considerable evidence of a belief that Tunis was turning away from piracy towards trade; this, as I have already said, was seen to be a sign of greater 'politeness'. Already in 1730 La Condamine considered Tunis to be richer than Algiers and her roads to be in better shape[17]. And Kokovtsov, again, remarks that the Tunisians are more reasonable and friendlier than the other Barbaresques, due to their commerce which puts them more in touch with the Europeans[18]. This opinion is particularly in evidence in Venture de Paradis's notes. He writes that the Europeans' trade with Tunis is increasing in a spectacular manner and he gives a certain number of details. He believes that this trade will encourage them to cease their piratical activities and become civilised. He even writes that, were Algiers no longer to exist, Tunis and Tripoli would rapidly become 'des peuples policés', for he considers that the elements of civilisation are already present and that there are more educated people in the Tunis Regency than in other Moslem countries. He does not even dispair of Algiers giving up her piracy if its practice is made too difficult, and turning towards agriculture; he considers that in the last forty years (that is, since the 1740s) the people have become more civilised and less barbaric as the soldiers, kept in better discipline, have turned to trade and agriculture. But despite such progress, Tunis is still ahead of Algiers[19]. The same opinion is expressed by Rehbinder, who, it should not be forgotten, had talked to Venture in Algiers; he too believes that the solution for Algiers is to develop her trade and agriculture, following the path already taken by her neighbour[20]. And this idea is echoed in the anonymous *Historical Memoirs of Barbary* published in 1816, whose author believes that the Tunisians, though indulging in plunder, are less cruel than the Algerines; he associates this characteristic with the fact that the former have more industry and better agriculture[21]. His contemporary, the American Noah, describes Tunis, unlike Algiers, as a port that has long been of great commercial importance[22]. Thus there was, at the turn of the century, a considerable body of opinion that considered Tunis, and even Tripoli, to be thanks to the development of their trade and agriculture turning away from piracy and becoming polite nations. Algiers, on the contrary, seemed much more fixed in her barbaric and uncivilised piracy, which made her a continuing danger to European trading nations. Indeed, her government's policies were considered to hinder actively any increase in its trade, which was not the case of the Tunisian government. This latter point is particularly made by Rehbinder who describes the restrictions on trade in the Algiers Regency and considers that under a different government commerce would flourish. He thinks it unlikely, though, that any change could come about in the attitude of the existing government, because of its greed[23]. Shaler likewise attributes the ruin of Algiers's trade and agriculture to its government's policy, as is evident from the remark already quoted concerning the Mitijah, which has become 'a perfect desert'. He gives the trade figures for 1823, indicating a deficit that is paid for in gold and silver. These figures make a striking contrast with the ones given by Rehbinder in the year 1800, which show a profitable balance, creating an influx of gold and silver. We also notice, incidentally, that Shaler's figures show the importance of East Indian and British goods among the imports[24]. According to A. Djeghloul, Algerian trade was by the end of the Eighteenth Century more and more controlled by foreign, especially French and Italian Jewish, merchants, and it tended more towards the export of raw materials and the import of manufactured goods[25]. It is therefore obvious why its development should be favoured by Europeans and also, perhaps, why the Algerians should see the continuation of 'piratical' activities and the exaction of tribute from the European nations (and also, now, the U.S.A.) as a surer source of revenue in gold and silver.

All of this goes a long way towards explaining the hostility which, by the beginning of the Nineteenth Century was more exclusively directed towards the Algerian Regency. Its two main sources were the Algerines'

continuing piratical activities and the Europeans' desire to develop their
trade with North Africa. To the extent that the Algiers government was
seen to be a hindrance to the development of European trade there, it
would be better to change the government. The result of this line of
reasoning was an upsurge of demands for European action against the
'nest of pirates'. Of course these demands were not new. D'Arvieux, as
we have already seen, called for action to punish the Algerians' 'insolence'. He even wrote a *Mémoire* for the Prince Regent of Portugal, ex-
posing the best way to go about it; he explains that it would be better to
destroy their ships and prevent them from acquiring others — a sure
means of destroying them — than to attempt to conquer the town itself,
which would be impossible to hold. If their fleet were destroyed they
would fight among themselves and the Moors would revolt against their
Turkish rulers, thus effectively bringing the pirates' activities to an
end[26]. No thought of conquest at this date, as we can see. D'Argens expresses the same point of view in 1738; he calls for concerted action on
the part of the European states to destroy the corsairs — the Tunisians
and Tripolitans as well as the Algerians — but again the aim should not
be conquest, merely the protection of European trade and the lives of
European sailors. Of course, d'Argens has another motive, namely to
draw attention to the self-interest of the Christian powers who refuse to
take action to curb the pirates' activities, which they find too useful. Each
state is willing to make a treaty and pay a tribute in order to ensure im-
munity for its own shipping, as this will leave the corsairs free to attack
her enemies. Thus the immediate commercial interest of each state (and
in particular the most powerful, namely the British, French and Dutch)
is stronger than their humanitarian feelings, and the English care little
if the Spaniards are enslaved as long as their own shipping and profits
are safe[27]. Here d'Argens is not only expressing the truth about the
European nations' hypocrisy, but also providing evidence that in the
early Eighteenth Century, hostility towards the corsairs was not necessarily a cover for desires of conquest. The corsairs — both Christian and
Turkish — were still an accepted fact of Mediterranean life, too useful
to be seriously challenged; the periodic expeditions against one or
another of their ports were not undertaken with the aim of destroying
them totally but usually, in the words of Peter Earle, had an 'ulterior and
sinister design' against one of their European enemies[28]. Thus, even in
1781, the French vice-consul Vallière proposes, not a conquest or even
a landing, but simply a bombardment which he believes will be sufficient
to ensure the pirates' respect for the French; moreover he considers that
the English are the Algerians' main allies and if the British bases at
Gibraltar and Mahon were destroyed, the Algerian corsairs would be

mastered[29]. Given such a context, it is clear that attacks such as that by d'Argens were an indictment of the cynicism of his own and other European governments, against whom they were primarily directed; they are also a sign of a growing humanitarian feeling and moral sense. The same point of view is expressed sixty years later by another 'enlightened' writer, the German Rehbinder, who considers the continued piracy of the Barbary states to be the shame of the age, pointing out that if they so wished the European powers could bring it to an end. Instead, thanks to the greed of the powerful nations like England, France and Spain, who prefer to protect their own shipping, the corsairs' activities are allowed to continue and probably will continue to flourish for a long time. The Europeans will never be able to come to an agreement on this matter. In addition, Rehbinder explains that the French African Company and the Marseille merchants do all they can to prevent a war with the Barbary states, which would harm their trade and thus they encourage the French government to pay the tributes demanded by the 'pirates'. The British, on the contrary, having a large fleet in the Mediterranean and few vital interests in the Regencies, are able to pay only small sums to keep the peace and consequently have no interest in going to war. By this period there was the added advantage for the British that the corsairs' activities hindered American shipping and kept this upstart ex-colony out of the Mediterranean. As for recommendations for future action, Rehbinder quotes the famous call for conquest made in the *Histoire des Deux Indes*, but he does not seem to think such a conquest likely, or perhaps even the best course to follow. He envisages the possibility of a Moorish government in Algiers to replace the existing Turkish one; if this government encouraged trade, the result would be, here as in Tunis, the decline of piracy. He apparently believes that the existing Turkish régime — which is 'monstrous' — contains the seeds of its own destruction but he does not think that improvement will come about as long as ignorance reigns and trade and industry are discouraged. He returns later to the same theme, saying that the policies of the present government prevent trade and that the government's harmful monopoly is an inevitable result of despotism[30]. This analysis of the situation is extremely interesting and shows that there were those who could, while stigmatising the backwardness and ignorance reigning in Barbary, envisage even if tentatively a new departure under a native government rather than the unavoidable necessity for foreign intervention. He thus goes much further than the abbé Raynal, who could only see their enlightenment as coming from Europe. Indeed, Rehbinder shows much greater scepticism as to the possibility of the European powers overcoming their narrow self-interest and rivalry than he does on the subject of the Algerians' capacity for self-regeneration.

The reference to Raynal brings us to the most frequently proposed solution to the question of the Barbary pirates by the end of the Eighteenth Century. In the famous passage which we have already mentioned several times — which may not indeed be by Raynal but which, after appearing in the *Histoire des Deux Indes*, is reproduced in the abbé's manuscript *Mémoires* on Barbary — he calls for the conquest of Barbary to put an end to despotism and ignorance. The aim of such a conquest should be not only to destroy the pirates, but also to bring freedom, enlightenment and progress. In the spirit of the Enlightenment, the author insists that this conquest should only be undertaken in the interests of the oppressed inhabitants of Barbary and that if it were not to improve their lot but instead to bring greater slavery, then it should not be undertaken; for all men are equal and the interests of some should not be subordinated to those of others. The sentiments are noble and their expression moving, but the passage is nevertheless an expression of Europocentrism, however enlightened. The North Africans cannot apparently civilise themselves, but must be taken in hand by the Europeans[31]. The same point of view is expressed by Volney during the same period; he claims that if the subjects of the Ottoman Empire continue in their ignorance and barbarism, it is the fault of the Europeans, and in particular the French and their commercial interests. He writes, "que les Maures de Barbarie restent pirates parce que cela favorise notre navigation"[32]. Thomas Paine, another representative of the Enlightenment, echoes the same concern with Barbary pirates, hardly surprising in view of the newly-independent Americans' problems with the Algerians. As I have said, the latters' attacks on United States' shipping were generally considered to be encouraged by the British. Paine sees this question as another occasion to attack the corrupt régimes of Europe and to call for their reform (the French are by now exonerated, having carried out their revolution and not being in a position at that moment to conduct a naval war in the Mediterranean). Paine writes in the second volume of his *Rights of Man* in 1792:

> As reforms, or revolutions, call them what you please, extend themselves among nations, those nations will form connexions and conventions and when a few are thus confederated, the progress will be rapid, till despotism and corrupt government be totally expelled, at least out of two quarters of the globe, Europe and America. The Algerine piracy may thus be commanded to cease, for it is only by the malicious policy of old governments, against each other, that it exists[33].

It is clear that for 'enlightened' opinion, the continuing existence of the Barbary corsairs was the fault of the European governments' narrow self-interest. The usual corollary of this belief was that they could only be destroyed by the action of the same European governments. With the exception of Rehbinder, the enlightened Europeans saw the population of Barbary, by the late Eighteenth Century as a passive mass, oppressed by despotism and sunk in barbarism, who could only be liberated by external intervention and not by their own unaided efforts. Such an attitude is completely in line with the developments we have seen in the second part of this book and, shorn of Raynal's proviso concerning the interests of the North African population, came to characterise European appeals to act against the pirates. The need for European action was from this period onwards universally recognised by all shades of opinion and comes to be associated with the desire for conquest and colonisation. Alexander Jardine is surprised by Europe's submission to the Barbary pirates and considers that a European nation should conquer them in order to encourage them to useful production, for "to be conquered by a civilised and generous nation would be a happy event for these poor Africans"; he is apparently proposing the setting up of military colonies on the Roman model in the whole of North Africa[34]. In contrast, James Grey Jackson a little later, while mainly concerned with Morocco, publishes the appeal to conquer Algiers, from which I have already quoted an extract. He reproduces the traditional hostility towards this Regency in particular, calling its governing Turks, 'the refuse of the Ottoman troops', an opinion we have frequently met already. He writes, "the first principle of this barbarous and sanguinary government, according to an African adage, is to 'Maintain the arm of power, by making streams of blood flow without intermission around the throne'". He claims that this government 'reflects disgrace on Christendom' and that a simple bombardment like that of Lord Exmouth in 1816 is insufficient punishment for "the repeated insults offered by these ruffians to civilised Europe"; in addition, it only punishes innocent subjects instead of the government. And nothing is to prevent the Dey from rebuilding his fleet and fortifications and retaliating. The only solution is therefore conquest, and the conquerors should then set up a firm government to quell the inhabitants' religious prejudices, until they are reconciled to a rational government, mild compared to the present despotism. The only reason for hostility on the part of the inhabitants is considered to be their religious fanaticism. Here again, the justification for conquest is both piracy and despotism; although Jackson admits that this conquest may not be welcomed by those who are supposed to be liberated, once their fanaticism and bigotry are overcome, they will realise how much their situation has improved. They are to be saved despite themselves[35]. Similar appeals for action are made by Pananti, Noah and Shaler, all with the same stated aim, namely to curb piracy and establish a just and civilised government which will encourage industry and commerce.

Another factor is introduced by Venture de Paradis, in a note on Raynal's manuscript concerning Barbary:

> Ne serait-il pas aussi à propos de dire, que dans ce moment où on s'occupe peut-être si impolitiquement de la liberté des nègres, personne ne s'est encore occupé d'assurer la liberté des blancs[36].

> (Would it not also be relevant to say that at a period when there is so much untimely interest in the freedom of the Negroes, no-one has yet been concerned to ensure the freedom of the whites.)

The same concern with 'white slavery' is found in Pananti's work — perhaps hardly surprising, in view of his own personal experience on the subject[37]. Both Venture and Pananti consider that the 'slavery of the whites' is a greater evil than that of the black Africans; their concern for suffering humanity — which for Raynal is equally valid whatever the race — is somewhat subordinated to their Europocentrism. And Venture even points out that the Africans will continue in any case to be enslaved. The comparison between black and white slavery is one that has frequently been made, both at the time and since. Sidney Smith attempted in the early Nineteenth Century to channel the growing demands for the abolition of the slave trade towards action against the Barbary corsairs, with the foundation of a society for liberating the slaves in Barbary[38]. One result was Lord Exmouth's expedition in 1816, whose aim was to force the Regencies to abandon slavery. It is, however, clear that the two cannot be put on the same level, either in terms of numbers, repercussions or suffering involved. One may perhaps infer from Venture's remark that the comparison between the two forms of slavery was in part a way of deflecting attention from the horrors of the Atlantic slave trade and of countering demands for its abolition. In support of this interpretation, we could also quote the remark attributed to Nelson in 1799, concerning the atrocities supposedly commited by the Barbary corsairs during their attacks on Christian shipping: "Never let us talk of the cruelty of the African slave trade while we permit such a horrid war"[39]. The same inference can also be drawn from Pananti's work on Algiers, for whatever his apparent concern to 'shed light and happiness on the degraded people of Africa', he seems more motivated by contempt for these 'degraded people' and by hatred for the "monsters who vie with each other in the deepest hatred and bitterest hostility towards Christianity and civilisation"[40]. His justification for the proposed conquest of Algiers is to destroy the pirates who enslave Christians, to convert the fanatical Moslems and to revive the classical past. The main colonial themes of the Nineteenth Century are present. As for the American Noah's violent denunciation of Algerian iniquity, I have already quoted the terms he uses, which are more violent than those of the authors whom we have already seen. He dwells at length on the horrors of Turkish slavery, giving a pathetic description of the miseries of the Christian slaves and claiming that few live long, as they die of oppression and despair. Here again it is Algiers that comes in for particular condemnation; in Tunis, he says, there are only six hundred slaves (he gives no figure for Algiers), they are not harshly treated and can make money. Noah's heart-rending description of the situation in Algiers leads naturally to a call for a crusade and to criticism of the European powers' inaction[41]. (Note that although Noah was in Barbary from 1813 to 1815, this appeal was published in 1819 and thus after the British bombardment.) His account of conditions in Algiers is not borne out by those of contemporary observers; the general consensus of opinion during this period was that the Algerian navy had considerably declined, that the number of Christian slaves was not great and also that they were in the main well-treated[42]. This has not prevented the theme of white slavery and barbaric piracy from being used throughout the colonial era. The appeal made in 1858 by Monseigneur Pavy, Bishop of Algiers, for the building of the cathedral Notre-Dame d'Afrique in Algiers uses the same argument; in a passage from this appeal reproduced in the *Revue africaine* he dwells at length on the horrors of 'la piraterie musulmane', using in particular the work written by the Père Dan, one of the Christian propagandists whose accuracy was put in doubt by eighteenth-century writers. The Bishop also mentions the passivity of the European states and concludes by insisting on the necessity for the conquest in 1830, which had brought these horrors to an end[43]. In 1925, Charles Tailliart opened his book, *L'Algérie dans la littérature française* with accounts of the cruelties towards the Christian slaves perpetrated by these barbarians[44]. And a recent book on Lord Exmouth's 1816 expedition, entitled *Gunfire in Barbary*, is subtitled "the story of the suppression of white Christian slavery"[45]. Studies by recent historians have shown that this is far from an accurate presentation of the facts; according to both L. Valensi and F. Braudel, the activities of the corsairs were at any rate by this period of no great importance and, such as they were, they were not stopped by Exmouth's expedition, as the fleet was rapidly rebuilt[46]. A. Temini has shown, by a study of documents from the Ottoman archives, that the corsairs' activity continued after 1816[47]. And by most accounts, the number of slaves at Algiers by 1830 was not very great; Shaler even tells us that there were none[48]. Despite all this evidence, European historiography long presented the seizure of Algiers, as L. Valensi writes, as a victory of civilisation over barbarism and as the final cleansing of the Mediterranean Sea of pirates. Enough has already been said by historians to disprove these claims and I do not intend to go further into the question. What I would like to show instead is that the more serious reasons for conquest appear clearly in the arguments given by contemporaries. Their works reveal that whatever the emotional charge held by evocations of pirates and white slavery, the real motives were elsewhere. By this, I am not referring to the immediate occasion of the French expedition in 1830, about which a number of myths have grown up, and which has been studied in a recent work[49]; nor am I claiming to discuss the motives of governments. Instead I am concerned with public awareness of the question and the perceptions that emerge from the writings on the subject. I am referring to the converging arguments in different European countries which all pointed to the interest residing in a conquest of Algiers. These arguments can be summed up in a single word: trade.

Trade, as we have already seen, was considered to be a stimulus to civilisation, whence the preference accorded to Tunis over Algiers. The former, whose trade was more developed, has even been called, thanks to its openness to international commerce, 'the Mediterranean Shanghai'[50]. But despite the fact that the Algiers government accorded less liberty to foreign traders and exercised a monopoly over foreign commerce, there was a growing awareness of the possibilities for European traders here as in the rest of the Barbary coast. Thus the *Encyclopédie* article on Algiers was concerned almost exclusively with its trade, including details concerning the exchanges with the peoples on the other side of the Sahara. By the end of the Eighteenth Century there was increasing pressure to exploit the possibilities offered by North Africa. It should not be forgotten that the abbé Raynal, whose appeal for the conquest of Barbary was made in the name of enlightenment and civilisation, was particularly interested in trade, as can be seen throughout his writings on Barbary. I have already mentioned his manuscript notes on the subject and on the activities of the French African Company[51]. And in the *Histoire des Deux Indes* the call for conquest comes in the middle of a discussion of trade in Barbary. The result of European control of North Africa would be the replacement of piracy by agricultural development; the agricultural produce would be exchanged for European manufactured goods, and this trade would be controlled by European merchants established in Barbary. Thus both sides would profit. According to the author of this passage, the European nations who support the pirates are unaware of their own long-term interests, which consist in forcing 'Africa' to have needs and the means to satisfy them[52]. The argument is clear: the justification for the conquest of Barbary is that it will bring enlightenment, but this enlightenment is synonymous with the development of trade which is to profit Africa of course, but also — and mainly — Europe. The honest and civilised activity which is to replace piracy is not manufacturing industry but agriculture; Barbary is to become a producer of raw materials and food and a market for European manufactured goods. The true nature of the Europeans' growing interest in North Africa is here starkly revealed. Whether or not this passage is by Raynal, the fact that it appears in the *Histoire des Deux Indes* is revealing enough. It is curious, to say the least, that the condemnation of European colonial enterprise in the West Indies could go hand-in-hand with similar colonial projects for Africa, however disguised as a humanitarian undertaking and shorn of the unacceptable aspects of European colonies in the Americas — namely the slaves. In North Africa the work-force already exists on the spot. It is also enlightening to read the *Mémoire* on the Compagnie royale de l'Afrique, established at La Calle; this text, as I have already said, is to be found among Raynal's manuscripts, although as it is not in his handwriting, its authorship is not certain. After general remarks on the Company and its history, the author describes its important role in providing corn for Marseille and Provence; in addition, as the main guarantee of French influence in the Algiers Regency, it is a vital asset for France. Thus she must maintain this company's monopoly. Nevertheless, the author discusses the possible advantages to be gained by allowing the 'Moors' to engage in trade at the expense of this monopoly. He concludes that in view of the low level of civilisation in Barbary, such a liberalisation remains a 'belle chimère' and it is therefore better to protect the position and interests of the French Company and of France at the Dey's court[53]. Commercial and national interests are here seen to override the possibility of improving the lot of the Moorish population by allowing them to control their own commerce. Such an argument throws a new light on calls for the enlightenment of these Barbary Moors. While it is no doubt true that the Europeans believed that their rule would be more beneficial to the population than the Turks' despotism, there was no question of their relinquishing the economic initiative. Their own commercial interests counted above all. The advantage of the plan of conquest proposed by the *Histoire des Deux Indes* was that it reconciled two aims: the civilisation of Barbary and the protection of European — and in this case French — economic interests went hand-in-hand. We note that the ultimate preoccupatons expressed here are the same as those shown by the far from enlightened Vallière, who believed that a government in Algiers which encouraged agriculture would thereby stimulate trade, from which the French African Company would profit. It is not clear who, in his opinion, would control the government, but he clearly believes that the existing Turkish régime was in inexorable decline and could not last[54]. The commercial interest of Barbary is less apparent in the writings of Venture de Paradis; this may be because we only possess his notes which were not intended to be published as they stood. His main reference to trade comes in the form of a table showing the revenues of the Algiers Regency. Nevertheless we have already seen the preference he accords the more commercially-minded Tunisian state. And a few remarks on Raynal's manuscript, concerning the interests of the French African Company at La Calle, indicate the same attitude. He too insists on the necessity to prevent foreigners from competing with this Company and, in addition, he seems to think that it should try to challenge the Algerian Jews' control of the important trade of Constantine in the East. He is evidently favourable towards a European attempt to conquer Algiers and even proposes a suitable site. He also remarks that if the Regency turned from piracy to trade, Arzew — a much better port but impossible to defend against enemies — should become the kingdom's capital[55].

The most blatant exposition of the commercial advantages attendant on the conquest of Algiers is to be found in the work by the Englishman James Grey Jackson concerning Morocco and Timbuctoo. I have already quoted from the letter he reproduces in this work, dated 1818 and signed 'Vasco da Gama', in which he calls for the conquest of Algiers. It is worth giving a more extensive quotation from this letter. He first exposes the pressing humanitarian reasons which necessitate the invasion of this Regency rather than a simple bombardment, and which concern the need to rid the Mediterranean of pirates. Such an invasion will result in the civilisation of the 'Berebbers' and their conversion to Christianity. He then remarks that the conquest of this state would lead to the occupation of her neighbours, and he enumerates the advantages that would follow:

1. An incalculable demand for spices and East Indian manufactures of silk and cotton.
2. A similar demand for coffees and for sugars, manufactured and un-manufactured; as well as for other articles of West Indian produce.
3. An incalculable demand for all our various articles of manufacture.

In addition, Britain would obtain 'from this fine country':

1. An immense supply of the finest wheat and other grain that the world produces.
2. Direct commerce with the interior of Africa [. . .][56].

Jackson here sets out clearly and directly the main reasons for civilised and commercial nations' interest in North Africa in general, and Algiers, the richest of the Regencies, in particular. His arguments are totally in line with those earlier expressed with less clarity, in the *Histoire des Deux Indes*. It was not only that Barbary was seen as a fertile agricultural region and, as has been pointed out many times, as the potential 'granary of Europe' — as it had supposedly been in Roman times — but, perhaps more importantly, she was considered to constitute an immense potential market for European and colonial produce. And, no less importantly, Barbary with her long-established trade routes across the Sahara, was the gateway to Africa, an even greater market, and a region thought to be immensely rich in gold. For Timbuctoo, as I have already said, continued to be an object of fascination due to its fabled wealth. According to Numa Broc, this trans-Saharan trade, which had slowed down somewhat during the Eighteenth Century, revived after 1815 due to the British Navy's activity against the slave trade on the West African coast; trade thus intensified with the Mediterranean overland[57]. This development serves to underline the importance of Jackson's argument, in which we see the significance of the greater awareness of Barbary as part of the African continent, discussed in chapter 1 above. Jackson's letter, already published in a newspaper, is apparently part of a campaign to arouse public opinion to call for energetic action against the pirates. Many people considered the British bombardment of 1816 to be inadequate; they demanded the acquisition of the area and its development in line with British interests. As we have seen, the 1816 expedition had not dealt a crushing blow to the corsairs, who simply rebuilt their ships. There was also a belief, expressed more recently by the two naval historians of Exmouth's exploit, that "the Algerines were committed by religion, custom and heredity to see life from a particular viewpoint" and would never become civilised unless forced to do so; thus "total conquest and permanent occupation" were the only solution[58]. We have already seen how to interpret such arguments. They disguised the true commercial motives and the perpetual chorus of regret (already present in Laugier de Tassy's work) that the Algiers government's monopoly of trade and insolence limited the European traders' activities. Such a regret is present even in the works of Poiret and Rehbinder, who do not call for a conquest[59].

But interested as Britain was in trade, she was not willing for the moment to become involved in new colonial responsibilities. It was true that the loss of her American colonies meant that she felt the need for new outlets for her produce, as is evident from Jackson's analysis. But it also meant that she was hesitant to repeat the American experience. Her naval supremacy after 1815 ensured that she felt strong enough to control the trade that was vital to her without the need for formal sovereignty and the responsibilities involved. A bombardment of Algiers, like that of 1816, was generally felt to be sufficient to establish her superiority and to force the Algerians to liberate their Christian prisoners, and no more was felt to be necessary. In addition, the corsairs were doubtless still felt to be useful as a curb to the revival of French power. The opposite case was argued in vain by those pressing for an expedition of conquest. L. Goldsmith, for example, argued forcefully in his *Anti-Gallican* for colonisation of the Barbary state, which would lead to the development of its agriculture and of British trade in North Africa, as well as reinforcing Britain's control of the Mediterranean[60]. And the short-sightedness (in terms of Britain's commercial interests) of her government's policy was pointed out not only by such anti-French propagandists or by enthusiasts for an African empire like Jackson, but even by Shaler, the United States Consul in Algiers. In 1826, he criticised British 'blunders' and the way she pandered to the 'pirates'. He insists that the British could have destroyed Algiers totally in 1816 had they so wished, but they omitted to do so, with the result that it remained 'a nest of banditti'. He contrasts this British pusillanimity with the Americans' vigorous action; the latter had refused to propitiate the Algerians by a tribute, forcing instead their respect by showing willingness to fight, with the result that American shipping was now respected. He considers that the only course open to civilised nations is to occupy and civilise 'this fine region'. Britain should found, not a colony on the old monopolistic principle (it would indeed have been difficult for an American in the early Nineteenth Century to propose this), but a colony 'on constitutional or chartered principles' which would instil 'a love of civil liberty' and would lead to self-government (under the control of the white colonists, as in the United States). In Shaler's opinion, Britain would inevitably lose her remaining colonies in North America, and the West Indies and India would not, in his view, add to her national strength. On the contrary, a 'nation of Englishmen in Numidia' with free institutions and a certain amount of independence would bring advantages for 'mankind at large' and, of course, Britain in particular. He has no doubt as to the importance of the region, which could provide abundant agricultural produce and absorbe Britain's surplus population[61]. As we have already seen, he explains elsewhere in his work his belief that Algiers's trade, at present ruined and of little importance (including her exchanges with the interior of the continent) would flourish under a different government. It is amusing to see this citizen of a former British rebel colony proposing the establishment of a new British colony of settlement, apparently on the lines of the United States of America, on North African territory and believing that its interests would coincide with those of the mother country. There is, at any rate, no doubt in his mind that the economic advantages for Britain would be great. The Italian Pananti, writing a little earlier, was of the same opinion. He describes the commercial advantages deriving from the occupation of Algeria, which would 'throw open the whole of that vast continent' and its inexhaustible resources. He too insists on the fertility of the land and its riches in precious metals. Interestingly enough, Pananti also sees Britain as the nation to lead the international league that, according to him, should be formed for the conquest of Barbary and the civilisation of Africa[62]. For such arguments, of course, Barbary is both a means to control the Mediterranean and the gateway to the interior of the African continent, and its population is of little account. These authors all insisted on the ease with which a conquest could be carried out and on the advantages to be drawn from the Moorish population's hostility towards their Turkish rulers; otherwise their existence is ignored. Others, however, who defended the British government's stance, struck a more cautious note. This is the case of the anonymous author of the *Historical Memoirs of Barbary*, published in 1816; he writes of the problems of fighting "a race of men, trained to habits of infamy, not residing in a single spot, but on the borders of an immense continent; the inhabitants of which, in their various connexions, are, to a great extent, unknown"[63]. Here is indeed Barbary as part of darkest Africa, striking terror into the heart of the white man! In addition, Barbary is for this author apparently inhabited exclusively by nomadic barbarians, although here such a perception has the effect, not of encouraging but of discouraging attempts at conquest. For the British government a factor that explains her unwillingness to engage on such a perilous undertaking was also no doubt the awareness that her trade with North Africa had never been vital (although according to Shaler her share of Algiers's foreign trade was rising in the years prior to the conquest).

For the French, on the contrary, and particularly for Marseille, trade with North Africa, mainly via La Calle, was seen to be of great importance. Hence the arguments concerning the vast commercial possibilities to be opened up by the occupation of this part of Barbary were not lost on them. The point of view expressed, as we have seen, in the *Histoire des Deux Indes*, was particularly put forward by the Marseille lobby, defending the town's commercial interests. We have already seen accusations that this lobby's concern for trade had encouraged the French government to conclude humiliating treaties with the Barbary states, and Algiers in particular. Now, doubtless because of the awareness of this Regency's weakness and the threat from the British navy, voices were raised in Marseille demanding an expedition. After the outbreak of hostilities in 1827 and the blockade, public opinion in the town was in favour of conquest and against a negotiated settlement. The importance of commercial interests comes out clearly in the articles in the Marseille newspaper *Le Sémaphore* quoted by Charles-André Julien in his article on the affair[64]. And more recently Henri Alleg, discussing the commercial motives behind pressure for conquest, quotes an article by Sismondi in the *Revue encyclopédique* to the same effect[65]. But these ulterior, and very real, motives tended to be concealed in the period leading up to 1830 behind more honourable and public ones. Thus the arguments put forward by Clermont-Tonnerre in 1827 related exclusively to the question of the French King's honour and the need for a crusade against the infidels[66]. As a result, traditional historiography has tended to take these declarations at their face value and consider that the crusading zeal and the desire to avenge the insult of the 'coup d'éventail' were the causes of the 1830 expedition. This is to ignore the long-standing pressure outside the government for action and the real commercial motives behind this pressure[67]. The role played by such motives can be seen by the fact that many of those who were against the expedition argued precisely that Algeria could not become a viable colony. This debate continued after 1830, for it was not at all evident that once the French army had expelled the Turks and seized the Dey's treasure, the government wished to establish a permanent colony. Many voices were raised claiming that a permanent establishment could only be a drain on France's resources. Those who were in favour of a permanent colonisation were again the Marseille lobbyists. Thus *Le Sémaphore*, immediately after the French landing, laid down as a principle that not only Algiers but also Oran and Constantine were henceforth French territory, and the arguments used were largely commercial[68]. Likewise, the principal justification for colonisation given by V.A. Hain — whose zeal for the annihilation of the natives we have already seen — concerned the commercial advantages that France could derive from the colony. On the one hand he praises, as so many had done before him, the fertility of the land which, properly cultivated, would produce large quantities of crops such as grain, wine, cotton; and on the other, he insists on the role of Algeria as the gateway to the interior of Africa, which could then be opened up to exploration and trade. This is one of the arguments refuted by the opponents of colonisation. We could quote, for example the author of a pamphlet published in 1835 entitled *La France doit-elle conserver Alger?*, by an 'Auditeur au Conseil d'Etat'. He claims that Algeria is useless as a route to penetrate the interior of the continent, as it is cut off from the rest of Africa by both the Atlas Mountains and the Sahara. In addition, the Algerian ports are poor and would not enable France to dominate the Mediterranean[69]. It is beyond the scope of this book to go any further into this discussion, which has already been studied by Ch.A. Julien[70]. My aim has simply been to show here that the potential commercial importance of Algeria was a factor that had led it, for at least half a century before the French expedition, to seem a likely candidate for colonisation. The question of the pirates or the need for a crusade against the infidels, or the liberation of the 'white slaves', however much they may have captured the popular imagination, were to a certain extent screens for the more down-to-earth motives of commercial interest. In addition, this conception of the possibilities of Barbary was closely linked to the different conceptions of its geographical situation. As a Mediterranean shore it was seen to be a key to control of the sea, a way to make it a 'French lake'. As part of Africa, it became both backward and unexplored, but also a gateway to the riches of the interior. The British were particularly open about the latter point, but we should not therefore suppose that it was absent from French calculations. As far as the former are concerned, the references we have seen in some British writings on Barbary to the African Association, founded by Joseph Banks, are particularly eloquent. We can also see the similarity between Jackson's arguments concerning Algeria and those put forward by the Secretary of the African Association in 1790:

> Of all the advantages to which a better acquaintance with the interior of Africa may lead, the first in importance is the extension of the commerce and the encouragement of the manufactures of Britain[71].

This awareness of Britain's trading interests was a constant factor in her attitudes towards Algeria, and to the rest of Africa, from the late Eighteenth Century onwards. Thus the Scottish poet Campbell discusses in 1837 the future of Algiers as a French colony; he considers the possible benefits to France (which he only sees as probable in the long run) and the harm that it is likely to cause to Britain. He plays down the latter danger as, in his opinion, the Mediterranean is unlikely to become a French lake as the French hope. He also believes that if France civilises Algeria, this country is likely to become a better customer for English manufactured goods. His conclusion is, "the retention of the country as a *point d'appui* for the entrance of European civilisation into Africa is a consummation devoutly to be wished for"[72]. Britain has no need to fear this French expansion because, in view of France's weaker navy and less developed industry, it is British trade that, in his opinion, will benefit from the French conquest of this part of Africa. He here reflects the view, shared by the British government, that the French conquest of Algiers could not harm Britain. The *Morning Chronicle*, in 1830, had welcomed France's expedition and praised the natural aptitude of the French for colonising[73]. Even Bannister, — who made an appeal to the French, published in 1833, against their establishment of a colony in Algeria and in favour of a government controlled by the native inhabitants — argues in terms of the interests of French trade. He claims that an independent colony would become France's friend, which would encourage the establishment of commercial links. He compares the situation in Algeria to that of the British in India, expressing his belief that less civilised peoples desire friendly relations with Christians; these favourable dispositions are, he claims, destroyed by violent conquest. As a result, France has more to gain by becoming the 'protectrice de l'Afrique' and her commercial partner rather than her ruler[74]. Such 'neo-colonialist' arguments, before the great era of European imperialism, are very interesting, and reflect the British view of the means to serve trading and manufacturing interests in the early Nineteenth Century.

But the French, being as yet less industrialised, saw their commercial interests more in terms of agriculture, which implied the need to establish permanent colonies of settlement, to seize and cultivate the land (although, as we have seen, agricultural development should lead to commercial expansion). This was indeed how the French colonisation of Algeria developed. We can, to terminate, quote Bugeaud, responsible for the 'pacification' of Algeria, who nevertheless considered its conquest to have been a grave error. He considered that the only interest there was agricultural, and that it would take a long time to develop the country's potential. In the mean time, the creation of a 'peuple nouveau' by colonial settlement would open up commercial relations with the Arabs of Algeria and the interior of Africa. For this soldier, however, this trade appears to be of only subsidiary interest[75]. This project for colonisation, while it implied the savage, African nature of Algeria, at the same time revived the idea of the Roman Empire in North Africa, to which the French were the heirs. The civilisation that the French were supposedly bringing to Africa did not, in this view of things, benefit the natives, as it was confined to fortified camps surrounded by hostile territory. Later it was to be emigrants from Europe who were to take and cultivate the land, while the indigenous inhabitants were denied any right to it, being, as we have seen, either highlanders or nomads. Thus the warning contained in the *Histoire des Deux Indes* can be seen to have been a prophecy as Africa did become, in the words of its author, the 'theatre of European barbarity'[76].

CONCLUSION

The French conquest of Algeria did finally, in the long run, open up the interior of the African continent, which was eventually explored and colonised. This process of colonisation both proceeded from and encouraged a conception of Africa as the Dark Continent, wild, backward and unknown. The Africans were considered to be no more than tribes of savages with no civilisation or even history, fixed in unchanging stupidity until awakened to the modern age by the white man. But while this had long been the Europeans' view of the mass of the African continent, due to their ignorance of the reality, such a view of North Africa was in the Nineteenth Century new. What I have tried to trace in this book is the process by which such a belief came about.

We have seen, in the attempts made by enlightened thinkers to make sense of, and dominate, the mass of new information collected about the rest of the world, how the region known as Barbary presented problems. It was difficult to fit into the new systems of classification that were elaborated in the Eighteenth Century. Barbary occupied a position which made it straddle these new categories; it was neither civilised nor savage, neither part of the European world nor really alien, and neither East nor West. In addition, as its inhabitants were obviously a long way from the state of Nature, it could teach the philosophers nothing concerning the origins of human society, philosophy or language. Despite attempts in this direction, the final conclusion was that it was characterised by despotism rather than by the presence of natural man. But when Algiers was conquered by the French in 1830, Barbary had been assigned to its 'proper' place; it was part of the backward, primitive and uncivilised African continent, its backwardness reinforced by its religious fanaticism, a land to be civilised by Europe. To arrive at this opinion, there had been a process not only of depreciation of the inhabitants of Barbary and their civilisation, but also, more radically, the establishment of a state of amnesia concerning most of what was known about North Africa. Thus after 1830, studies of 'Africa' (a term used frequently by the French to refer to their new colony of Algeria rather than the continent as a whole) could be carried out on a totally new basis without taking account of previous studies. Earlier works on the country were either ignored or reduced to insignificance. In this way a new classification of the natives into Arabs and Kabyles — considered to be radically different and mutually antagonistic — could be elaborated. The usefulness of this way of dividing up the population and the extent to which it contrasted with previous attempts at classification are clear. But we have also seen that such a transformation of perceptions, and of the way that knowledge about Barbary was interpreted, did not only occur after 1830. One thing that emerges clearly from the texts that we have studied is the fact that a change of attitudes towards the Maghreb is perceptible around the turn of the century, that is, some time before the conquest of Algiers. It cannot therefore be attributed solely to the colonisation of part of North Africa by a European nation; instead, it precedes it and, to a certain extent, prepares the way for it. This gradual and uneven transformation of ways of looking at the region and its inhabitants accompanies ever more insistent calls for an expedition against the corsairs, ending finally in demands for a conquest and then colonisation of Algeria. While, as we have seen, this mutation is not uniform, there being considerable differences between individual authors, the general tendency is indisputable. There is thus an evident connection between the depreciation of North Africans, both racially and in terms of their degree of civilisation, on the one hand, and the growing desire to exercise control over the region, on the other. But we should be wary of seeing a simple and direct relationship of cause and effect between the two, however much we may consider them to be linked. We are after all not concerned here with government policy or the activities of pressure groups but with a movement of opinion among thinkers, which is a reflection of diverse factors. The new depreciation of Barbary was part of a more general transformation of the ways in which Europeans looked at the rest of the world. Belief in the uniformity of human nature gave way to theories of the existence of irremediably inferior peoples with smaller brains, and reaction against the idealisation of the noble savage reinforced belief in the superiority of European civilisation[1]. At the same time, the very nature of awareness of the Eighteenth Century as an Age of Enlightenment could reinforce a belief in the Europeans' inherent superiority. Thus we see, in the *Histoire des Deux Indes*, the justification of what is in effect a colonial enterprise in the name of the need to enlighten the miserable victims of Turkish despotism, despite the proviso that the only justification for colonisation is the good of the inhabitants.

Which brings us back to the problem of Islam, which coloured all attitudes to the Maghreb. Despite the Enlightenment's greater sympathy towards this religion and the civilisation it inspired, anti-clericalism could unite with long-standing Christian prejudices to reinforce a belief in the need for European intervention against the Turks. Instead of being perceived as a tolerant, even philosophical religion, Islam was now seen as a factor of immobility, backwardness and ignorance. This image of Moslem civilisation was reinforced by the fact that the Ottoman Empire was by the late Eighteenth Century thought to be less of a threat to Europe and a civilisation in decline. Its subjects were considered to be kept forcibly in misery and darkness by its despotic rule. In this view of things, enlightened thinkers could agree with Christian propagandists as to the need to liberate these peoples. Furthermore, awareness of trade as a factor leading to civilisation coincided with the new awareness of the commercial possibilities of the region and the desire to take advantage of them. Despite the fact that the great period of colonisation in Africa did not begin until the third quarter of the Nineteenth Century, the upsurge in interest in the exploration of the continent which is visible at the end of the Eighteenth Century corresponds already to an awareness of the commercial possibilities to be exploited there. Thus perceptions of Barbary were gradually transformed in accordance with a complex set of factors. On one hand, the disappearance of the Eighteenth Century's attempt to understand Islam and the development of a new aggressivity towards the Ottoman Empire, seen to have lost the initiative in the Mediterranean; on the other, the emerging realisation of the perspectives to be opened up by the penetration of Africa, in view of the declining importance of European colonies in the New World and the revival of the trans-Saharan trade routes following British action against the slave traders on the West Coast. However mutually contradictory these two perceptions of Barbary might seem to be, the 'Oriental' and the 'African' image combined in the early Nineteenth Century to produce a belief in the inferiority of North Africa and its availability for conquest. To enlightened thinkers the awareness of Barbary as part of the Islamic world precluded interest in it as providing examples of primitive or 'natural' man; attempts to find specimens of natural man, among the Bedouins or elsewhere, were short-lived. It was finally their religion that proved an obstacle; North Africans could only be good savages to the extent that they were not thought to be Moslems. Thus after the abandonment of Philosophes' attempts to use Islam in order to condemn Christian superstition and intolerance, it was finally Moslem superstition and intolerance that became the enemy as the peoples of Barbary became the degraded victims of Turkish despotism, in need of enlightenment at the hands of Europeans. This interpretation of the situation also enabled enlightened thinkers to condemn the self-interest of the Christian governments who permitted, and even helped, Turkish despotism to continue. But at the same time the North Africans were, so to speak, the victims of a new preoccupation that emerged from another aspect of enlightened thought. The systems of racial classification that were developed in the late Eighteenth Century divided mankind according to physical characteristics; in this view of things, primitive peoples were not so much the representatives of the childhood of mankind as beings with an inferior constitution, incapable of reaching the same degree of civilisation as the white Europeans, endowed with a superior organisation. The Maghreb, as part of Africa, was for the partisans of such systems, who turned their backs on the Enlightenment's belief in the universality of human reason, a region peopled by beings incapable of developing its immense potentialities. Colonisation by the superior race was the only way to bring prosperity to North Africa.

Thus there was, in the late Eighteenth and early Nineteenth Century, a set of factors involving both material interests and intellectual developments which, despite their apparently contradictory aims, could combine to produce a belief in the need for European intervention in North Africa. It is true that the intellectual framework of the author of *L'Histoire des Deux Indes* is far removed from that of a colonial propagandist like Hain; nevertheless they share a common belief in the necessity for European control of North Africa's destiny. And while the victory of the latter's beliefs meant the rejections of the former's ideals, there remains some common ground concerning France's commercial interests. For the representative of the late Enlightenment, the furtherance of European commercial interests could only contribute in equal measure to the well-being of the North Africans, seen to have the same rights as the Europeans; for the men of the imperial era, on the contrary, the former was all that counted, as there was no question of considering the African natives as even potentially equal. This book has, I hope, gone some way towards explaining how this new way of looking at non-European peoples in Barbary emerged and how a different view was once possible.

NOTES

INTRODUCTION

1. I have explained in my Preface the way in which my aim is different from that of Denise Brahimi's book, *Voyageurs français au XVIII° siècle en Barbarie*, which deals mainly with four French travellers to Algeria, although I inevitably cover some of the same ground as this author.

2. See for example Lucette Valensi, *Le Maghreb avant la prise d'Alger* (Paris, 1969), pp.11 ff. This opinion is repeated by Wadi Bouzar, *La Mouvance et la pause. Regards sur la société algérienne* (Alger, 1983) vol.I, p.91. Numa Broc, in *La Géographie des Philosophes* (Paris, 1975), p.59, also talks of the difficulties encountered by travellers in North Africa.

3. Peyssonnel and Desfontaines, *Voyages dans les Régences de Tunis et d'Alger*, published by Dureau de la Malle (Paris, 1838).

4. *Réfutation de l'ouvrage de Hamdan Khoja intitulé Aperçu historique et statistique sur la Régence d'Alger*, (Paris, 1834), p.57. The book by the Algerian notable Hamdan ben Othman Khodja entitled *Le miroir* attacked the behaviour of the French authorities following the conquest of Algiers. It has recently been reedited with an introduction by A. Djeghloul (Paris, 1985).

5. *Note sur la Commission exploratrice et scientifique d'Algérie*, présentée à son excellence le Ministre de la Guerre par le colonel Bory de Saint Vincent de l'Institut (16th October 1838), p.9.

6. Playfair's *Bibliography* lists a considerable number of books. In order to see how widely they circulated, one would need to undertake systematic investigations into private library catalogues. An indication can perhaps be given by the catalogue of the sale of the books owned by La Mettrie (together with some other books) in Berlin on 17th April, 1752; among the "Voyages", there are those of Shaw (in French), Laugier de Tassy, Brooks, Tollot and several others concerning Barbary.

7. For example, Laugier de Tassy's history of Algiers was plagiarised by Le Roy in French and Morgan in English.

8. See the article concerning d'Argens in the *Dictionnaire des Journalistes (1600–1789)*, ed. Jean Sgard (Grenoble, 1976), p.10ff. D'Argens's *Lettres juives* were a great success and were frequently reedited and translated for much of the century.

9. *Histoire philosophique et politique des établissements et du commerce des Européens dans l'Afrique*, 2 vols., (Paris, 1826). The title was chosen by Peuchot to remind the reader of the famous *Histoire philosophique et politique des établissements et du commerce des Européens dans les Deux Indes*, first published in 1770 and attributed to Raynal. In fact there were numerous contributors, including Diderot.

10. Denise Brahimi, Introduction to *Opinions et regards des Européens sur le Maghreb aux XVII° et XVIII° siècles* (Alger, 1978), p.8.

11. In a recent article in the *British Journal for Eighteenth-Century Studies* (vol.8, n°1, spring 1985, pp.1–15), John Lough has argued vigorously in favour of dropping the term 'Enlightenment' altogether; but insofar as these eighteenth-century writers were aware of themselves as embodying a new way of thinking about the world, I believe that its use is justified.

12. In using the word 'Man' to refer to the human race, I am simple following eighteenth-century usage. On this subject, see Gérard Leclerc, *Anthropologie et colonialisme* (Paris, 1972), annexe, "Les Lumières, préanthropologie et précolonialisme".

13.   See for example, Thomas Pellow, *The History of the Long Captivity and Adventures* . . . , 1739; or J. Foss, *A Journal of the Captivity and Sufferings of J. Foss, several Years a Prisoner at Algiers* (2nd.ed. Newburyport, 1798).
14.   *Narrative of a Residence in Algiers* . . . *by Signor Pananti*, (London, 1818).
15.   For example, Pierre Dan, *Histoire de Barbarie et ses corsaires* (Paris, 1637); or *Relation en forme du voyage pour la rédemption des captifs aux Royaumes de Maroc et d'Alger* . . . (Paris, 1726) by several authors.
16.   *Voyage fait par ordre du Roy Louis XIV dans la Palestine* . . . , published by La Roque (Paris, 1717); concerns Palestine and contains remarks on the 'Arabs' in general. *Mémoires du chevalier d'Arvieux* . . . by J.B. Labat, 6 vols. (Paris, 1735), concerning Barbary as well as the Levant.
      For complete titles of these works and those following, see the Bibliography.

PART ONE — PRECONCEPTIONS

1. See for example R.L. Playfair, *The Scourge of Christendom. Annals of British Relations with Algiers prior to the French Conquest* (London, 1884); E. Dupuy, *Américains et Barbaresques (1776—1824)* (Paris, 1910); Godfrey Fisher, *The Barbary Legend. War, Trade and Piracy in North Africa (1515—1830)*, (Oxford, 1957); John B. Wolf, *The Barbary Coast. Algeria under the Turks* (New York, 1979).
2. *Bibliothèque orientale ou Dictionnaire universel contenant tout ce qui fait connaître les Peuples de l'Orient* . . . , article BERBER. This was the standard reference work on all things Islamic in the Eighteenth Century and was frequently reedited.
3. Edward Gibbon, *Decline and Fall of the Roman Empire*, edited by J.B. Bury (London, 1909), vol. I, p.499, n.190.
4. *Histoire des Etats barbaresques qui exercent la piraterie* . . . (Paris, 1757), pp.1—2. See also the remarks by Hebenstreit in 1732, quoted by M. Fendri in *Revue d'Histoire maghrebine*, n°35—6 (Tunis, Dec. 1984), p.34.
5. M. Canard, "Une description de la côte barbaresque au XVIII° siècle par un officier de la Marine russe", in *Revue africaine*, n°95 (1951), p.147—8. I have translated into English Canard's text, which is translated from the Russian.
6. Paul Coles, *The Ottoman Impact on Europe* (London, 1968), p.145.
7. Peter Earle, *Corsairs of Malta and Barbary* (London, 1970), p.8.
8. *Bibliothèque orientale* (1777 edition), vol.I, p.xvij.
9. *Voyage* . . . (1717), p.162; cp. *Mémoires* . . . (1735), vol.III, p.188.
10. "It is through these barbarians that these scourges have arrived; it is they who, by their stupid fanaticism, perpetuate the contagion by renewing its germs". Volney, *Oeuvres complètes* (Paris, 1864), p.765. All of these hostile stereotypes are developed in Tott's *Mémoires sur les Turcs et les Tartares* (Amsterdam, 1785).
11. Werner Krauss, *Zur Anthropologie des 18. Jahrhunderts* (Berlin, 1978), pp.176—189. See also D. Brahimi, *Voyageurs français*, pp.676—9.
12. Laugier de Tassy, *Histoire des états barbaresques* . . . (1757), p.iij.
13. In the title of the latter work, 'Oriental' means largely, but not exclusively, Islamic. I shall come back in the next chapter to the problems surrounding this term. On these works, and this problem in general, see Edward Said's *Orientalism* (London, 1978).
14. This text, which circulated in manuscript form throughout the Eighteenth Century, was first published in Holland in 1719; see I.O. Wade, *The Clandestine Organisation and Diffusion of Philosophic Ideas in France from 1700 to 1750* (Princeton, 1938, reprinted New York, 1967).
15. H. Djait, *L'Europe et l'Islam* (Paris, 1978), p.23. Notice the distinction made here between 'Oriental' and 'Barbaresque', which I shall discuss in the next chapter.
16. Laugier de Tassy, *Op.cit.*, p.iv.
17. D'Arvieux, *Mémoires*, vol.IV, p.55.
18. *Mémoires*, vol.I, pp.40—41.
19. Abbé Poiret, *Voyage en Barbarie*, Letter XVI; ed. D. Brahimi (Paris, 1980), pp.126ff.
20. *Nachrichten und Bemerkungen über den algierischen Staat* (Altona, 1798—1800), vol.III, pp.282ff. and 308.
21. Venture de Paradis, *Tunis et Alger au XVIII° siècle*, ed. Joseph Cuoq (Paris, 1983), p.90.

22. Thomas Shaw, *Travels or Observations relating to Several Parts of Barbary and the Levant* (Oxford, 1738), p.261.
23. D'Argens, *Lettres juives* (La Haye, 1738), vol.V, p.99.
24. Voltaire, *Essai sur les Moeurs*, in *Oeuvres complètes* ed. Moland (Paris, 1878), vol.XII, ch. CLXI, CLXII.
25. Rehbinder, *Nachrichten* ..., Vol.I, pp.231–2.
26. Shaw, *Travels*, p.303.
27. See for example, Letter XVIII (ed. 1980, p.133).
28. *Journal de Campagne de l'Amiral de Bauffremont ... dans les pays barbaresques (1766)*, ed. M. Chirac (Paris, 1981), p.43.
29. *Letters from Barbary, France, Spain, Portugal* ... (London, 1788), vol.I, p.105.
30. H. Djait, *L'Europe et l'Islam*, p.24.
31. On Volney, see D. Brahimi, *Arabes des Lumières et Bédouins romantiques* (Paris, 1982), passim. Diderot's lack of sympathy was brought out clearly during the recent "Journées Diderot" at Tunis University (November 1984), particularly in the paper given by Roger Kempf.
32. Maxime Rodinson, *La fascination de l'Islam* (Paris, 1981), pp.68ff.
33. Laugier de Tassy, *Histoire* ..., p.iij-vj.
34. Poiret, Letter I (p.51).
35. E. Gibbon, *Decline and Fall of the Roman Empire*, vol.IV, p.362.
36. *Ibid.* p.481ff.
37. *Decline and Fall*, vol.III, p.55.
38. James Grey Jackson, *An Account of the Empire of Morocco*, 3rd.ed. (London, 1814, reprint, London, 1968) pp.191, 208.
39. *Essai sur les moeurs*, ch.XCIII; *Candide*, Conclusion, ch.30 (*Romans et Contes*, ed. H. Bénac, Paris, 1960, pp.219ff).
40. *Lettres juives*, vol.V, p.106–7.
41. *Ibid.*, p.110.
42. D'Arvieux, *Mémoires*, vol.I, p.444 and vol.IV, p.4.
43. *Mémoires*, IV, p.56.
44. Laugier de Tassy, *Histoire*, ch.VII; Le Roy, *Etat général et particulier du Royaume et de la ville d'Alger* (La Haye, 1750), p.xij.
45. Desfontaines, *Fragments d'un voyage* ... (Paris, 1838), p.120; Kokovtsov, *Description* ... (*Revue africaine*, n°.95, 1951), p.162; Vallière, *Mémoire* (ed. L. Chaillou, Toulon, 1974), p.30.
46. William Shaler, *Sketches of Algiers* ... (Boston, 1826) p.56.
47. *Bibliothèque orientale*, 1777 edition, vol.I, pp.604–5.
48. See P.J. Marshall and Glyndwr Williams, *The Great Map of Mankind. British Perceptions of the World in the Age of Enlightenment* (London, 1982), pp.14, 102.
49. *Essai sur les moeurs*, ch.XCIII (*Oeuvres complètes*, vol.XII, p.95).
50. D'Arvieux, *Mémoires*, vol.I, pp.457–8.
51. *Nachrichten*, vol.I, pp.9f.
52. *Lettres juives*, vol.V, pp.77–80.
53. *Candide*, ch.XI (*Romans et contes*, p.159).
54. L. Valensi, *Le Maghreb avant la prise d'Alger* (Paris, 1969), p.94f.
55. M. Emerit, "Le voyage de La Condamine à Alger", *Revue africaine*, 1954, p.380.
56. Desfontaines, *Fragments* ..., p.38; Peyssonnel, *Voyages dans les Régences de Tunis et d'Alger* (Paris, 1838), p.29.
57. Laugier de Tassy, *Histoire*, ch.VI; Venture de Paradis, *Tunis et Alger* ... p.154.
58. Vallière, *Mémoire*, p.43.
59. Tott, *Mémoires sur les Turcs et les Tartares* (Amsterdam, 1785), vol.II, pp.367ff.
60. Shaler, *Sketches of Algiers*, p.76.
61. Jackson, *An Account of the Empire of Morocco*, p.293.
62. Mordecai M. Noah, *Travels in England, France, Spain and the Barbary States* ... (New York and London, 1819), pp.365f.
63. Roger Perkins and Captain K.J. Douglas-Morris RN, *Gunfire in Barbary* (Havant,

1982), subtitled, "Admiral Lord Exmouth's battle with the Corsairs of Algiers in 1816 − the story of the suppression of white christian slavery"; see pp.24−30.

64. M. Rodinson, *La fascination de l'Islam*, p.84.
65. Venture de Paradis, *Tunis et Alger au XVIII° siècle*, p.34.
66. Ibid., p.235.
67. Poiret, Letter XX, p.143.
68. *Histoire philosophique et politique des établissements et du commerce des Européens dans les Deux Indes* (Amsterdam, 1773), vol.I, p.62 note. It should however be remembered that the attribution of the different parts of this work is problematic, and much of it is not in fact by the abbé Raynal. See esp. Denis Diderot, *Contributions à l'Histoire des deux Indes* ed. Gianluigi Goggi (Siena 1977).
69. *A Historical and Philosophical Sketch* . . . (Edinburgh, 1799), p.25.
70. *Narrative of a Residence in Algiers* . . . (London, 1818), p.xx.
71. Noah, *Travels*, p.394.
72. *Histoire philosophique et politique des établissements et du commerce des Européens dans l'Afrique* (Paris, 1826), vol.I, pp.106f and 137.
73. Thomas Campbell, *Letters from the South* (London, 1837), Vol.I, p.198 and vol.II, pp.112ff.
74. M.P. Rozet, *Alger*, in *L'Univers, ou Histoire et description de tous les peuples, de leurs religions, moeurs, coutumes, etc.* (reproduced in *Algérie, Etats tripolitains*, Paris, 1846, reprint Tunis, 1980), p.32.
75. For recent examples of prejudices concerning the Islamic world, see Edward W. Said, *Covering Islam* (London, 1981).

PART TWO — INTRODUCTORY

1. Carl Linnaeus, *Systema naturae*, 1735.
2. D'Arvieux, *Mémoires*, vol.III, p.188; *Voyages*, p.163.
3. Laugier de Tassy, *Histoire*, p.v (see above, p.24).
4. Ibid., vol.II, pp.73—4, 125.
5. D'Argens, *Lettres juives*, vol.V, pp.53, 112—3.
6. Ibid., p.56.
7. Letter from Joel Barlow to the American Secretary of State, 18th October 1796, quoted by H.G. Barnby, *The Prisoners of Algiers. An Account of the Forgotten American-Algerian War, 1785—1797* (Oxford, 1966), p.316.
8. D'Argens, *Lettres juives*, vol.V, p.119.
9. Mounir Fendri, "Trois voyageurs allemands en Tunisie au XVIII° siècle", in *Revue d'histoire maghrebine*, n°35—6 (Tunis, Dec. 1984), p.34. See also the passage in Voltaire's *Candide* already quoted.
10. See for example, Vallière's *Mémoire*, pp.7, 18, 29, 72.
11. Poiret, Letter V, p.71. I shall discuss this question in Chapter 3 below.
12. Rehbinder, *Nachrichten* . . . , vol.III, pp.671ff.
13. Jackson, *An Account of the Empire of Morocco*, p.xi.
14. Shaler, *Sketches of Algiers*, vol.I, p.58.
15. Campbell, *Letters from the South*, vol.I, p.141, 191.
16. E.g. vol.I, p.43.
17. Philippe Lucas and Jean-Claude Vatin, *L'Algérie des anthropologues* (Paris, 1975), pp. 90—94.
18. Victor-Armand Hain, *A la Nation. Sur Alger* (Paris, 1832), pp.31, 58ff.

CHAPTER I — LOCATION

1. Michèle Duchet, *Anthropologie et histoire au siècle des Lumières* (Paris, 1971); P.J. Marshall and Glyndwr Williams, *The Great Map of Mankind* (London, 1982).
2. Numa Broc, *La géographie des Philosophes* (Paris, 1975), p.54.
3. See Fernand Braudel, *La Méditerrannée et le monde méditerrannéen à l'époque de Philippe II* (Paris, 1949).
4. Thomas Shaw, *Travels or Observations* . . . , Preface, p.i.
5. Ibid., p.viii.
6. But N. Broc has great praise for Shaw's work and considers that nothing comparable was published on North Africa in France (*La Géographie des Philosophes*, p.60). Shaw and his work have hitherto been frequenlty quoted but never studied; this situation should soon be remedied as a postgraduate student at Algiers University, Ms Zhor Zizi, is currently working on this author.
7. Poiret, Letter XX, p.142.
8. Gibbon, *Decline and Fall*, vol.III, p.429.
9. Pananti, *Narrative*, p.412.
10. Campbell, *Letters from the South*, vol.I, pp.269—70.
11. The *Revue africaine* was published by the Société historique algérienne from 1856 onwards; it is at present being reprinted by the Office des Publications Universitaires, Alger.
12. Louis Bertrand, *La Cina* (1901), p.53; quoted by Martine Astier Loutfi, *Littérature et colonialisme 1871—1914* (The Hague, 1971), p.76.
13. H.G. Barnby, *The Prisoners of Algiers* (Oxford, 1966), p.22.
14. Desfontaines, *Fragments d'un voyage* . . . (Paris, 1838), p.141.
15. Vallière, *Mémoire*, p.25.
16. D'Argens, *Lettres juives*, vol.V, p.53.
17. Simon Ockley, *An Account of South-West Barbary, containing what is most Remarkable in the Territories of the King of Fez and Morocco* (London, 1713), Preface of the Editor, p.xix.
18. Laugier de Tassy, *Histoire*, vol.II, ch.VII, and Conclusion, p.93.
19. Gibbon, *Decline and Fall*, vol.III, pp.53ff.
20. See for example, vol.IV, p.315.
21. Poiret, Letter I, p.53.
22. Letter V, p.70.
23. *Letters from Barbary, France, Spain, Portugal* . . . (London, 1788), vol.I, p.55.
24. Ibid., p.103.
25. Valliére, *Mémoire*, p.16.
26. *Historical and Philosophical Sketch*, Chapter I.
27. *Narrative of a Residence*, p.xix ff.
28. Shaler, *Sketches*, p.91.
29. Speech on 10th July 1829, quoted by André Julien, "Marseille et la question d'Alger à la veille de la conquête", in *Revue africaine*, 1919, p.31.
30. Campbell, *Letters from the South*, vol.I, pp.15, 56, 166.
31. See Denise Brahimi, "Un informateur de l'abbé Raynal: l'abbé Poiret, auteur du *Voyage en Barbarie*", in *Dix-huitième Siècle*, n°4 (1972), pp.237—254; and Ann Thomson, "Raynal, Venture de Paradis et la Barbarie" in *Dix-huitième Siècle*, n°15 (1983), pp.329—333.

32. "Mémoire sur la Compagnie royale d'Afrique", B.N., ms.fonds français, 6431, f° 1–12.
33. Louis Moreau de Maupertuis, *Lettre sur le progrès des sciences* (Berlin, 1752), p.47.
34. Pananti, *Narrative of a Residence*, p.412.
35. Letter dated 1818, in *An Account of Timbuctoo* (London, 1820), p.463.
36. *Histoire des Deux Indes* (Amsterdam, 1773), vol.IV, pp.115ff. e.g.: "Ces conquêtes deviendraient d'autant plus sûres que le bonheur des vaincus en devrait être la suite. Ce peuple de pirates, ces monstres de la mer, seraient changés en hommes par de bonnes lois et des exemples d'humanité. Elevés insensiblement jusqu'à nous par la communication de nos lumières, ils abjureraient avec le temps un fanatisme que l'ignorance et la misère ont nourri dans leurs âmes ..."
    According to Yves Benot (in a private conversation), this passage is not in fact by Raynal, but there is no proof one way or another, and he reproduces it in his manuscript "Mémoires" on Barbary.
37. Leyden, *A Historical and Philosophical Sketch*, ch.I. The Association for Promoting the Discovery of the Interior Parts of Africa was founded in 1788. See Marshall and Williams, *The Great Map of Mankind*, pp.252–4.
38. Mungo Park, *Travels in the Interior Districts of Africa in the Years 1795, 1796 and 1797* (London, 1799); René Caillié, *Journal d'un Voyage à Tembouctou et à Jenné, dans l'Afrique centrale ... pendant les années 1824, 1825, 1826, 1827, 1828* (Paris, 1830).
39. Jackson, *An Account of the Empire of Morocco*, Preface, pp.vii, viii.
40. D'Argens, *Lettres juives*, vol.V, p.53.
41. Venture de Paradis, *Tunis et Alger*, p.35.
42. Wadi Bouzar, *La Mouvance et la pause* (Alger, 1983), vol.I, p.157. The question of "Orientalism" is a vast subject; I am simply concerned here with the question of how far in the Eighteenth Century the Maghreb was seen to be part of the Orient and how far Oriental stereotypes were applied to it, not with the question of whether or not it was Oriental. And of course the Orient is not necessarily a geographical concept.
43. Ibid., p.220.
44. Cherbuliez, *La Vocation du comte Ghislain* (Paris, 1888), p.209, quoted by M.A. Loutfi, *Littérature et colonialisme* (The Hague, 1971), p.48.
45. V.A. Hain, *A la Nation. Sur Alger*, p.2.
46. See E.W. Said, *Orientalism* (London, 1978).
47. See R. Schwab, *La Renaissance orientale* (Paris, 1950).
48. D'Arvieux, *Voyage*, pp.279ff. *Mémoires*, vol. V, p. 235.
49. See her letter to the abbé Conti, written from Tunis, 31st July, 1718.
50. *Letters from Barbary*, vol.I, pp.15–16.
51. Montesquieu, *De l'Esprit des Lois*, Livre XXII, Ch.II, note.
52. Ibid., Livre V, ch.XIV.
53. Helvétius, *De l'Esprit*, ch.XVI (ed. F. Châtelet, Verviers, 1973, p.299).
54. Adam Ferguson, *An Essay on the History of Civil Society 1767*, ed. D. Forbes (Edinburgh, 1966), p.67.
55. *Candide*, ch.XI (*Romans et Contes*, Paris, 1960), pp.159–60.
56. Shaw, *Travels*, p.311.
57. D'Argens, *Lettres juives*, vol.V, p.57.
58. Gibbon, *Decline and Fall*, vol.I, p.207.
59. Emerit, "Le voyage de La Condamine à Alger", *Revue africaine*, 1954, p.374.
60. Ockley, *An Account of South-West Barbary*, p.78; Peyssonnel, *Voyage ...*, pp.411, 416.
61. B.N. ms. fonds français 6429, 6430; see my article "Raynal, Venture de Paradis et la Barbarie", in *Dix-huitième Siècle*, n°15 (1983), pp.329–333.
62. Venture de Paradis, *Tunis et Alger*, p.135.
63. B.N. ms. 6429, f°8, f°46.
64. *Tunis et Alger*, p.75ff.
65. "It is rare to see, not only in despotic countries of the Orient, but even among the most civilised peoples, a wiser man or one with more regular morals"; *Tunis et Alger*, p.81–2.

66. See for example Shaw, *Travels*, pp.111, 261f.; Ockley, *An Account* ..., p.36; d'Argens, *Lettres juives*, vol.V, p.86.
67. Rehbinder, *Nachrichten*, vol.III, p.371.
68. Ibid., vol.I, pp.284, 286.
69. Ibid., vol.III, pp.409f.
70. Poiret, Letter XXVII, p.191.
71. See for example, his *Histoire*, vol.I, p.183.
72. Peyssonnel, *Voyage*, pp.67, 174.
73. Quoted by W. Bouzar, *La Mouvance et la pause*, vol.I, p.378.
74. See Lucas and Vatin, *L'Algérie des anthropologues* (Paris, 1975), p.21.
75. *The History of the Long Captivity and Adventures of Thomas Pellow in South Barbary* (London, 1739).
76. See Ockley, *An Account*, ch.VI; Shaw, *Travels*, p.303; Poiret, Letter XXI, p.151; Desfontaines, *Fragments*, p.22.
77. Vallière *Mémoire*, p.35; Rehbinder, *Nachrichten*, vol.I, p.514; Jackson, *An Account of the Empire of Morocco*, p.159; Rozet, *Alger*, p.19.
78. Rehbinder, *Nachrichten*, vol.I, p.595.
79. D'Argens, *Lettres juives*, vol.V, pp.58—9.
80. Rehbinder, *Nachrichten*, vol.I, p.638.
81. Poiret, Letter XXI, p.154.
82. Peyssonnel, *Voyage*, p.216.
83. Shaw, *Travels*, p.303; Poiret, Letter XXI, p.151; Rehbinder, *Nachrichten*, vol.I, p.545.
84. Poiret, Letter XXI, p.151.
85. Shaw, *Travels*, p.303.
86. Vallière, *Mémoire*, pp.35, 44.
87. Pananti, *Narrative*, p.415.
88. *Réfutation de l'ouvrage de Hamdan Khoja intitulé Aperçu historique et statistique sur la Régence d'Alger* (Paris, 1834), p.47.
89. Jackson, *An Account of the Empire of Morocco*, p.163; Shaler, *Sketches*, p.60.
90. Paul Raynal, *L'Expédition d'Alger. 1830. Lettres d'un témoin* (Paris, 1930), quoted by Lucas and Vatin, *L'Algérie des anthropologues*, p.97.
91. M.E. Carette, *Algérie* in *Algérie; Etats tripolitaines* (Paris 1846, reprint, Tunis, 1980), p.31. This contrast between town and mountain is already found, though expressed in different terms, in Poiret's Letter XXI.
92. Lucas and Vatin, *L'Algérie des anthropologues*, pp.98—99.
93. Marek Alloula, *Le Harem colonial* (Geneva, 1981).
94. G.W.F. Hegel, *The Philosophy of History* (ed. C.J. Friedrich, New York, 1956), Introduction, 'Geographical basis of History', pp.92—3.

CHAPTER II – RACE

1. The term 'race' is one that presents problems and is frequently used very loosely; in this chapter I shall be discussing, first, the question of race in its true acceptation, namely the classification of mankind according to its different 'varieties' or 'races'. I shall then move onto the subject of the composition of the Barbary population, whose different groupings are improperly called races.

2. There is a large literature and a diversity of opinions on this subject; see, for example, J.S. Spink, *French Free Thought from Gassendi to Voltaire* (London, 1960); John W. Yolton, *Thinking Matter. Materialism in Eighteenth Century Britain* (Oxford, 1984).

3. See my article, "From *L'Histoire naturelle de l'Homme* to the Natural History of Mankind" in *British Journal for Eighteenth-Century Studies*, vol.9 (1986), pp.73–80.

4. See Buffon, *De l'homme*, présentation de Michèle Duchet (Paris, 1971) p.223ff.

5. See for example, Barrère, *Dissertation sur la cause physique de la couleur des nègres*, (Paris, 1741); Maupertuis, *Vénus physique*, (1745); J.H.S. Formey's article NEGRES in the *Encyclopédie*.

6. Henry Home, Lord Kames, *Sketches of the History of Man*, (Edinburgh, 1774); David Hume, "Of National Characters", first published in *Essays*, 1742, (see *The Philosophical Works*, Edinburgh, 1826, vol.III, p.236); Edward Long, *The History of Jamaica*, (London, 1774).

7. See Buffon, *De l'homme* (Paris, 1971), p.313.

8. J.B. Robinet, *Considérations philosophiques de la gradation naturelle des formes de l'être ou les Essais de la Nature qui apprend à faire l'homme* (Paris, 1768), p.186.

9. J.F. Blumenbach, *De generis humani varietate nativa* (Göttingen, 1775); was frequently translated and reedited throughout the Eighteenth Century.

10. Pieter Camper wrote several works on anatomy, on the orang-utang and so on in the 1760s and 1770s; see in particular, *Ueber den natürlichen Unterschied der Gesichtszüge . . .*, trans. Sömmering, Berlin, 1792.

11. Blumenbach, *De l'unité du genre humain et de ses variétés* (Paris, an XIII), pp.303–4.

12. Jean-Léon l'Africain, *Description de l'Afrique* (Paris, 1981), vol.I., p.4.

13. See for example Poiret, Letter VI, p.74; Desfontaines, *Fragments*, p.26; Vallière, *Mémoire*, p.11; Rehbinder, *Nachrichten*, vol.I, p.317.

14. Rehbinder, *Nachrichten*, vol.I, p.318.

15. By racism, I mean the phenomenon in its true sense, which is hatred based on (real or imagined) biological differences; on the definition of racism, see the useful discussion in Christian Delacampagne, *L'invention du racisme* (Paris, 1983), pp.35–50.

16. E. Gibbon, *Decline and Fall of the Roman Empire*, vol.III, pp.54ff.

17. Peyssonnel, *Voyage*, p.74.

18. See D. Brahimi, *Opinions et regards des Européens sur le Maghreb aux XVII° et XVIII° siècles* (Alger, 1978), pp.8ff, and "Approches sociologiques de la Régence d'Alger (vers 1725)", *Dix-huitième Siècle*, n°7 (1975), pp.101f.

19. Shaw, *Travels*, p.viiii.

20. Gibbon, *Decline and Fall*, vol.IV, pp.337ff.

21. Ibid., vol.V, p.501.

22. Pananti, *Narrative*, pp.192–197.

23. Ibid., p.416.

24. Venture de Paradis, *Alger au XVIII° siècle* (Paris, 1898, reprinted Tunis, n.d.),

pp.131, 129; these passages have been omitted from Cuoq's edition, *Tunis et Alger au XVIII° siècle*, where they should be found on pp.226–7. No explanation is given by the editor for this omission.

25. Bibliothèque nationale, ms. fonds français, 6430, f°76.

26. See my article, "Raynal, Venture de Paradis et la Barbarie", *Dix-huitième siècle*, n°15 (1983), p.332.

27. Poiret, Letter IV, p.67.

28. *A la Nation. Sur Alger*, pp.78, 94.

29. See Lucas and Vatin, *L'Algérie des anthropologues* (Paris, 1975), esp. pp.104ff.

30. Virey, *Histoire naturelle du genre humain* (Paris, an IX), vol.I, p.120.

31. J.B.G.M. Bory de Saint-Vincent, *L'Homme* (2nd ed. Paris, 1827), vol.I, p.171; this appears to be the same Bory de Saint-Vincent who led the scientific commission in Algeria after the conquest and whose *Note* for the War Ministry, dated 16th October 1838 we have already quoted.

32. See Philip D. Curtin, *The Image of Africa. British Ideas and Action 1780–1850* (London, 1965), chapter 2 passim.

33. See G. Cuvier, *Leçons d'anatomie comparée* (Paris, an VIII). See also Jean Copans, Jean Jamin, *Aux origines de l'anthropologie française* (Paris, 1978).

34. James Cowles Prichard, *Researches into the Physical History of Man* (London, 1813); *The Natural History of Man* (London, 1843).

35. *The Natural History of Man*, section xxiv.

36. Shaler, *Sketches*, p.174.

37. Ibid., p.58.

38. Shaw, *Travels*, p.261.

39. D'Argens, *Lettres juives*, vol.V, p.119.

40. Kokovtsov, *Description*, p.148.

41. Vallière, *Mémoire*, pp.11, 17, 18.

42. *A Historical and Philosophical Sketch*, p.24.

43. Rehbinder, *Nachrichten*, vol.I, p.275.

44. Ibid., vol.III, pp.473, 561.

45. John B. Wolf, *The Barbary Coast. Algeria under the Turks* (New York, 1979), p.109.

46. Shaler, *Sketches*, p.84. This subject has been discussed, for the early part of the Eighteenth Century, by D. Brahimi, "Approches sociologiques de la Régence d'Alger (vers 1725)", *Dix-huitième Siècle*, n°7 (1975), pp.87–104.

47. Noah, *Travels*, p.300.

48. M. Canard, "Une description de la côte barbaresque ...", *Revue africaine*, n°95 (1951), p.141.

49. *Revue africaine*, n°66 (1925), p.484, note 2.

50. Ibid., p.540.

51. Venture de Paradis, *Tunis et Alger au XVIII° siècle*, p.270.

52. Bibliothèque nationale, f.fr. 6430, f°47, 81.

53. L. Chénier, *Recherches historiques sur les Maures* (Paris, 1787).

54. Venture de Paradis, *Tunis et Alger*, pp.78–9.

55. D'Arvieux, *Mémoires*, vol.II, pp.144ff and vol.IV, p.25.

56. Peyssonnel, *Voyage*, pp.81, 171, 176.

57. Ibid., p.475.

58. Ibid., p.378.

59. Shaw, *Travels*, p.288.

60. Ibid., p.120.

61. Laugier de Tassy, *Histoire*, pp.84ff.

62. Poiret, Letter I, pp.53–4.

63. pp.73–4.

64. Desfontaines, *Fragments*, pp.142–4.

65. Vallière, *Mémoire*, pp.9–11.

66. Venture de Paradis, *Alger et Tunis*, pp.48–51.

67. We may wonder whether perhaps Venture was influenced by Ibn Khaldun's

Muqaddima, whose second chapter develops the distinction between the nomadic and sedentary way of life; there is unfortunately no reference by Venture to this work.

68. *Histoire philosophique et politique des établissements et du commerce des Européens dans l'Afrique*, vol.I, pp.56ff.
69. Rehbinder, *Nachrichten*, vol.I, pp.314ff; 337ff.
70. Ibid., p.357.
71. See for example, *Nachrichten*, vol.III, p.371.
72. *Nachrichten*, vol.I, ch.5.
73. Jackson, *An Account of the Empire of Morocco*, pp.140–143.
74. Shaler, *Sketches*, ch.4.
75. *Sketches*, p.85.
76. Pananti, *Narrative*, pp.152–169.
77. Ibid., p.187.
78. See D. Brahimi, "L'éloge de l'Arabe", in *Revue de l'Histoire et Civilisation du Maghreb*, n°10 (1973), pp.89–97.
79. Noah, *Travels*, pp.300ff.
80. Lucas and Vatin, *L'Algérie des anthropologues*, pp.96–99.
81. Jackson, *An Account of the Empire of Morocco*, p.v.
82. See for example the article BÉDOUINS in the *Encyclopédie*, vol.II, p.189.
83. Campbell, *Letters from the South*, vol.I, p.165.
84. Rozet, *Alger*, pp.8–12.
85. Hain, *A la Nation*, p.26.
86. Carette, *Algérie*, p.107.
87. Note that the use of the word 'Moor' to refer to the people of Algeria vanished, except for its derogatory use to refer to the women as 'Mauresques'.
88. Charles-Robert Ageron, *Les Algériens musulmans et la France (1871–1919)* (Paris, 1968), vol.I, pp.267ff.; Lucas and Vatin, *L'Algérie des anthropologues*, pp.27–8.
89. Yves Lacoste, *Unité et diversité du tiers monde* (Paris, 1984), pp.471ff.
90. *Letters from Barbary*, p.54.
91. Raynal's texts on Barbary were published even before the conquest, in 1826; Shaler's *Sketches* were published in French in 1830; extracts from Shaw's *Travels* concerning Algeria were translated into French by MacCarthy (Paris, 1830); and the works by Peyssonnel and Desfontaines were published by Dureau de la Malle in 1838.
92. Shaw, *Travels*, p.288.
93. Shaler, *Sketches*, p.91.
94. Rozet, *Alger*, p.11.
95. Campbell, *Letters*, vol.I, p.159.
96. See Lucas and Vatin, *L'Algérie des anthropologues*, pp.104ff.
97. H.G. Barnby, *The Prisoners of Algiers* (Oxford, 1966), p.21.
98. Ageron, *Les Algériens musulmans et la France*, p.267.
99. *Le Sémaphore*, 17th June and 24th July 1829; quoted by A. Julien, "Marseille et la question d'Alger à la veille de la conquête", *Revue africaine*, 1919, 32–3.
100. Ibos, *Le general Cavaignac*, p.23; quoted by Mostefa Lacheraf, *L'Algérie; nation et société* (Paris, 1976), p.219.
101. D'Arvieux, *Mémoires*, vol.I, p.301.
102. Shaler, *Sketches*, p.65.
103. La Condamine, *Voyage*, p.371.
104. Laugier de Tassy, *Histoire*, chapter IV.
105. Poiret, Letter XX, p.146, mentions the Moors who come to the synagogue in 'Bonne' (Annaba) to be healed; see also Shaler, *Sketches*, p.65, Rehbinder, *Nachrichten*, p.364.
106. Laugier de Tassy, *Histoire*, vol.I, p.122.
107. Ibid., vol.II, p.58.
108. Peyssonnel, *Voyage*, p.82.

109. Vallière, *Mémoire*, pp.10–12.
110. Jackson, *An Account of the Empire of Morocco*, p.63.
111. Rehbinder, *Nachrichten*, vol.I, p.364.
112. Rozet, *Alger*, p.12.
113. Campbell, *Letters*, vol.I, pp.148ff.
114. M. Eisenbeth, "Les Juifs en Algérie et en Tunisie à l'époque turque (1516–1830)", in *Revue africaine*, 1952, pp.114ff and 343ff.
115. This is what Noah claims in his *Travels*, p.376.
116. Venture de Paradis, *Tunis et Alger*, p.60.
117. Noah, *Travels*, pp.307–310.
118. Pananti, *Narrative*, p.158.
119. Rehbinder, *Nachrichten*, vol.I, p.370.

CHAPTER III — SOCIETY AND GOVERNMENT

1. Lucas and Vatin, *L'Algérie des anthropologues*, p.48, note 84.
2. Hobbes, *Leviathan*, Part I, ch.13 (ed. C.B. Macpherson, Harmondsworth, 1968, p.187).
3. Locke, *Second Treatise of Government*, chapter II, par.14.
4. David Hume, *A Treatise of Human Nature*, Book III, Part II, section II (Oxford, 1888, p.493).
5. See his *Supplément au voyage de Bougainville; Fragments échappés du portefeuille d'un philosophe* (*Oeuvres complètes*, ed. Assézat-Tourneux, vol. VI, pp.445, 457); *Histoire des Deux Indes* (Amsterdam, 1773), vol.VI, p.200.
6. Montesquieu, *De l'Esprit des Lois*, Livre LXVIII, ch.xi.
7. J.J. Rousseau, *Discours sur l'origine de l'inégalité parmi les hommes*; see especially, in *Du Contrat social et autres oeuvres politiques* (Paris, 1975), pp.66ff.
8. Adam Ferguson, *An Essay on the History of Civil Society* (Edinburgh, 1966) pp.81ff.
9. Ibid., pp.272ff.
10. Laugier de Tassy, *Histoire*, vol.II, p.73.
11. Ibid., vol.I, p.162.
12. D'Arvieux, *Mémoires*, vol.V, pp.70, 108.
13. Laugier de Tassy, *Histoire*, vol.I, p.2; see also Le Roy, *Etat général et particulier du Royaume et de la ville d'Alger* (La Haye, 1750), pp.xij-xiij.
14. Shaw, *Travels*, p.310; Peyssonnel, *Voyage*, p.384; La Condamine, *Voyage*, pp.380—1; see also Vallière, *Mémoire*, p.61.
15. Venture de Paradis, *Tunis et Alger*, p.84.
16. Kokovtsov, *Description*, pp.148—9.
17. Rehbinder, *Nachrichten*, vol.I, p.314.
18. Peyssonnel, *Voyage*, p.384.
19. Ibid., pp.485, 174.
20. See *Essai sur les moeurs*, chapters CLXI and CLXII.
21. *Histoire philosophique et politique des établissements et du commerce des Européens dans l'Afrique*, vol.I, p.81.
22. Venture de Paradis, *Tunis et Alger*, p.103.
23. Poiret, Letter VIII, p.83.
24. *Letters from Barbary*, pp.34, 42.
25. Pananti, *Narrative*, pp.198, 423.
27. Shaler, *Sketches*, pp.52, 58, 104.
28. Campbell, *Letters*, vol.I, p.259.
29. Desfontaines, *Fragments*, p.221; Kokovtsov, *Description*, p.177.
30. Rehbinder, *Nachrichten*, vol.III, pp.216—224.
31. Tott, *Mémoires*, vol.II, p.366; Shaler, *Sketches*, p.56.
32. Ibid., p.83; see also Vallière, *Mémoire*, p.24—5, who points out that there was a famine due to bad harvests in 1775—8, although he says that the harvest was abundant in 1781, the year in which he was writing.
33. Peyssonnel, *Voyage*, p.174.
34. Hain, *A la Nation*, p.27.
35. Gibbon, *Decline and Fall*, vol.IV, p.311.
36. Ibid., vol.V, p.501, note 193.

37. Shaw, *Travels*, p.300; *Histoire des Deux Indes*, (Amsterdam, 1773), vol.IV, p.112.
38. *Letters*, p.14.
39. Rehbinder, *Nachrichten*, vol.I, p.597.
40. *Nachrichten*, vol.III, p.671ff.
41. Poiret, Letter V, p.70—71; *Voyage en Barbarie ou Lettres écrites de l'ancienne Numidie pendant les années 1785 et 1786* (Paris, 1789), Discours préliminaire, pp.vj, xxij. This 'Discours' is not reproduced in the edition of 1980, although no reason is given for this omission.
42. Letter XIX, p.140—1; VI, p.79.
43. Vallière, *Mémoire*, p.11.
44. Poiret, Letter XIII, p.112.
45. D'Argens, *Lettres juives*, vol.V, p.365; on the conception of a 'Philosophe' see my article, "Le philosophe et la société", in *Studies on Voltaire and the Eighteenth Century*, n° 190 (1981), pp.273—284.
46. J.J. Rousseau, *Discours sur les Sciences et les Arts*, in *Du Contrat social et autres oeuvres politiques* (Paris, 1975), p.8; D. Diderot, *Supplément au voyage de Bougainville* in *Oeuvres philosophiques* (Paris, 1964), p.469; *Histoire des Deux Indes*, vol.VI, p.200.
47. D'Arvieux, *Mémoires*, vol.IV, p.30.
48. See my article, "Bédouins et bons sauvages", read at the *Journées Diderot* at the University of Tunis (November, 1984), to be published in the Acts.
49. *De l'Esprit des Lois*, Livre XVIII, ch.XIX.
50. *Histoire des Deux Indes*, vol.IV, p.10.
51. Volney, *Oeuvres complètes* (Paris, 1864), pp.199—208.
52. Rehbinder, *Nachrichten*, vol.III, p.619.
53. Jackson, *An Account of Timbuctoo*, pp.130—1, 43.
54. Pananti, *Narrative*, p.175.
55. Noah, *Travels*, p.302.
56. *Note sur la colonisation d'Alger*, p.4; quoted by Charles Tailliart, *L'Algérie dans la littérature française* (Paris, 1925), pp.59—60.
57. Noah, *Travels*, p.300.
58. Peyssonnel, *Voyage*, p.378—9.
59. James Bruce *Travels to Discover the Sources of the Nile in 1768, 1769, 1770, 1771, 1772* (London, 1790), Introduction, vol.I, p.xxxi.
60. Ageron, *Les Algériens musulmans et la France*, vol.I, p.267.
61. *Histoire philosophique et politique* . . . , vol.I, pp.65ff.
62. *Tunis et Alger*, pp.119, 49.
63. Rehbinder, *Nachrichten*, vol.I, pp.337ff.
64. Pananti, *Narrative*, p.150.
65. Shaler, *Sketches*, p.91.
66. Campbell, *Letters*, vol.I, p.159.
67. *Réfutation de l'ouvrage de Hamdan Khoja intitulé Aperçu historique et statistique sur la Régence d'Alger*, p.11.
68. Hain, *A la Nation*, pp.28—33.
69. *Note sur la commission exploratrice et scientifique d'Algérie* (16th October 1838), p.13.
70. Carette, *Algérie*, p.112.
71. Peyssonnel, *Voyage*, p.348.
72. Rozet, *Alger*, p.11.
73. *La Grande Kabylie* (Paris, 1847), in Lucas and Vatin, *L'Algérie des anthropologues*, p.109.
74. Volney, *Oeuvres complètes*, pp.208—214.
75. Hain, *A la Nation*, p.30.
76. Carette, *Algérie*, p.112.
77. Quoted by Wadi Bouzar, *La Mouvance et la pause* (Alger, 1983), vol.I, pp.216—7.
78. Rozet, *Alger*, p.32.
79. Gibbon *Decline and Fall*, vol.I, p.28.
80. Bibliothèque nationale, ms., f.fr., 6430, f° 140, 8.

81. Venture de Paradis, *Tunis et Alger*, p.35.
82. *De l'Esprit des Lois*, Livre II, ch.III-V.
83. La Condamine, *Voyage*, p.374.
84. *Essai sur les Moeurs*, ch.CLXI, CXCI, CXCII (*Oeuvres complètes*, vol. XII, p.454, XIII, pp.137, 149). The ruler of Algiers was called the Dey, while the ruler of Tunis was known as the Bey.
85. See the articles BEY and DEY, by Mallet.
86. D'Arvieux, *Mémoires*, vol.IV, pp.50, 242–9.
87. D'Argens, *Lettres juives*, vol.V, pp.51–3.
88. Ferguson, *An Essay on the History of Civil Society*, p.67.
89. See Shaw, *Travels*, p.311.
90. Gibbon, *Decline and Fall*, vol.I, p.207, note 69.
91. *De l'Esprit des Lois*, Livre XXII, ch. II.
92. Laugier de Tassy, *Histoire*, 'du Dey'.
93. Le Roy, *Etat général et particulier*, p.xij.
94. Peyssonnel, *Voyage*, p.56.
95. Poiret, Letter XXIX, pp.200–212.
96. Rehbinder, *Nachrichten*, vol.III, pp.1–6.
97. Ibid., vol.III, p.441.
98. Venture de Paradis, *Tunis et Alger*, p.75; and see my discussion above, chapter 1.
99. See especially pp.82ff; do not forget that this text, *Observations sur le gouvernement de Tunis*, was written in 1788, that is before the Revolution.
100. Pananti, *Narrative*, pp.287, 56.
101. Noah, *Travels*, p.365.
102. See for example pp.2ff.
103. Shaler, *Sketches*, pp.18, 24–5, 45, 56.
104. Rozet, *Alger*, p.14.
105. Shaw, *Travels*, p.328.
106. Ibid., p.310.
107. Peyssonnel, *Voyages*, p.325.
108. Kokovtsov, *Description*, p.177.
109. D'Arvieux, *Mémoires*, vol.V, p.236.
110. Venture de Paradis, *Tunis et Alger*, p.118.
111. Shaler, *Sketches*, p.92.
112. Lucas and Vatin, *L'Algérie des anthropologues*, pp.111–114.

PART THREE — TOWARDS THE CONQUEST

1. D'Arvieux, *Mémoires*, vol.III, pp.391 onwards.
2. Ibid., vol.V, p.108.
3. Ibid., vol.V, pp.288—9.
4. Peyssonnel, *Voyage*, pp.297, 367, 383—4, 418.
5. Shaw, *Travels*, p.328.
6. Poiret, Letter XXIX, pp.199ff.
7. Bruce, *Travels to Discover the Sources of the Nile* ... (London, 1790), Introduction, pp.xxiii.
8. Noah, *Travels*, p.365. See also the remarks by Rehbinder and Tott quoted in the previous chapter.
9. See Peter Earle, *Corsairs of Malta and Barbary* (London, 1970), p.10.
10. *Candide*, ch.XI (*Romans et contes*, p.159).
11. Godfrey Fisher, *The Barbary Legend. War, Trade and Piracy in North Africa (1515—1830)*, (Oxford, 1957).
12. For example, Salvatore Bono, *I Corsari barbareschi* (Turin, 1964); Peter Earle, *Corsairs of Malta and Barbary* (London, 1970).
13. Fernand Braudel, *Civilisation matérielle, Economie et Capitalisme, XV°-XVIII° siècle*, vol.3, *Le Temps du Monde* (Paris, 1979), p.42.
14. D'Arvieux, *Mémoires*, vol.III, pp.430—433, vol.V, p.109.
15. Vallière, *Mémoire*, p.22; Venture de Paradis, *Tunis et Alger*, p.42ff.
16. D'Argens, *Lettres juives*, vol.V, p.103; Kokovtsov, *Description*, p.177.
17. La Condamine, *Voyage*, pp.73ff.
18. Kokovtsov, *Description*, p.162.
19. Venture de Paradis, *Tunis et Alger*, pp.102—3, 224—5.
20. Rehbinder, *Nachrichten*, vol.III, p.453.
21. *Historical Memoirs of Barbary* (London, 1816), p.59.
22. Noah, *Travels*, p.252. See also Tott, *Mémoires*, vol.II, p.366.
23. Rehbinder, *Nachrichten*, vol.III, p.453.
24. Shaler, *Sketches*, p.83; Rehbinder, *Nachrichten*, vol.III, p.403.
25. Abdelkader Djeghloul, "La Formation sociale algérienne à la veille de la colonisation", *La Pensée*, n° 185 (1976), pp.61—81.
26. D'Arvieux, *Mémoires*, vol.V, pp.363—412.
27. D'Argens, *Lettres juives*, vol.V, p.85.
28. Peter Earle, *Corsairs of Malta and Barbary*, p.40.
29. Vallière, *Mémoire*, pp.67, 46ff.
30. Rehbinder, *Nachrichten*, vol.III, pp.153ff, 441.
31. *Histoire philosophique et politique des établissements et du commerce des Européens dans l'Afrique*, vol.I, pp.100ff; *Histoire des Deux Indes* (1773), vol.IV, pp.115ff. I have reproduced part of this passage above, chapter 1, note 36.
32. *Considérations sur la guerre des Turcs* (1788), *Oeuvres complètes*, p.766.
33. Thomas Paine, *Rights of Man*, Part II, chapter 5 (Harmondsworth, 1969, p.292).
34. *Letters from Barbary*, pp.103, 182.
35. Jackson, *An Account of Timbuctoo*, pp.457—463.
36. B.N., f.fr. 6430, f° 140.
37. See Pananti, *Narrative*, p.xxi.

38. See E. Dupuy, *Américains et barbaresques (1776—1824)*, (Paris, 1910), p.317.
39. Quoted by Perkins and Douglas-Morris, *Gunfire in Barbary* (Havant, 1982), p.37.
40. Pananti, *Narrative*, pp.416, xx.
41. Noah, *Travels*, pp.365—8.
42. See for example, Rehbinder, *Nachrichten*, vol.I, pp.381—425; vol.III, pp.114ff.
43. *Revue africaine*, vol.2 (1858), pp.337—352.
44. Tailliart, *L'Algérie dans la littérature française*, p.3.
45. Perkins and Douglas-Morris, *Gunfire in Barbary*, title page.
46. See Lucette Valensi, *Le Maghreb avant la prise d'Alger*, (Paris, 1969), pp.68—9.
47. Abdeljelil Temimi, "Le bombardement d'Alger en 1816", in *Recherches et Documents d'Histoire maghrébine* (Tunis, 1980), pp.40—41.
48. Shaler, *Sketches*, p.76.
49. A. Hamdani, *La vérité sur l'expédition d'Alger* (Paris, 1984).
50. L. Valensi, *Le Maghreb*, p.78.
51. B.N. ms. f.fr. 6431, f° 1—12, see above, chapter 1.
52. *Histoire des Deux Indes*, vol.IV, pp.116ff.
53. B.N. ms. f.fr. 6431, f° 8.
54. Vallière, *Mémoire*, pp.64ff.
55. B.N. ms. f.fr. 6429, f° 19—20.
56. Jackson, *An Account of Timbuctoo*, p.463. The rest of the passage has already been quoted above in chapter 1.
57. N. Broc, *La Géographie des Philosophes* (Paris, 1975), p.63.
58. Perkins and Douglas-Morris, *Gunfire in Barbary*, p.175.
59. Poiret, Letter IV, pp.65f; Rehbinder, *Nachrichten*, vol.III, p.453.
60. Quoted by Dupuy, *Américains et Barbaresques*, pp.63ff.
61. Shaler, *Sketches*, pp.167—176.
62. Pananti, *Narrative*, pp.412, 426.
63. *Historical Memoirs of Barbary*, ch.VI.
64. A. Julien, "Marseille et la question d'Alger à la veille de la conquête", *Revue africaine*, 1919, pp.16—61.
65. Henri Alleg, *La Guerre d'Algérie* (Paris, 1981), vol.I, pp.18ff.
66. See Charles-André Julien, *Histoire de l'Algérie contemporaine*, vol.I, *Conquête et colonisation* (2nd edition, Paris, 1979), p.31.
67. This is not to deny the role played in the 1830 expedition by the French King's desire to seize the Dey's fabulous treasure, as is shown by A. Hamdani in his book *La vérité sur l'expédition d'Alger* (Paris, 1984).
68. See *Revue africaine*, 1919, p.59.
69. Hain, *A la Nation*, pp.49—56; *La France doit-elle conserver Alger?* (Paris, 1835), pp.47ff.
70. Julien, *Histoire de l'Algérie contemporaine*, vol.I, ch.II passim.
71. Quoted by Marshall and Williams, *The Great Map of Mankind* (London, 1982), p.253.
72. Campbell, *Letters*, vol.I, pp.193—202.
73. *Morning Chronicle*, 23, 24 July, 1830; quoted by E. Halévy, *A History of the English People in the Nineteenth Century*, vol.2, *The Liberal Awakening (1815—1830)* (English translation, London, 1961), p.302.
74. *Appel en faveur d'Alger et de l'Afrique du nord* par un Anglais (Paris, 1833), pp.10—16.
75. *De l'établissement de légions de colons militaires dans les possessions françaises du nord de l'Afrique* (Paris, 1838), in *Par l'épée et par la charrue. Ecrits et discours de Bugeaud* (Paris, 1948), p.53.
76. *Histoire des Deux Indes*, vol.IV, pp.115—6.

CONCLUSION

1. See the discussion in Part II, chapter II and the texts published by Jean Copans and
    Jean Jamin, *Aux origines de l'anthropologie française* (Paris, 1978); also F. Babié, *Voyages
    chez les peuples sauvages ou l'Homme de la Nature*, (Paris, an IX), 3 volumes.

BIBLIOGRAPHY

List of the main works on which this study is based

Bibliothèque nationale, Paris, Manuscripts, fonds français, nos.6429—6431.

ARGENS, Jean-Baptiste d', *Lettres juives*, 6 vol., La Haye, 1738.
ARVIEUX, chevalier d', *Mémoires du chevalier d'Arvieux, envoyé extraordinaire du Roy à la Porte, consul d'Alep, d'Alger, de Tripoli, et autres Echelles du Levant. Contenant ses voyages à Constantinople, dans l'Asie, la Syrie, la Palestine, l'Egypte et la Barbarie, la description de ces Pays, les Religions, les moeurs, les coutumes, le Négoce de ces Peuples et leurs Gouvernemens, l'Histoire naturelle et les événemens les plus considerables, recueillis de ses Mémoires originaux* et mis en ordre avec des réflexions par le R.P. Jean-Baptiste Labat de l'ordre des Frères Prêcheurs, 6 vol., Paris, 1735.
ARVIEUX, chevalier d', *Voyage fait par ordre du Roy Louis XIV dans la Palestine, vers le Grand Emir, chef des Princes Arabes du Desert, connus sous le nom d'Arabes scenites, qui se disent la vraie postérité d'Ismael, fils d'Abraham, Où il est traité des Moeurs et des Coutumes de cette Nation . . .*, par Monsieur, D.L.R., Paris, 1717.
BANNISTER, S. *Appel en Faveur d'Alger et de l'Afrique du nord*, par un Anglais, Paris, 1833.
BAUFFREMONT, *Journal de campagne de l'Amiral de Bauffremont, prince de Listenois, dans les pays barbaresques (1766).* Manuscrit inédit, établi et présenté par Marcelle Chirac, Paris, 1981.
BLUMENBACH, J.Fr., *De l'Unité du genre humain et de ses variétés*, traduit du latin sur la troisième édition par Fr. Chardel, Paris, an XIII.
BORY DE SAINT-VINCENT, J.-B.-G.-M., *L'Homme (homo), Essai zoologique sur le genre humain*, deuxième édition, 2 vol., Paris, 1827.
BORY DE SAINT-VINCENT, *Note sur la Commission exploratrice et scientifique d'Algérie*, présentée à son excellence le Ministre de la Guerre par le colonel Bory de Saint-Vincent de l'Institut, 16 octobre 1838.
BUFFON, *De l'homme*, Présentation de Michèle Duchet, Paris, 1971.
CAMPBELL, Thomas, *Letters from the South*, 2 vol., London, 1837.
CARETTE, M.E., *Algérie* in *Algérie* par MM. les capitaines du génie Rozet et Carette, *Etats tripolitains* par M. le Dr Ferd. Hoefer, Paris, 1846, reprint, Tunis, 1980.
DESFONTAINES, Louiche René, *Fragmens d'un voyage dans les Régences de Tunis et d'Alger fait de 1783 à 1786*, in *Voyages dans les Régences de Tunis et d'Alger* publiés par M. Dureau de la Malle, Paris, 1838, vol.II.
Encyclopédie, ou Dictionnaire raisonné des Sciences, des arts et des métiers, par une société de gens de lettres, 1751 onwards.
FERGUSON, Adam, *An Essay on the History of Civil Society 1767*, edited, with an introduction, by Duncan Forbes, Edinburgh, 1966.
FOSS, J. *A Journal of the Captivity and Suffering of J. Foss; several years a Prisoner at Algiers*, second edition, Newburyport, 1798.
GIBBON, E., *Decline and Fall of the Roman Empire*, edited by J.B. Bury, 7 vol., London, 1909 (founded on the edition of 1896).
HAIN, Victor-Armand, *A la Nation. Sur Alger*, Paris, 1832.
HELVÉTIUS, Claude-Adrien, *De l'Esprit*, présentation de François Châtelet, Verviers, 1973.

HERBELOT, Barthélemy d', *Bibliothèque orientale ou Dictionnaire universel contenant Tout ce qui fait connoître les Peuples de l'Orient*, 4 vol., Paris, 1777—1779.

Histoire philosophique et politique des établissements et du commerce des Européens dans les Deux Indes, 6 vol., Amsterdam, 1773.

Historical Memoirs of Barbary, as connected with the Plunder of the Seas, including a Sketch of Algiers, Tripoli, Tunis and Considerations of their Present Means of Defence, London, 1816.

JACKSON, James Grey, *An Account of the Empire of Morocco and the Districts of Suse and Tafilet, compiled from miscellaneous observations made during a long residence in, and various journeys through, these countries*, 3rd edition, London, 1814, reprint, London 1968.

JACKSON, James Grey, *An Account of Timbuctoo and Hausa ... to which is added Letters descriptive of Travels through West and South Barbary and across the Mountains of Atlas*, London, 1820.

JARDINE, Alexander, *Letters from Barbary, France, Spain, Portugal ...* by an English officer, London, 1788.

KOKOVTSOV, M.G., *Journal de voyage*, 1776—7 in: M. Canard, "Une description de la côte barbaresque au dix-huitième siècle par un officier de la Marine russe", *Revue africaine*, 95 (1951), pp.120—180.

La Condamine, account of his visit in 1731, in: M. Emerit, "Le voyage de La Condamine à Alger", *Revue africaine*, 98 (1954), pp.354—381.

La France doit-elle conserver Alger? par un Auditeur au Conseil d'Etat, Paris 1835.

LAUGIER DE TASSY, *Histoire des Etats barbaresques qui exercent la piraterie contenant l'origine, les Révolutions et l'Etat présent des Royaumes d'Alger, de Tunis, de Tripoli et de Maroc, avec leurs forces, leurs revenus, leur politique et leur commerce*. Par un auteur qui y a résidé plusieurs années avec caractère public, 2 vol., Paris, 1757. (First edition 1725).

LE ROY, *Etat général et particulier du Royaume et de la ville d'Alger. De son Gouvernement, de ses forces de terre et de mer, Revenus, Justice, Police, Commerce, Politique ...*, La Haye, 1750.

LEYDEN, J., *A Historical and Philosophical Sketch of the Discoveries and Settlement of the Europeans in Northern and Western Africa at the Close of the Eighteenth Century*, Edinburgh, 1799.

MONTESQUIEU, *De l'Esprit des Lois*, édition de R. Derathé, 2 vol., Paris, 1973.

NOAH, Mordecai M., *Travels in England, France, Spain and the Barbary States in the years 1813—14 and 15*, New York and London, 1819.

OCKLEY, Simon, *An Account of South-West Barbary: containing what is most Remarkable in the Territories of the King of Fez and Morocco. Written by a Person who had been a Slave there a considerable Time*, London, 1713.

PANANTI, Filippo, *Narrative of a Residence in Algiers, comprising a geographical and historical account of the Regency, biographical sketches of the Dey and his ministers, anecdotes of the late war, observations on the relations of the Barbary States with the Christian Powers & c*, translated by E. Blaquiere, London, 1818.

PELLOW, Thomas, *The History of the Long Captivity and Adventures of Thomas Pellow, in South Barbary*, London, 1739.

PEYSSONNEL, *Relation d'un voyage sur les côtes de la Barbarie fait par ordre du Roi*, in *Voyages dans les Régences de Tunis et d'Alger*, publiés par Dureau de la Malle, Paris, 1838, vol.I.

POIRET, abbé, *Voyage en Barbarie, ou lettres écrites de l'ancienne Numidie pendant les années 1785 et 1786*, Paris 1789, reedited as *Lettres de Barbarie 1785—1786*, Préface de Denise Brahimi, Paris, 1980.

PRICHARD, James Cowles, *The Natural History of Man, Comprising Inquires into the Modifying Influence of Physical and Moral Agencies of the Different Tribes of the Human Family*, London, 1843.

RAYNAL, abbé, *Histoire philosophique et politique des établissemens et du commerce des Européens dans l'Afrique*, publiée et augmentée par Peuchot, 2 vol., Paris, 1826.

Réfutation de l'Ouvrage de Hamdan Khoja intitulé Aperçu historique et statistique sur la Régence d'Alger, extrait de *l'Observateur des Tribunaux* Paris, 1834.

REHBINDER, *Nachrichten und Bemerkungen über den algierischen Staat*, 3 vol., Altona, 1798—1800.

ROZET, M.P., *Alger*, in *Algérie par MM. les capitaines du génie Rozet et Carette, Etats tripolitains par M. le Dr. Ferd. Hoefer*, Paris, 1846, reprint Tunis, 1980.

SHALER, William, *Sketches of Algiers, Political, Historical and Civil, containing an account of the Geography, Population, Government, Revenues, Commerce, Agriculture, Arts, Civil Institutions, Tribes, Manners, Language and Recent Political History of that Country*, Boston, 1826.

SHAW, Thomas, *Travels or Observations Relating to Several Parts of Barbary and the Levant*, Oxford, 1738.

TOTT, Baron de, *Mémoires du Baron de Tott, sur les Turcs et les Tartares*, 2 vol., Amsterdam, 1785.

VALLIÈRE, Césaire-Philippe, *Mémoire*, in: L. Chaillou, *L'Algérie en 1781*, Toulon, 1974.

VENTURE DE PARADIS, Jean-Michel, *Tunis et Alger au XVIII° siècle*, Mémoires et observations rassemblés et présentés par Joseph Cuoq, Paris, 1983; *Alger au XVIII° siècle*, edited by E. Fagnan, Alger, 1898, reprinted Tunis, n.d.

VIREY, J.J., *Histoire naturelle du genre humain*, 2 vol., Paris, an IX.

VOLNEY, C.F. de Chasseboeuf, comte de, *Considérations sur la Guerre des Turcs, Voyage en Egypte et en Syrie*, in *Oeuvres complètes*, Paris, 1864.

VOLTAIRE, *Candide* in *Romans et contes*, édition de H. Bénac, Paris, 1960; *Essai sur les Moeurs* in *Oeuvres complètes* edited by Moland, Paris, 1878, vol. XI, XII, XIII.

INDEX